CHOOSE YOUR OWN MASTER CLASS

URGENT IDEAS TO INVIGORATE YOUR PROFESSIONAL LEARNING

BETH PANDOLPHO & KATIE CUBANO

Solution Tree | Press

a division of
Solution Tree

555 North Morton Street
Bloomington, IN 47404
800.733.6786 (toll free) / 812.336.7700
FAX: 812.336.7790

email: info@SolutionTree.com
SolutionTree.com

Visit **go.SolutionTree.com/teacherefficacy** to download the free reproducibles in this book.

Printed in the United States of America

Library of Congress Cataloging-in-Publication Data

Names: Pandolpho, Beth, author. | Cubano, Katie, author.
Title: Choose your own master class : urgent ideas to invigorate your
    professional learning / Beth Pandolpho, Katie Cubano.
Description: Bloomington, IN : Solution Tree Press, [2023] | Includes
    bibliographical references and index.
Identifiers: LCCN 2023020275 (print) | LCCN 2023020276 (ebook) | ISBN
    9781954631472 (paperback) | ISBN 9781954631489 (ebook)
Subjects: LCSH: Teachers--In-service training. | Career development. |
    Transformative learning. | Educational sociology. | Professional
    learning communities.
Classification: LCC LB1731 .P337 2023 (print) | LCC LB1731 (ebook) | DDC
    370.71/55--dc23/eng/20230426
LC record available at https://lccn.loc.gov/2023020275
LC ebook record available at https://lccn.loc.gov/2023020276

Solution Tree
Jeffrey C. Jones, CEO
Edmund M. Ackerman, President

Solution Tree Press
President and Publisher: Douglas M. Rife
Associate Publishers: Todd Brakke and Kendra Slayton
Editorial Director: Laurel Hecker
Art Director: Rian Anderson
Copy Chief: Jessi Finn
Senior Production Editor: Tonya Maddox Cupp
Proofreader: Elijah Oates
Text and Cover Designer: Fabiana Cochran
Acquisitions Editor: Hilary Goff
Assistant Acquisitions Editor: Elijah Oates
Content Development Specialist: Amy Rubenstein
Associate Editor: Sarah Ludwig
Editorial Assistant: Anne Marie Watkins

In the mists and fog of life find
your way to the rainbow by the
sound of your own voice.

—Ntozake Shange

ACKNOWLEDGMENTS

To educators everywhere, we hope this book offers you what you so generously give to your students. —Beth and Katie

Solution Tree Press would like to thank the following reviewers:

Heather Bell-Williams
 Author and Consultant
 ConsultHBW
 St. Stephen, New Brunswick, Canada

Lindsay Carey
 AVID Coordinator and Teacher
 McKinney High School (MISD)
 McKinney, Texas

Erin Kruckenberg
 Fifth-Grade Teacher
 Harvard Community Unit School
 District 50
 Harvard, Illinois

Peter Marshall
 Education Consultant
 Burlington, Ontario, Canada

Rachel Swearengin
 Fifth-Grade Teacher
 Manchester Park Elementary School
 Olathe, Kansas

Kim Timmerman
 Middle School Principal
 ADM Middle School
 Adel, Iowa

Visit **go.SolutionTree.com/teacherefficacy** to download the free reproducibles in this book.

TABLE OF CONTENTS

ABOUT THE AUTHORS

Beth Pandolpho is an instructional coach at the West Windsor-Plainsboro Regional School District in New Jersey. She has taught English at the high school and college levels for over twenty years. She taught a summer social justice series to high school students in her community and trained at the Moth Teacher Institute to learn how to cultivate students' ability to speak and write about issues that matter to them and tell their own stories. Her mission is to find ways for educators to positively impact student learning while at the same time taking care of their own needs and infusing joy into the profession.

Beth has written for *Education Week, Educational Leadership*, and *The New York Times Learning Network* and is a frequent Edutopia contributor.

Beth earned a bachelor's degree in English language and literature at the University of Maryland, a master of science in reading at Adelphi University, and her supervisory certification for curriculum and instruction at Rutgers University.

To learn more about Beth's work, follow @bethpando on Twitter.

Katie Cubano is an educator interested in teacher leadership toward curriculum and instruction that effectively and equitably meet students' needs. After teaching English for over a decade, she became an instructional coach in 2019. Katie is passionate about providing each student access to their civil right to education, and supporting teachers and schools toward expanding their vision of what it means to teach for a more civil, sustainable, and just future. Throughout her career, she has worked to improve educational outcomes for underserved student populations through her own practice, collaboration with colleagues, and partnerships with school communities and district leaders.

In 2018, Katie and friend and colleague Carolyn Ross's article titled "A Legacy of Collaboration: Supporting Reflective Practitioners Through Teacher Work Groups," which examines a case study on teacher leadership, was published in *English Leadership Quarterly*. Katie has been an active member of the National Council of Teachers of English (NCTE) for her entire career, and is an active member of NCTE's Conference on English Leadership (CEL). She was the program chair for the 2023 CEL Convention.

Since earning the Robert Mehlman Award for Excellence in Student Teaching upon graduation in 2008, Katie has maintained a strong relationship with the teacher education program at her alma mater, the College of New Jersey. She has served on assessment panels for student teaching capstone presentations and returned often to provide and participate in professional development for preservice and novice teachers.

To book Beth Pandolpho or Katie Cubano for professional development, contact pd@SolutionTree.com.

INTRODUCTION

Shortly before writing this book, we began a new journey together as instructional coaches serving the cross-disciplinary needs of teachers of grades 6–12. Before we moved into these roles, Beth was already working in our district as a high school English teacher. Katie was working as a high school English teacher in a neighboring district.

When we learned we would be working together as teammates in our new roles, we began to connect via social media. Our partnership seemed fated from the start—through our early connection on Twitter, we quickly discovered that we shared a favorite podcast, Krista Tippett's *On Being*. As our colleagueship and friendship grew, we discovered that while we had many other favorites in common, what really united us was a way of thinking, a curiosity that drives us to explore ideas, philosophies, research, and science from a wide range of disciplines. That curiosity drives us to make meaning. To find connections. To explore contradictions, paradoxes, and parallels. And to synthesize the deeper insights we gain and apply them to our work in service of teaching and learning, in service of students. In so many ways, both of us design our reading and listening experiences to create our own unique *master class*—a class comprising a series of experts of our choosing who share their wisdom about some of our most urgent concerns. Such a class provides educators the opportunity to connect to their agency, creates tools to ease the challenges inherent in the position, and supports educators to positively impact student learning and well-being while taking care of their own needs. For both of us, this ability to customize our learning experiences and share them with each other feels like the optimal professional learning opportunity.

It was this discovery, and the knowledge that so many K–12 educators share this way of thinking, that prompted us to consider how we could write a book that offered educators the kind of experience we find most transformative: exploring emerging, evolving ideas that span a wide range of disciplines and considering how those ideas can positively impact teaching and learning. We also contemplated how, in doing so, we could honor the complex and creative nature of our profession to enable educators to grow in both the art and science of their craft. It has been a significant undertaking, but one we have approached with an abundance of curiosity and a desire to serve, grounded in an abiding friendship.

Foundational to our purpose, and at the heart of what we do, are a deep love for students and the practice and promise of education, a profound respect for the teaching profession, and a desire to empower educators to meet the needs of their students most effectively.

Toni Morrison (as cited in Associated Press, 2019) famously said in a 1981 speech to the Ohio Arts Council, "If there's a book that you want to read, but it hasn't been written yet, then you must write it."

For us, this is that book.

Our Aspirations for This Book

The demands inherent in the education profession often make it difficult for us to read widely during the school year and to engage in common reading experiences and the resulting conversations that can shift our thinking and impact our teaching. Consequently, we sometimes don't encounter ideas until years after they emerge in their fields and they begin to filter through the education bubble. Because we believe so deeply in the power of reading and learning, we wanted to offer educators direct access to timely and urgent ideas from thought leaders working outside the silo of education so you can contemplate for yourself how these ideas might inform a different approach to pedagogy and practice. To that end, this book features thought leaders from organizational psychology, sociology, economics, neuroscience, literature, and more to inspire you to consider how you might apply these lenses to gain new insights about teaching and learning.

Journalist David Epstein (2019), in his book *Range: Why Generalists Triumph Specialized World*, explains how everyone can benefit from seeking wisdom outs their own discipline:

> Nobel laureates are at least twenty-two times more likely to partake as an amateur actor, dancer, magician, or other type of performer. Nationally recognized scientists are much more likely than other scientists to be musicians, sculptors, painters, printmakers, woodworkers, mechanics, electronics tinkerers, glassblowers, poets, or writers, of both fiction and nonfiction. . . . The most successful experts also belong to the wider world. (p. 33)

cool!

We imagined writing one book that could invite you into this wider world while both fitting into your busy life and meeting your needs, just as you meet the needs of your students and school community.

We imagined one book that could do the following.

- Offer you choice so the book could appeal to a wide range of interests and needs.

- Withstand long stretches of time between readings and remain relevant.

- Offer you new insights so you could spark discussion and circle up with colleagues to devise creative approaches that could both impact student learning and ease lesson design.

- Give you what you give to your students: differentiation, choice, time to reflect and process, and scaffolding to engage in conversation about what feels most relevant to your teaching practice.

- Invite you to design the learning experience you need most and, in essence, create a master class that is all your own.

As writers and coaches, we've been thinking a lot about how educators seem expected to toil endlessly to meet students' needs and then, in their free time, practice educator self-care. We can't help but wonder, Why do these practices have to be mutually exclusive? Being an educator may be a labor of love, but there is only so much you can read, research, implement, and master before you entirely deplete your resources. Yet, it seems even when educators give everything they have, they may fear that at best, they are insufficient, and at worst, they are failing. Our hope through this book is to offer ideas that can enhance students' learning experiences and at the same time support your needs and infuse joy into the profession to help you reconnect with why you became an educator in the first place. The question that has been deeply resonating with us is, What if serving students and taking care of some of our own needs can sometimes actually be the very same thing?

What Makes This Book Different

This book features a series of stand-alone chapters, each of which focuses on a concept, perspective, or field of research that holds great promise for the work educators do every day. It is designed to free you from the burden of marching through a text from cover to cover, while offering you the opportunity to begin with the chapter that feels most relevant and fulfills your most urgent need. You may choose to read in whatever order makes sense to you, and perhaps you'll choose to skip a chapter that doesn't seem to apply to your practice at all. Only you know the proper sequencing, content, and subsequent conversations that would make up your very own master class.

Each chapter follows the same structure, beginning with an exploration of insights from thought leaders in diverse fields outside of education, ranging from the arts to the sciences and beyond. We culled and curated these ideas from books, podcasts, articles, and blogs that not only moved us but shifted our thinking and transformed in some crucial way how we view teaching and learning. After we guide you through that exploration, the Implications for the Classroom section will expand on our vision of how you might apply those insights in your work. For example, you will learn how to align your practice with your values by examining lessons from organizational leaders, how to increase and leverage students' emotional intelligence to positively impact learning with research from the sciences, and how to create more equitable classrooms by drawing on cross-disciplinary wisdom, strategies, and approaches that advance civil discourse.

After Implications for the Classroom, three types of tools are provided to guide you as you consider how those ideas apply to your practice and your students. First, there are introspective exercises designed to support you in examining how the ideas explored in the chapter and your own values and beliefs can anchor and inform your instructional decisions. Next, there are classroom strategies designed for immediate use based on the chapter's focus so students can engage in activities inspired by the wisdom of the chapter's thought leaders. Last, there are three sets of questions. The first are chapter-specific questions for individual reflection. The second are chapter-specific questions to guide conversations with colleagues who have also read that chapter. The third are questions to facilitate conversations with colleagues who have read other chapters, similar to a jigsaw activity. You'll notice that this last set of questions is the same each time, as the questions can apply to any chapters you are discussing.

This book offers readers choice and flexibility, differentiation, and access.

Choice and Flexibility

Each of the six chapters is completely independent of the others with a unique focus, so they can be read in any order based on interest level, available time, and most urgent need. The chapters are of varied lengths based on their depth, breadth, content, or focus, so this may factor into your choices. Additionally, each chapter includes an estimated read time to support you in anticipating the time commitment to read it from start to finish.

Differentiation

You can engage with this text in a variety of ways depending on your individual preferences. Perhaps you only want to read one chapter, reflect on your learning independently, and decide for yourself what will work best with your students. Maybe you want to do a chapter study as part of a professional learning community, team, or departmental initiative and collaborate to decide how these ideas can inform that endeavor. Maybe it can be a book study for your whole school with individuals reading the chapter that sparks their own interest, and you will engage in conversations across chapters to generate creative solutions tailored to meet your school's needs.

Access

This book offers you access to ideas from a diverse range of thought leaders spanning various fields that you might not otherwise have the time to engage with during the school year considering the demands inherent in the profession.

In offering this format, we hope that you will enjoy a unique reading experience that infuses new ideas into your practice during the school year, the time when educators need inspiration most. We hope that by tailoring this experience to your own needs, you can indeed follow the "sound of your own voice."

A Note to Administrators

This book works as a One School, One Book initiative (https://readtothem.org /one-school-one-book) with teams or departments as a professional learning initiative, or as a summer book club. All these initiatives have the capacity to increase collective teacher efficacy, which is a top factor related to student achievement (Visible Learning, 2018). This book can also serve as a shared text for administrative teams to read and reflect on together. The introspective exercises; the questions for reflection, conversation, and jigsawing across chapters; and the classroom strategies lend themselves to collaboration. They also offer ideas and frameworks for reimagining how to best meet the needs of students in the classroom and the larger school community.

Chapter Contents and Elements

Chapter 1 dives into research from thought leaders in the fields of psychology, neuroscience, and parenting on why fostering emotional intelligence and fluency in the classroom is essential to students' academic achievement and overall well-being. The introspective exercises will allow educators to consider how to build the skills of emotional intelligence into lessons, assignments, classroom culture, and classroom strategies designed to help students recognize, understand, and manage their emotions so they can more effectively engage in learning.

Chapter 2 explores perspectives from writers in the fields of art, journalism, and computer science to examine how the design and function of addictive technology have come to absorb people's time and attention. These perspectives help educators think critically about the impact of the digital world on students' ability to focus, think critically, and manage their well-being. The chapter offers introspective exercises designed to help educators reflect on and leverage this knowledge in order to make decisions about when and how to implement technology in ways that both mitigate negative effects and support student learning. The classroom strategies invite students to co-create classroom norms around technology use and foster authentic, face-to-face, student-to-student communication.

Chapter 3 explores how people often struggle to communicate with those with whom they disagree and to find value in opposing viewpoints. It offers approaches for working alongside students to cultivate more civil classrooms and school communities toward a more civil society. It offers introspective exercises for educators to reflect on their current practices and classroom strategies that can support increased civil discourse to empower students to learn how to work together toward mutual understanding and a greater capacity to problem solve together.

Chapter 4 walks readers through ideas from thought leaders in the fields of social work, organizational leadership, and philanthropy to explore how a nuanced understanding of human behavior can support more effective leadership and successful outcomes. It offers introspective exercises to help you apply these insights to your practice, as well as classroom strategies designed to support students in establishing good habits, harnessing their individual genius, and exploring how their values can help them shape their identities and long-term goals.

Chapter 5 offers insights from thought leaders in the fields of economics and psychology about how to manage the abundant decisions inherent in modern life that often lead to uncertainty, guilt, and regret. Decision fatigue is particularly resonant for educators because they need to make hundreds of instructional, curricular, administrative, and interpersonal decisions on a daily basis. The chapter departs from the others in that while it offers introspective exercises, it includes no classroom strategies. The introspective exercises facilitate reflection on how you can apply research-based techniques to simplify and reduce the number of required decisions to both ease decision fatigue and create more equitable outcomes for students.

Chapter 6 explores ideas from writers and thought leaders to help both students and educators think about the stories they tell about themselves and their lives, and consider how they can tell truer stories that can lead to greater personal growth and freedom. It includes introspective exercises so you can reflect on the kinds of stories you tell yourself and the impact of the language that you use, along with ready-to-use activities for students to do the same.

Spotlight On is a recurring feature throughout the book that highlights a practical strategy or approach inspired by the ideas in the chapter. Spotlight On is designed to offer clear examples of what these ideas might look like in a classroom so that you can replicate them, adapt them, or use them to inspire your own.

Our collective years in education have taught us that the most impactful learning experiences for educators go beyond the latest buzzwords and trends and instead prioritize choice, relevance, inquiry, and conversation. Further, they immerse us in a wider scope of philosophies and research on which we can draw to inspire and inform our practice and reconnect to the underlying principles that have shaped our commitment to education and to students.

It is our hope that this book will offer some new ideas to invigorate your practice, affirm your foundational reasons for becoming an educator, and empower you to positively impact student learning.

We invite you to begin with the chapter that most interests you, apply these cross-disciplinary ideas to devise your own solutions, and choose your own master class.

CHAPTER 1

CULTIVATING SELF-AWARENESS AND EMOTIONAL INTELLIGENCE

Estimated Read Time:

40 Minutes

Another world is not only possible, she is on her way. . . .
On a quiet day, if I listen very carefully, I can hear her breathing.

—Arundhati Roy

Cultivating emotional intelligence was decidedly not a main feature of our (Beth's and Katie's) K–12 educational experiences. As adults, we came to value the importance of emotional intelligence. For Katie, the gift of becoming a parent led her to the work of early childhood educational philosopher Magda Gerber. Gerber (1979) and her student Janet Lansbury (2014) both advocate for a relationship that allows children to feel seen, validated, and heard—one that respects their right to access the full range of human emotions, and one that sees the experience and expression of this range as healthy and necessary to growth and development. For Beth, her collective years both in the classroom and as a parent taught her that learning is inextricably connected to one's emotional life. Anxiety leads to poorer test performance, and frustration affects the ability to pay attention, whereas positive emotions can enhance motivation and engagement. Again and again, research supports the fact that "emotions and learning are inseparable. Emotions can both enhance and interfere with learning depending on which ones are driving or colouring the experience" (Osika, MacMahon, Lodge, & Carroll, 2022). This understanding led us to seek out thinkers from across disciplines to determine how we could most effectively leverage our intuition and insight toward better decision making and more enduring learning experiences. We invite you to join us in exploring this topic, along with Leonard Mlodinow, Shawn Ginwright, and Marc Brackett, and think about how it may resonate with you.

Ideas to Consider

You've likely observed wide variability in the degree to which educators attend to and nurture students' self-awareness and emotional intelligence. Is it enough to offer students time to reflect on their learning and ensure they treat their classmates with respect, or do all of us, as educators, need to go further and integrate metacognitive thinking and the language of emotions into everyday lesson design? The latter seems to be the response from the Collaborative for Academic, Social, and Emotional Learning (CASEL, n.d.) because CASEL identifies self-awareness as an essential part of its framework necessary to "cultivate skills and environments that advance students' learning and development." In addition to addressing these skills in instruction, educators must model these skills for students. Educator Colt Turner and counselor Dhanya Bhat (2022) write for the Center for Responsive Schools that "teachers and leaders have significant opportunities to model the rhetoric and behavior that we desire our students to adopt." If we want our students to become increasingly self-aware and grow in their emotional intelligence, we need to do the same.

The more we read and learn about these dispositions and skills, the clearer it becomes how these skills have implications for both our students and our lives beyond the classroom. Meditation teacher Oren Jay Sofer (2018) writes, "Self-awareness is the basis for empathic connection. As we experience the inner landscape of our life with more detail and richness, so grows our ability to understand the inner lives of others" (p. 103). Research supports the connection between self-awareness and empathy, with two studies revealing that "empathic people aren't just skilled at navigating other people's emotions. They're in touch with their own feelings, too—which means that self-awareness may be one of the foundations of empathy" (Newman, 2018). When we support our students to cultivate self-awareness, it impacts their learning trajectory and improves their relationships. Expanding our self-awareness as educators makes us better role models for our students and enhances our personal well-being.

In addition to increasing empathy, cultivating our emotional intelligence enables us to communicate more clearly about our inner lives, our experiences, and our needs. Vulnerability researcher Brené Brown (2021) offers the analogy of the importance of clearly expressing physical symptoms to a doctor (enabling the doctor to determine the tests that support a conclusive diagnosis) to help us understand how crucial it is to hone our ability to accurately communicate our emotional realities to one another in order to get what we need:

> When we don't have the language to talk about what we're experiencing, our ability to make sense of what's happening and share it with others is severely limited. Without accurate language, we struggle to get the help we need, we don't always regulate or manage our emotions and experiences in a way that allows us to move through them productively, and our self-awareness is diminished. (Brown, 2021, p. xxi)

In our classrooms, it is essential that we model emotional intelligence in our instruction and relationships with students and also incorporate activities that support students to grow in their emotional intelligence. Understand that spending classroom time attending to students' emotional intelligence and fluency has a powerful impact on student achievement; developing the language of emotions benefits students and makes educators more effective in their practice. This stance that embraces the wholeness of our own and our students' emotional lives is the pathway to healthier classroom communities—to stronger connections, increased well-being, fewer disruptions, and deeper, more meaningful learning. As Paulo Coelho (1988) writes in *The Alchemist*, "You will never be able to escape from your heart. So it's better to listen to what it has to say" (p. 134).

It is worth noting that self-awareness and emotional intelligence are foundational to many of the other issues explored in this book. Chapter 2 (page 41), which examines technology use in the classroom, requires that educators be mindful of their decisions about when students are using technology during school. Further, self-awareness and emotional intelligence are integral parts of engaging in civil conversations, which is covered in chapter 3 (page 79), and of making decisions and fostering equity, which are addressed in chapter 5 (page 143). Last, self-awareness and fluency in the language of emotions are necessary if we want to tell truer stories about ourselves toward increased personal freedom, which is explored more deeply in chapter 6 (page 173).

This chapter offers an exploration into the emotional realm, based on scientific research, that reveals how our emotions affect our decision making, attention, memory, creativity, and behavior regulation. It examines how, through these understandings, you can sharpen your emotional intelligence with an eye toward improving experiences in your classroom for both yourself and your students.

Leonard Mlodinow on Understanding Our Emotional Lives

Leonard Mlodinow is an author and theoretical physicist who earned a PhD from the University of California, Berkeley. In his book *Emotional: How Feelings Shape Our Thinking*, which draws on scientific research in evolutionary biology, psychology, and neuroscience, Mlodinow (2022) explores the idea that when we better understand how our emotional lives affect our behavior and decision making, we can more effectively leverage our emotions to better inform our decisions. We can also begin to empathize more deeply with and feel more connected to others.

Contrary to popular belief, we cannot separate our emotions from our thinking and decision making. As Mlodinow (2022) explains, "The human brain is often compared to a computer, but the information processing that this computer executes is inextricably intertwined with the deeply mysterious phenomenon we call feelings" (p. xi).

Mlodinow's early childhood experiences sparked a curiosity about how our emotional lives affect who we are and how we think, act, react, and connect with others. As the son of Holocaust survivors, he found that some of his earliest memories with his mother profoundly align with what the research suggests—that our emotional lives and past experiences impact our present thoughts and subsequent actions. Mlodinow (2022) recounts in the introduction to his book:

> When I made a big mess or tried to flush the transistor radio down the toilet, my mother would work herself into a frenzy, erupt in tears, and start to scream at me. "I can't take it!" she'd shout. "I wish I were dead! Why did I survive? Why didn't Hitler kill me?" (p. ix)

At the time, as he lacked perspective, Mlodinow (2022) thought his mom's reaction was typical of all mothers. Yet, when he was in high school, and a psychiatrist who had met with his mother indicated that her reactions were a result of the emotional trauma of her past, he began to think differently. He offers another anecdote from a family dinner when he was a child that illustrates this deeper understanding. He remembers his mom saying:

Finish your chicken. . . . Eat it. . . . Someday you might wake up and find that your whole family was killed! And you, with nothing to eat, will have to crawl on your belly through the mud in order to drink stinking, filthy water from mud puddles! Then you'll stop wasting food but it'll be too late. (Mlodinow, 2022, p. x)

As his mother's outburst seemed to be evidence of the psychiatrist's diagnosis, Mlodinow began to see his mother's behavior in a different light. He began to understand, for the first time, how his mother's emotional past impacted her thinking and decision making. Mlodinow (2022) writes, "Even when you believe you are exercising cold logical reason, you aren't. . . . People aren't usually aware of it, but the very framework of their thought process is highly influenced by what they're feeling at the time—sometimes subtly, sometimes not" (p. 72). To make matters more complicated, Mlodinow's father, who was also a Holocaust survivor, was "always being full of optimism and self-confidence" (p. xi). This glaring contradiction led Mlodinow to consider a series of questions. Perhaps the one most pertinent to our work as educators is this: "How do [our emotions] affect our thoughts, judgments, motivation, and decisions, and how can we control them?" (p. xi). Another question that comes to our minds is, How might our students be similarly impacted by the emotional realities of their own lives, and what can we do as a result of this understanding?

The following sections address how emotions affect decision making and emotional regulation.

How Emotions Affect Decision Making

As educators, we sometimes wonder why our students make the choices they do. Why don't they do their homework, why do they arrive late to class, or why don't they participate in class discussions? These behaviors often don't make logical sense, because our students' decisions, like our own, are impacted by emotions that are invisible to others, and sometimes even to oneself. Research across disciplines examines the role emotions have in decision making, and the results are clear. Not only do our emotions affect our minor decisions, but also "many psychological scientists now assume that emotions are, for better or worse, the dominant driver of most meaningful decisions in life" (Lerner, Li, Valdesolo, & Kassam, 2015).

Mlodinow offers a series of stories and anecdotes to illustrate this phenomenon—how our emotional states affect our cognitive abilities and can heighten or hinder our decision-making skills. He writes, "Each emotion represents a different mode of thinking and creates corresponding adjustments to your judgments and reasoning" (Mlodinow, 2022, p. 75). He notes, for example, that research subjects are more likely to overestimate the likelihood of future misfortune when they are afraid; their senses are heightened toward reaching safety. When they are anxious, they are more likely to interpret an ambiguous situation with a negative bent. Similarly, positive emotions also affect people's decision making. For example, when we feel proud, we are bursting to share our news with others, and when we are happy, we are more "creative, open to new information, and flexible and efficient in [our] thinking" (p. 87). Mlodinow (2022) writes, "We all interpret the world and our options within it through the calculations of our mind. Emotions evolved as an aid to tune those mental operations to the specific circumstances we find ourselves in" (p. 77).

For educators, that begs the questions, How much control do we have over our emotional lives, which have such a profound impact on our decision making? and How can we support our students to become more aware of their emotional lives to positively impact learning? Based on this evidence that our emotions are inextricably linked to our decision making, it seems wise to prioritize learning more about these emotions and how they impact our thinking, and that of our students, toward enhanced self-regulation and more positive outcomes.

Mlodinow's (2022) analysis of how our emotional lives affect our decision making also demonstrates that becoming better stewards of our emotional lives is the path toward both greater personal freedom and "our ability to cooperate and live together in societies" (p. 80). These understandings can support us, as educators, to build stronger classroom communities in which students are accepted for the unique people they are while they learn to interact more productively and in greater connection with others.

How Emotions Affect Emotional Regulation

When thinking about emotional regulation, we (Beth and Katie) view it in two ways: (1) How can we be attuned to our emotional lives toward increased self-awareness and personal well-being? and (2) How can we manage our emotions and their impact on our actions and reactions to other people? These are not simple questions to answer, but a deeper understanding of our emotional lives can help us ensure that we are not ruled by our emotions.

Keeping emotions in check is not an easy task. Meaningfully responding to students' needs while providing an environment conducive to learning for everyone is a constant juggling act. However, the more self-aware we are about our *own* needs and triggers as educators, the more we can remain balanced and calm in the classroom and model self-regulation. According to a research study in primary schools in Norway:

> Competent self-regulation develops progressively through the child's interactions with caregivers as part of a multifaceted process termed, co-regulation. . . . As part of this process, "support, coaching, and modelling are provided to facilitate a child's ability to understand, express and modulate their thoughts, feelings and behaviour." (Kostøl & Cameron, 2021)

When faced with a challenge in the classroom, you can co-regulate with students many ways. For example, you can model a think-aloud about how you navigated a situation. You might say something like, "When everyone was talking at the same time, I had the urge to yell, but sitting quietly at my desk until you all noticed and quieted down was more calming for me and I hope for you as well." Or when a student seems frustrated, you can coach them through it by saying something like, "It looks as though you're frustrated. When I'm frustrated, sometimes it helps to write down what is bothering me. If you'd like to do that, I'm here to listen when you're ready."

Mlodinow recounts a few evidence-based examples that indicate how our emotional reactions are shaped in relation to other people in ways that are often out of our control. For example, if a coworker recounts a particularly painful injury, we often wince as if we feel it in the same spot in our body. Similarly, when they tell us about an uncomfortable encounter they had with the principal, we begin to feel that same anxiety; when we see a ball aimed toward someone else's head during a sporting event, we duck in response. Mlodinow (2022) explains, "We are hardwired to feel what others do" (p. 184). Scientists call this *emotional contagion* (Baldwin, 1897; Herrando & Constantinides, 2021; Reber, 1985). What makes this tricky is that we are exposed to emotional contagion even when the company we keep is beyond our control: we don't choose our colleagues, the students in our classrooms, or the content that news outlets and social media companies amplify to manipulate our emotions to achieve their desired ends.

According to Mlodinow (2022), the extent to which our emotions affect our decision making is also strongly correlated with our emotional profile, which is influenced greatly by our early childhood experiences. His mother's emotions and behaviors are a perfect example of this. Research has demonstrated, though, that when we have a clear understanding of our emotional lives, we do have the capacity to transform ourselves; we can cultivate ways to regulate our emotions in order to strengthen our decision making in situations that *are* in our control. Put another way by Harvard Medical School psychologist Susan David (2017), "Emotions are data, they are not directives. We can show up to and mine our emotions for their values without needing to listen to them."

Mlodinow (2022) offers in his book what he calls *inventories*, based on research, that can help you characterize your emotional profile in the areas that he believes are the most influential in our lives (shame, guilt, anxiety, anger, aggression, happiness, and romantic love. Your scores can help you determine how who you are may impact your responses to emotional events in everyday life. Regardless of your emotional profile, Mlodinow does offer three approaches that anyone can use to regulate their emotions toward greater self-control: (1) stoicism, (2) reappraisal, and (3) expression.

Table 1.1 illustrates the three most effective approaches to regulating our emotions as identified by Mlodinow, along with brief descriptions and examples of what each approach might look like in action.

TABLE 1.1: Mlodinow's (2022) Emotional Regulation Approaches

Approach Description	Possible Ways to Regulate Emotions Using This Approach
Stoicism requires accepting, even welcoming, what may happen. When we release ourselves from the impulse to control what is already out of our control, it enables us to respond more positively rather than increase our suffering in an effort to rail against it.	Practice acceptance of negative events, thoughts, and emotions. Cultivate an understanding that change is inevitable.
Reappraisal calls on us to challenge our negative patterns of thinking and consider more positive alternatives.	Consider positive outcomes even when the negative ones appear more glaring.
Expression means talking or writing about our feelings to attempt to achieve greater clarity and calm.	Keep a journal to write about your feelings, or talk through them with a trusted confidant.

It is important to understand that not just our experiences impact how we perceive the actions and reactions of others; our emotional makeup also determines how easy or difficult it will be to regulate our emotions and control our internal and external responses. This dynamic interplay of who we are and what happened to us in the past, and our commitment to learning how to regulate our emotions, accounts for the variation in people's emotional reactivity, particularly in stressful situations.

As educators, we can appreciate how a classroom of students with different personal histories and personalities may have had little opportunity to practice emotional regulation and can benefit from becoming more in tune with their emotional lives. In learning how to recognize when and why their emotions negatively impact their decisions, and learning how to apply self-regulation strategies, these students can strengthen their emotional regulation abilities toward more positive outcomes and better decision making.

In addition to benefiting from Mlodinow's insights, we can learn strategies from professor and activist Shawn Ginwright that can help us and our students become increasingly self-aware of our emotional lives and lead to greater success both on our own and in relation to each other.

Shawn Ginwright on How to Sharpen Emotional Intelligence

Shawn Ginwright is an author, an activist, and a professor in the Africana studies department at San Francisco State University. His work primarily focuses on ways to create more equitable conditions in urban communities. In his book *The Four Pivots: Reimagining Justice, Reimagining Ourselves*, Ginwright (2022) explores how people who work to sharpen their emotional intelligence through self-awareness and personal reflection can more effectively collaborate toward successful outcomes. Ginwright is writing specifically about social justice movements and community activism, but his work has broader implications for how we can all work together in greater harmony. Throughout his work, Ginwright underscores the idea that individuals' ability to engage productively with others begins with a focus on themselves.

The following sections address developing self-awareness through reflection and building connection through emotional intelligence.

Developing Self-Awareness Through Reflection

Ginwright (2022) examines how we can strengthen our emotional intelligence and self-awareness by sharpening our ability to see clearly. He describes this as moving *from lens to mirror*—shifting from focusing on what we are trying to do, and how others might be impacting our ability to do that, to looking carefully at our own motivations and actions and applying this internal understanding to guide us. To further articulate this idea, he uses terminology he learned from activist Ruby Sales: "true sight, the real ability to see, involves hindsight, foresight, and insight" (Ginwright, 2022, p. 44).

Hindsight

Ginwright acknowledges that we often view *hindsight* as something that enables us to understand what we might have done differently in a past situation. Yet, he contends that we can leverage our hindsight to learn important lessons that can positively impact our future decision making. Ginwright (2022) offers questions that can help us "lean into hindsight as a tool for reflection":

> » *Knowing what I know now, would I have done anything differently?*
>
> » *What is the major lesson or takeaway from this situation?*
>
> » *What could I have done better, or where might I have grown?*
>
> » *How will this help me in the future? (p. 45)*

By reflecting on our past actions and reactions, we can gain the self-awareness we need to self-regulate and positively impact our future behavior. Reflecting on our past behavior can be a powerful lever for both teachers and students as we learn from it and use these lessons to inform future decisions. For example, getting a speeding ticket often results in adhering to the speed limit in the future; a student who didn't spend enough time on an assignment to earn the desired competency or grade may make a different decision in the future toward a better outcome.

Foresight

Foresight is commonly understood as the ability to predict or imagine a possible future. Ginwright (2022) describes foresight as the "capacity to take key lessons from the past and combine them with a passion to create a possible future" (pp. 45–46). Foresight requires us to draw on hindsight and then envision a future that is vast and expansive, one in which a dose of reality is bathed in a dreamlike vision.

Ginwright (2022) offers some reflective prompts that can help us build our muscle for foresight:

> » *Where is my life going, and what will it take to get me there?*
>
> » *What do I really want in life? What have I been settling for?*
>
> » *If I could have any three things ten years from today, what would they be? (p. 50)*

Cultivating foresight is generative; it can help us envision a future full of possibilities that extend beyond what might feel like our current limitations. And having foresight to dream and imagine fosters motivation and determination in the present and in the work toward this hopeful future.

Insight

Ginwright (2022) discusses how we often undervalue the power of our own *insight*—the ability to be still and listen to our thoughts in order to find answers—in favor of more outward-facing, tangible solutions that often ignore our instincts and intuition. In other words, too often, we just don't give ourselves the time and space for truth to surface and guide our decisions. He writes, "What I am suggesting is that we've become a culture where terms like *innovation, strategic planning*, and *design thinking* have replaced terms like *moral compass, ethical decisions, gut feelings*, and *spirit*" (p. 48). Ginwright maintains that instead of obsessing over our strategic plans, which are too often associated with our cerebral effort rather than introspective work, we are better served by fortifying our powers of insight through reflecting and using accurate language to describe our emotional experiences. This will allow us to become more self-aware and make more informed decisions, individually and collectively.

Susan David (2017) supports Ginwright's assertion, as she indicates that it is insufficient to simply acknowledge and be tuned in to our emotions; our emotional fluency matters. She writes:

> *I found that words are essential. We often use quick and easy labels to describe our feelings. "I'm stressed" is the most common one I hear. [But] when we label our emotions accurately, we are more able to discern the precise cause of our feelings. And what scientists call the "readiness potential" in our brain is activated, allowing us to take concrete steps. But not just any steps—the right steps for us. Because our emotions are data. (David, 2017)*

Ginwright further advises that we can develop all three of these abilities to see—(1) hindsight, (2) foresight, and (3) insight—not only by sharing what we learn about ourselves through reflection, but by asking trusted friends for feedback about things we may need to work on. Cultivating these abilities through reflection provides us with a compass to guide us as we begin to develop a comprehensive approach to tuning in to our emotional lives and using these understandings to inform our words and actions.

Building Connection Through Emotional Intelligence

Ginwright (2022) offers that as we cultivate our emotional intelligence, it can lead us to become more grounded and authentic versions of ourselves, as well as lead us to satisfy the basic human need to belong. Belonging is what most of us hope to achieve in our classroom culture—as educators, we want our students to feel both welcomed as their authentic selves, in all their messiness and imperfection, and connected to the rest of the classroom community:

> Belonging . . . requires agreement among groups to form meaningful connection and purposeful membership. Belonging provides us with an identity, a sense of meaning, connection, and purpose. It happens when we join clubs in college, civic groups to solve tough problems in our cities, and movements that improve the conditions of our society. (Ginwright, 2022, p. 94)

To cultivate this sense of belonging, we need our relationships with each other to be what Ginwright (2022) calls *transformative* rather than *transactional*:

> Transactional relationships are based on the performance of roles and the execution of tasks . . . . Transformative relationships, on the other hand, are based in those features of life like care, vulnerability, love, curiosity, connection. Transformative relationships are formed when we exchange pieces of our humanity with each other. When we do that, we give permission to others to do the same. (pp. 114–115)

As messy and complicated as this reality might be, Ginwright expands on this concept in a way that really drives his point home. On Brené Brown's (2022) podcast *Unlocking Us*, he discusses how schools responded to the COVID-19 pandemic in 2020:

One of the things I suggested that they do is, when you reopen schools, allow for the adults to tell their stories. . . . Because when you do that, you're giving permission for people to be human with each other. And this experience . . . all experiences of human species together cannot be dealt with only in a transactional way.

Those who were working in the profession during the years 2020–2022 know that Ginwright is correct. Across the country, school reopenings were handled in a transactional way, and teachers seemed to be just another cog in the wheel required for schools to operate efficiently. When schools began reopening during the pandemic, many districts continued prioritizing compliance and control, ensuring that teachers abided by their contractual obligations instead of extending some grace and listening to their teachers' needs. Faculty meetings remained as scheduled; observation processes remained unchanged. And during intermittent school closures as new COVID-19 variants emerged, many teachers were required to report to their school buildings to teach from their classrooms even when students were attending school virtually.

We know that what teachers needed at the time was to be seen and heard in the fullness of their humanity in order to do the transformative work that is required of educators. And this is the kind of transformative work we need to do with our students, encouraging them to build self-awareness and examine their ways of knowing to inform their decision making. Districts could have listened to and leveraged teachers' hindsight, insight, and foresight based on teaching during the pandemic to inform schoolwide decisions. When districts empower teachers as the valuable stakeholders they are, they benefit from teachers' wisdom and model for students and the community how working in collaboration and being responsive lead to wiser decision making and better outcomes for all. As we consider how we can apply this in our classrooms, there is much we can learn from psychologist Marc Brackett, whose work focuses on how we can welcome our students' emotional lives into our classes to support learning.

Marc Brackett on How Emotions Affect Student Learning

Marc Brackett is a research psychologist at Yale and the founder and director of their Center for Emotional Intelligence, a strong advocate for building social and emotional intelligence skills in schools, and a member of the board of directors for CASEL. His work can help us more fully consider how Mlodinow's and Ginwright's research on emotional intelligence and increased self-awareness applies to our teaching practice. Brackett (2019) writes, "classroom research shows that where there is an emotionally skilled teacher present, students disrupt less, focus more, and perform better academically" (p. 20). Brackett further explores how emotional intelligence and fluency have a profound impact on students, noting that emotions affect students' memory, learning, creativity, and ability to pay attention, as well as their capacity to forge relationships and make decisions. These findings are "based on the past five decades of research into the roles—plural—that emotions play in our lives" (Brackett, 2019, p. 26). Brackett's research clearly demonstrates how a deeper understanding of our emotional lives can support our teaching practice and students' ability to learn.

Sometimes, we may view emotions as stumbling blocks toward our goals, and elevate reason and logic as the only worthy areas of focus for our cognitive processes. However, as both Mlodinow and Brackett would likely agree, when we pay attention to our emotions, we can use them as information to guide our responses and help us find a way forward. It is when we are *unaware* of our emotional lives that we are more often hampered. Brackett (2019) writes:

> We believe that our ability to reason and think rationally is our highest mental power, above our unruly emotional side. This is but a trick our brains play on us—in fact, our emotions exert a huge, though mostly unconscious, influence over how our minds function. . . . In reality, our emotions largely determine our actions. (p. 31)

If we leave our emotional lives unchecked and attempt to make decisions solely by focusing on logic and reason, we are fooling ourselves. Emotions are information—if we remain unaware of them, they will inevitably cloud our judgment and, in fact, make it *more* difficult for us to accurately perceive situations, paradoxically leading us away from reason and logic entirely.

Brackett's (2019) research demonstrates that if we cannot understand and articulate our emotions, our decision making is impaired; even our ability to pay attention and retain and recall information is hindered:

> Strong, negative emotions (fear, anger, anxiety, hopelessness) tend to narrow our minds—it's as though our peripheral vision has been cut off because we're so focused on the peril that's front and center. . . . This inhibits the prefrontal cortex from effectively processing information, so even at a neurocognitive level our ability to focus and learn is impaired. (p. 28)

If we consider how negative emotions might affect our students (whether they are experiencing trauma at home, navigating a complex social dynamic in class, or simply experiencing performance anxiety on a test), it is clear that we have an important opportunity—perhaps even a responsibility—to help them fine-tune their emotional intelligence. These efforts will benefit the students holistically, improving their personal, social, and academic lives and helping them grow as learners and thinkers.

Emotions also have a role in supporting our students' access to their creativity, which is critical to meaningful engagement. According to Brackett (2019), "Emotions rule the whole creative process, from motivating creative work to idea generation to persisting toward the actualization of our own ideas" (p. 47). Students' ability to be creative is contingent on their connection to and understanding of their emotions and the encouragement they receive to hone their skills of creativity. We often assume creativity is "an all-or-nothing gift, rather than a set of skills that can be improved with practice" (Brackett, 2019, p. 43). But we can provide our students with opportunities to practice the skills of creativity all the time by conducting experiments, solving problems, testing proposed hypotheses or theories, and envisioning solutions that may have never before existed. To engage in this kind of divergent thinking, students need to use the information from their ever-changing emotions, and the freedom to act (or not act) on these emotional cues, as they likely make many mistakes on the path to reaching viable solutions. As we work to help students become more emotionally intelligent, we help them access their creativity toward amplifying their overall learning and academic success.

Implications for the Classroom

When you began reading this chapter, you likely did so with the understanding that, of course, students' emotional lives are critical to learning. Educators likely understood long before the term *social-emotional learning* gained a foothold in the educational sphere that students' emotional lives are central to the classroom experience and that relationships between students and teachers are foundational to learning. And yet, as these insights from Mlodinow, Ginwright, and Brackett have helped us more fully recognize how our students' emotional lives are connected to their ability to learn, it has become abundantly clear that curricula, instructional decisions, lesson design, and our teaching practice need to include emotional skills. *What* we do in our classrooms and *how* we do it can support students in deepening their understanding of how to recognize, express, regulate, and leverage their emotions toward better decision making, increased connection, and more meaningful learning.

Implications for the classroom include transformative relationships, emotional fluency, and effective decision making.

Transformative Relationships

Though they have the potential to be truly transformative, our relationships with our students can very easily be relegated to the transactional. We offer instructions, students complete the work, we offer feedback and grades—repeat. And yet, if we want our students to experience transformative results, transformative relationships are where we need to begin. And in order to enter into these relationships, which are essential to growth and learning, we must be willing to mutually explore the complexity of our own emotional lives.

With the deepening understanding that our students' emotional lives are critical to their ability to learn, we first need to ensure that our students feel accepted in our classrooms for who they are. We may feel strongly that this is something we already do, but *feeling* that you care for your students and explicitly *showing* them that you care are two very different things. When you think about your students, how much do you know about them? Do you know about their home lives? Do you know if they have any pets? Do you know what they do outside of school that brings them joy? Do you know who they look up to or what sports teams or musicians they follow? Do you know what movie or book has made them cry? Do you know what they worry about the most? Of course, we have so many students—and if you teach in the upper grades, you have exponentially more students.

Connecting with our students in this more personal way may seem daunting, but we can integrate opportunities to develop these understandings about one another into curriculum and instruction over time, and these small moments will grow into profound knowledge of one another. During the first five days of school, this may look like a series of introductory activities that involve self-exploration. It may sound like a series of short exchanges when students enter your classroom. It may be an exit ticket that asks students to complete the sentence starter, "If there's one thing I'd like you to know about me, it's . . ."

If we want to have transformative relationships and learning experiences with our students, that quite simply begins with knowing them, not just during the first five days but throughout the school year. Being curious about one another and showing

Spotlight On: Building Transformative Relationships

Consider offering these sentence starters as an exit ticket.

- I'm wondering . . .
- I'm worrying . . .
- I'm celebrating . . .
- One thing I'd like to ask you is . . .

a bit of our humanity is how we build connection. And when our students feel connected to us and know that we value them for who they are, they will be more open to sharing their emotional lives, which will lead to deeper and more meaningful learning experiences and greater overall well-being.

Beyond these interpersonal shares, it is critical that we develop a cultural awareness of our students' lives, especially when we teach in a school where our students' cultural backgrounds are very different from our own. A lack of awareness in this realm may cause us to misinterpret a student's means of self-expression as odd or disrespectful. If we knew the student better, we might learn that what may seem like idiosyncrasies are instead deeply held cultural beliefs and norms that have a powerful impact on students' sense of who they are and what matters to them. We may think that we have a sense of these cultural realities, but as figure 1.1 (page 26) clearly shows, there are many underneath the surface that can become barriers to true connection.

In examining the iceberg concept of culture, you may find that there are aspects of your own culture that you've taken for granted as the universal norm; this is human nature. For example, you may be surprised to discover that your concept of time may differ widely from your students' (or even from the concepts of time of people in your personal life). *On time*, to you, may translate to when the bell rings. For a student, *on time* could mean a rough two- to three-minute window around when the bell rings. In becoming aware of aspects that lie farther beneath the water and carry a higher emotional load, we can begin to understand how the self-expression of students with whom we do not share a common culture may be perplexing or vexing to us, and even create a barrier to connection.

Like an iceberg, the majority of culture is below the surface.

Surface culture (above sea level)

Emotional load: Relatively low

Examples: Food, dress, music, visual arts, drama, crafts, dance, literature, language, celebrations, games

Unspoken rules (partially below sea level)

Emotional load: Very high

Examples: Courtesy, contextual conversation patterns, concept of time, personal space, rules of conduct, facial expressions, nonverbal communications, body language, touching, eye contact, patterns of handling emotions, notions of modesty, concept of beauty, courtship practices, relationships to animals, notions of leadership, tempo of work, concepts of food, ideas of child-rearing, theory of disease, social interaction rate, nature of friendships, tone of voice, attitudes toward elders, concepts of cleanliness, notions of adolescence, patterns of group decision making

Unconscious rules (completely below sea level)

Emotional load: Intense

Examples: Definition of insanity; preference for competition or cooperation; tolerance of physical pain; concept of self; concept of past and future; definition of obscenity; attitudes toward dependents; problem solving; roles in relation to age, sex, class, occupation, kinship

Source: Adapted from Hall, 1976.

FIGURE 1.1: The iceberg concept of culture.

By reflecting on how much we *don't* know about students' cultural identities, we can create opportunities in our curriculum, instruction, and classroom community to surface these realities and bring about greater mutual understanding.

Emotional Fluency

The task of learning how to engage in meaningful dialogue about feelings, at its core, entails language and data—areas with which, as educators, we already have considerable expertise. Our task is to expand our teaching savvy into the emotional realm.

When students are empowered with the language and schema to understand and regulate their emotions, and the time, space, and encouragement to practice expressing their emotions during the school day, they will become less inhibited by their emotions, more connected to their experience at school, and less likely to be unduly distracted by stressors in their personal lives. We can support students in their emotional fluency in ways large and small. We can design welcoming activities that incorporate emotional check-ins, and we can invite students to reflect regularly on their experience with content, tasks, and group work. We can offer students choices that allow them to listen to their emotions and follow their instincts to guide their choices. And we can take off our teacher hats and model our own vulnerability and human experience. If policies prohibit you from encouraging your students to bring their whole selves to school, ask yourself, "What in my sphere of control can I do to support my students' overall wellness that doesn't violate any rules I'm bound to uphold?"

A classroom that supports and nurtures students' emotional fluency may have a two-word check-in at the beginning of class to gauge how students are feeling. It can normalize language that guides student choice by tapping into emotions. That may sound like, "What feels most urgent to you?" "What do you feel most passionate about sharing?" or "What matters to you that you want to express?" As teachers, when we are struggling or overwhelmed, we can model vulnerability with our students. We may do so by sharing a bit of our experience in an appropriate way that shows them how we bring our whole selves to school and communicates that we welcome them to do the same.

We can humanize ourselves for our students, sharing some of our challenges and imperfections to a degree that is appropriate and in our comfort zone. Often, our students only witness our confidence and competence, so we need to also let them see that we are vulnerable and make mistakes. This can look like telling your students when you're behind on grading and returning their exams and explaining to them why. It can sound like telling students if you earned a C (or worse!) on your paper in your graduate course, how you feel about it, and what you plan to do to try to improve your grade. Maybe you dented your car when pulling it into the garage or you regret how you handled a situation at the store.

The more we can show our humanity, the more our students can embrace their own imperfections. When the language of emotions becomes part of our classroom, our students can develop a more nuanced vocabulary to describe how they're feeling. This more accurate picture will help the students be more connected to their emotional experience and also determine and ask for the support they need. These understandings are also critical because the way we support a student who is feeling sad is quite different from how we may talk to a student who is feeling guilty or afraid.

ficity of language is critical for self-awareness, self-regulation, and connection. roscientist Lisa Feldman Barrett (2018) refers to this facility with language as *emotional granularity*:

> One of the best things you can do for your emotional health is to beef up your concepts of emotions. . . . You've probably never thought about learning words as a path to greater emotional health, but it follows directly from the neuroscience of construction. . . . Each word is another invitation to construct your experiences in new ways.

Another consideration that supports students' emotional fluency is coursework that is engaging and relevant to their lives. We can ensure our instruction is worthy of students' attention when we adapt our curriculum so that it is responsive to the students in front of us. Students should be reading books that feature characters who reflect their experiences, solving the kinds of problems they encounter in their lives, and engaging in activities that align with their passions and interests. When students feel connected to the work they are doing, it is generative; there is much more to explore and discuss, and the learning transcends the school day because it matters to students. They will continue reading a novel that speaks to their experience beyond what is required because they are invested. They will research how to solve a compelling problem after school because the solution is consequential. They will reach out to you to discuss a topic in greater depth or seek feedback when they care about the topic at hand. Teachers support fluency in the language of emotions, and academic fluency in general, when they allow students to communicate when they have something they want to talk about. And that happens when students are self-aware, motivated, and engaged in the work they are doing in school.

Effective Decision Making

It is critical that our students learn how to identify and understand their emotions to preserve their limited bank of self-control (already compromised due to their underdeveloped access to their prefrontal cortex). According to neuroscience research, the prefrontal cortex isn't done developing until one's mid-twenties. The prefrontal cortex is "responsible for neurobehavioral excitement," which means that "adolescents are risk-taking and novelty-seeking individuals and they are more likely to weigh positive experiences more heavily and negative experiences less so than adults" (Arain et al., 2013, p. 450). Students need to actively cultivate self-awareness to make well-informed decisions, from completing assignments and managing their time to communicating their needs to the teacher and working with others.

One way we can support our students in learning how to recognize and leverage their emotions toward more effective decision making is through reflection. Since people are all guided by their emotions, they often have difficulty recognizing their actions and reactions from moment to moment; this is especially true for students powering through their long school days. However, if we prioritize time for student reflection and draw on the questions Ginwright offers to harness hindsight, we can help our students steadily improve their capacity to make better decisions by reflecting on the outcomes of past decisions. These questions are useful and relevant to many aspects of teaching and learning. Students can use them for individual reflection after completing tasks or projects. You can use the questions to facilitate small- and whole-group discussions, including restorative conversations when classroom norms are not upheld. You can even use the questions for reflection on your own instructional decisions and practices.

Spotlight On: Engaging in Reflective Practice

Consider these questions from Ginwright (2022):

- *Knowing what I know now, would I have done anything differently?*
- *What is the major lesson or takeaway from this situation?*
- *What could I have done better, or where might I have grown?*
- *How will this help me in the future? (p. 45)*

One question we might add to Ginwright's list for the purpose of restorative conversations is this: What was the precise emotional state that informed this decision? This additional question can give our students (and us) a more nuanced understanding of how particular emotional states tend to impact our decisions.

Beth uses the following guidepost (from an unknown author) to help her pause before making important decisions: "Between stimulus and response, there is a space. In that space is our power to choose our response. In our response lies our growth and our freedom." This mantra reminds her to give herself time before responding too quickly in a way she might later regret, whether that response involves writing an email, volunteering for something she may not have time for, or even deciding whether to invest time in cooking dinner or to order takeout. She also shares this mantra with her students. When we all prioritize reflection, take time to pause, or simply become more intentional in our decision making, it truly does impact our growth and freedom. Chapter 6 (page 173) explores more deeply the power of listening to our inner voice and how the stories we tell ourselves can lead to our liberation.

As we solidify this understanding that prioritizing our students' emotional intelligence and fluency is critical to their academic success and overall well-being, it follows that we carefully consider how we define and measure success by asking ourselves broader questions like these: What is it that we value most for our students? Is it that they are content-area specialists? High scorers? Or is it that they are well-rounded and self-aware individuals, ready to use their gifts to adapt and find joy in an ever-changing world? We likely already know the answer, and Brackett (2019) frames it this way: "Is it math skills, scientific knowledge, athletic ability? Or is it confidence, kindness, a sense of purpose, the wisdom to build healthy, lasting relationships?" (p. 20). If our aspirations for our students are this lofty and comprehensive, then we need to consider both what kind of classroom will nurture these outcomes and what roadblocks might be standing in our way.

It's understandable that attending to our students' emotional lives might feel overwhelming and even beyond our area of expertise. Teachers are already expected to meet ever-changing programming demands, and social-emotional learning initiatives can often feel like just one more thing to be responsible for. And although it may be tempting to consider whether a greater focus on social-emotional learning initiatives is creating more sensitive and less emotionally resilient students, tending to our students' emotional lives is not what is causing students to be more sensitive. Brackett (2019) notes that in reality, our students just *are* more sensitive these days, but he asserts this is not a detriment.

Sensitivity is an *asset* for learning, and neuroscientist Mary Helen Immordino-Yang says it well: "It's literally neurobiologically impossible to remember or think deeply about anything that you haven't felt emotion about" (Varlas, 2018).

What our students most need are the skills and abilities to harness their sensitivity and articulate the information they gather from being in touch with their emotions, which are precisely the skills and dispositions of emotional intelligence and fluency. Although it might seem counterintuitive, the path to more resilient students lies in welcoming emotions into our classrooms—both positive and negative. With students' increased emotional intelligence and fluency, we will have a greater facility to be honest with them about their progress and build their capacity to receive and act on our feedback, which is necessary for learning and increasingly successful outcomes. As we strengthen our ability to integrate our students' emotional lives into our instructional decisions, the payoffs for both learning and overall well-being will be immeasurable.

Introspective Exercises for Teachers

Engage in the following exercises to examine how the ideas in this chapter could impact and inspire your teaching practice and inform your instructional decisions.

Introspective Exercise One: Building Educator Self-Awareness Pathways

Much of the work of cultivating emotionally literate classrooms is rooted in our own self-awareness, our ability to look objectively at our teaching practice, and our ability to be compassionate with ourselves when we fall short of achieving our goals. The strategies and resources offered in table 1.2 represent intersections between Marc Brackett's (2019) philosophy of staying curious and open about emotions (what he terms being an *emotion scientist*) and familiar, tried-and-true research-based practices. Consider incorporating one or more of these into your own life to further connect with your emotional experiences for your personal well-being and to be a model for students.

TABLE 1.2: Pathways to Building Educator Self-Awareness

Strategy: Increase your knowledge of emotional intelligence and emotional fluency.
Read: • *Atlas of the Heart* by Brené Brown (2021) • *Permission to Feel* by Marc Brackett (2019) **Listen:** • *Ten Percent Happier* podcast with Dan Harris (www.tenpercent.com/podcast) • *We Can Do Hard Things* podcast with Glennon Doyle (http://wecandohardthingspodcast.com) **Practice:** • Exercises by Byron Katie (https://bit.ly/3Z8SpRR)

continued ▶

Strategy: Incorporate a five- to ten-minute mindfulness action into your daily schedule.
Practice:
• Connecting with a friend, a family member, or nature • Practicing mindful breathing or meditation
Access:
(Access the following in Google Play or the Apple App Store. Some offer free introductory subscriptions for educators; some are entirely free.)
• Breethe (https://breethe.com) • Headspace (www.headspace.com) • Sanctuary With Rod Stryker (https://bit.ly/3YveMk6) • Smiling Mind (www.smilingmind.com.au)
Strategy: Implement a daily practice of keeping a written, digital, or voice journal.
Access:
• Built-in recording apps (already installed on your smartphone or tablet) • Google Keep (https://keep.google.com; part of Google Workspace) • Day One app (https://dayoneapp.com)
Strategy: Seek out a therapist or critical friend or group with whom you can work to reflect on your practice.
Practice:
• National School Reform Faculty resource on the Critical Friends Groups protocol (https://bit.ly/3JQd6h4)

Introspective Exercise Two: Increasing Overall Well-Being and Creativity

Cultivating happiness in your own life will have a positive effect on you and will also increase your capacity to support your students in their emotional growth and pursuit of happiness. As Leonard Mlodinow (2022) writes, "research shows that happy people are more creative, open to new information, and flexible and efficient in their thinking" (p. 87). Mlodinow's assertion is supported by *positive psychology*, which is a "scientific approach to studying human thoughts, feelings, and behavior" that focuses on strengths versus weaknesses (Ackerman, 2018). Positive psychology suggests that "a relatively small change in one's perspective can lead to astounding shifts in well-being and quality of life" (Ackerman, 2018).

Use table 1.3 to focus on increasing your own happiness, and share these ideas with your students.

TABLE 1.3: Ideas for Increasing Overall Well-Being and Creativity

Question for Identification (Mlodinow, 2022)	Practice
What is going well for you?	Express gratitude. Celebrate small (and large) wins. Either can be done quietly to yourself, in writing, or to someone else.
What are some small, simple things you enjoy?	Reflect on what small joys get you through the day—a cup of coffee and National Public Radio on your drive to work, a can of seltzer with lunch, or a scenic route home at the end of the day? Fit one or two of these into your daily life. Consider what about the natural world fills you with awe or wonder. Expose yourself to these elements directly or follow your curiosity to learn more about them.
What relationships in your life help you feel seen and understood?	Make time to talk or visit with these people often. Asynchronous voice apps can help with keeping in touch (such as Voxer or iPhone in-text voice memos).
What social activities do you enjoy?	Identify two or three social activities you enjoy, and reflect on how you currently spend your time so you can be intentional about engaging in them on a more regular basis.
What fills your cup when you're feeling depleted?	Identify what activities, people, or aspects of the natural world help you feel recharged. When you need to restore your energy supply, let your intuition guide you toward increased wellness.
What is your favorite kind of physical movement?	Move your body and enjoy the stress relief, elation, and health benefits.

Classroom Strategies

These strategies are inspired by the ideas in this chapter and designed for immediate classroom use. Use these strategies with your students to cultivate qualities that empower them to gain greater self-awareness and lead their own learning.

Classroom Strategy One: Co-Creating an Emotional Intelligence Charter

Many of us are familiar with setting norms or expectations for students, either for our classrooms or for particular discussions or activities. These norms are generally more effective when we co-create them with students, so students feel included and integral to the process. Brackett (2019) offers this same idea, but he says it is "how everybody . . . wishes to feel" (p. 181). Figure 1.2 presents a way to create a class-room charter that combines Brackett's idea with some more traditional classroom norming ideas.

	What is a one-word description?	What might this look like?	What might this sound like?	What might this feel like?
How do we want to feel as a class?				
What can we do to experience these feelings as often as possible?				
What can we do when we are not living the charter?				

Source: Adapted from Brackett, 2019.

FIGURE 1.2: Chart for co-creating an emotional intelligence charter.

*Visit **go.SolutionTree.com/teacherefficacy** for a free reproducible version of this figure.*

Offer this chart to students and give them time to independently consider a one-word description for each entry in the first column. Students can then discuss their responses in small groups to co-create a more robust list of words. You may want each group to share the words they came up with and then have the groups decide what each one-word description might look like, sound like, and feel like. Capture student responses either digitally or on chart paper so you can display these norms as a reminder and a guide for you and your students.

Classroom Strategy Two: Strengthening Emotional Literacy

Finding the words to express how we feel is the first step to understanding our emotions and noticing how they affect our actions and reactions. Brackett (2019) notes, "Emotional skills are the missing link in a child's ability to grow up to be a successful adult" (p. 66). Helping students develop accurate ways to express their emotions empowers them to advocate for the kind of support they need. In a visible place in your classroom, display Marc Brackett's *RULER* acronym along with either Brackett's Mood Meter (www.marcbrackett.com/the-colors-of-our-emotions) or the extensive list of emotions from education author Elena Aguilar (2018). Visit https://tinyurl.com/34hf6zuu for the full list of emotions that fall under each of these categories.

- Anger

- Disgust

- Fear

- Happiness

- Jealousy

- Love

- Sadness

- Shame

 The RULER acronym stands for the following.

- **R**ecognize what we're feeling.

- **U**nderstand what we've discovered.

- **L**abel our emotions.

- **E**xpress our feelings.

- **R**egulate our emotions (for example, use them wisely to achieve our goals).

Build in regular time to practice noticing and labeling emotions. Visit http://mood meterapp.com for a Mood Meter app and www.rulerapproach.org if you want to learn more about Brackett's RULER approach for social-emotional learning.

Then, because emotions are important information, you can invite students to reflect on their emotional experience at key times during lessons—for example, after receiving direct instruction, while working independently or in groups, or after completing a task. Helping them decode what those emotions might be telling them is a powerful way to help them navigate their academic and social lives. Table 1.4 (page 36) shows an example of how you might facilitate this kind of reflection.

Note that when using this approach, you may want students to have a dedicated space to stop and jot as they practice their emotional fluency.

TABLE 1.4: Example of Strengthening Emotional Literacy

RULER Framework (Brackett, 2019)	Example One	Example Two
Recognize what we're feeling. *Right now, in my body . . .*	My head feels like there are too many things going on. My stomach is tense.	I feel light and energetic.
Understand what we've discovered. *I feel . . .*	I feel like I've totally spaced out and missed the lesson my teacher just did.	The lesson made sense to me, and I was able to connect it to yesterday.
Label our emotions. *My core emotions are . . .*	I am uncertain and a little uneasy.	I am excited and cheerful.
Express our feelings. *When I put this information together, I can tell that . . .*	I was unsure of what was going on, so I lost track of the concepts being covered. Now, I don't know what to do.	I am feeling ready to take on the next part of the lesson.
Regulate our emotions (use them wisely to achieve our goals). *Now I can . . .*	Remember that everyone gets confused sometimes, check my resources, and ask my teacher to meet if I can't figure it out.	Focus on the first task ahead.

Classroom Strategy Three: Incorporating Affective Statements

Restorative practices in schools arose out of the restorative justice movement as a way to resolve conflicts through communication and healing. Restorative justice practices are deeply rooted in Indigenous cultures and they prioritize "strengthening relationships between individuals and ties to one another in their communities" (Marsh, 2019). As defined in *The Restorative Practices Handbook*, the movement "seeks to develop good relationships and restore a sense of community in an increasingly disconnected world" (Costello, Wachtel, & Wachtel, 2009, p. 7).

We can model emotional fluency for our students by incorporating affective statements. *Affective statements* seek to honor our feelings that occur in our daily interactions, and they can be used whenever we want to effectively acknowledge desirable behavior in students. By using affective statements, we model the specificity involved in emotional fluency, and students learn to communicate in an objective and meaningful way, which will establish trust and psychological safety. A well-crafted affective statement consists of a description of a behavior and precisely how it makes you feel or the observable quality it demonstrates.

Table 1.5 lists some types of behavior you might respond to, along with examples and non-examples of affective statements you might use when responding.

TABLE 1.5: Implementing Affective Statements

Type of Behavior	Example	Non-Example
Successful (at an attempt or task)	"When I heard that you scored the winning goal in the soccer game, I was proud of you because I know how hard you worked."	"Congratulations on scoring the winning goal in the soccer game. Well done!"
Hardworking	"I see how dedicated you are to solving that problem. I am impressed by your ability to persevere through such challenging work."	"Nice work on solving that problem. It was really difficult."
Collaborative	"I'm noticing how well you're listening to and building on each other's ideas. It means a lot to me that you are working so well together."	"You're really working so well together."

Visit the International Institute for Restorative Practices website at https://bit.ly/4311wql for information about restorative justice.

Questions for Reflection and Discussion

In this section, you will find three different types of questions: questions for individual reflection, questions for conversation, and jigsaw questions across chapters.

Each offers you a specific way to think through additional questions about concepts from the chapter.

Questions for Individual Reflection

Consider the following questions to think more deeply about how the ideas in this chapter apply to your practice.

- In what ways did this chapter shift your thinking about the importance of cultivating students' emotional intelligence in your classroom?

- Based on the research- and evidence-based examples in this chapter, it is clear that recognizing and supporting our students' capacity to become more emotionally intelligent are critical to their learning and overall well-being. Which strategies or ideas discussed here feel the most relevant or hold the most promise for your practice?

- Notice how the suggestion to adapt curriculum and instruction toward nurturing students' emotional intelligence feels to you. Consider what factors—from your personal life, your experiences within your district, and your history in the classroom—might shape your response to this suggestion. What else do you need to know or what resources do you need to have in order to feel more willing or able to make these changes?

Questions for Conversation

Consider the following questions to converse about the ideas in this chapter and to leverage these insights toward improving your school.

- Leonard Mlodinow (2022) provides a wealth of evidence to demonstrate how our feelings impact our thinking. Can you share a particular instance when your emotional state clearly impacted one of your actions, reactions, or decisions and how it might have differed if at the time you had dedicated time to increasing your capacity to regulate your emotions? Which of the strategies or approaches might have worked in this instance?

- Shawn Ginwright (2022) offers that the way to transform our relationships and our desired outcomes is through building greater self-awareness. If you agree, discuss the extent to which you are already doing this in your life or classroom. Brainstorm ways you might extend your efforts even further for your own benefit and your students'. If you disagree, what about this idea brings up resistance? What are your thoughts about how best to transform relationships and achieve the outcomes we're looking for?

- Marc Brackett (2019) explores how attending to our students' emotional lives is critical to student learning. Share about a time when you've noticed evidence of how students' emotions affect their ability to learn. Based on these anecdotes, discuss what strategies from the chapter hold the most promise for your students.

- Discuss how the skills and competencies explored in this chapter help cultivate more equitable learning environments.

Jigsaw Questions Across Chapters

Consider the following questions for conversation with individuals who read a different chapter. Share insights and discover how the intersection of these ideas might spark creative solutions to both impact student learning and improve your experiences as educators.

- Can you summarize an inspiring idea from this chapter in your own words? In what way did this idea cause you to think differently about your practice? How might this idea offer insight to you personally?

- What word or quote from this chapter resonates with you?

- What voices and perspectives are not represented in this text?

- What idea, introspective exercise, or strategy from the chapter holds the most promise for you, and why and how would you implement it in your classroom?

- What is one takeaway from this chapter that you'd like to share with students, colleagues, or your team?

- What additional readings can you bring to the conversation? What other texts or articles could further advance everyone's thinking on this topic?

Conclusion

The insights offered in this chapter support the belief that attending to students' social-emotional well-being is essential to learning. Mlodinow helps us understand, from a neuroscientific perspective, why people behave the way they do; Ginwright offers unique approaches from his experience as a social justice advocate; and Brackett connects these understandings to the classroom.

If this is an area you are interested in exploring further, visit the CASEL website at https://bit.ly/3zyJLBp for ready-to-use classroom strategies and resources to implement as professional development. Visit https://bit.ly/40Ztcdk for Brené Brown's list of terms and phrases that can help you establish a common language to develop the emotional intelligence of a group and enhance relationships and collective efforts.

CHAPTER 2

BALANCING TECHNOLOGY USE IN THE CLASSROOM

> People will come to adore the technologies
> that undo their capacities to think.
>
> —Neil Postman

Our interest in exploring the impact of the rush of digital technology into the classroom grew from direct experience in our teaching and our personal lives. For Katie, once again, the work of becoming a parent compelled her to grow deeply invested in understanding the nuances of the impact of digital technology on humans' brains. Becoming a parent in 2016, she felt a pressing need to understand the risks associated with screen exposure and other elements of living in a digital world, especially those related to attention and mood. For Beth, frustration stemmed from students' distractibility resulting both from phone use and district-issued one-to-one devices, which continually challenged teachers. Similar to Katie, she looked to the research to try to understand ways to proceed that were in the best interest of students. We invite you to join us in exploring this topic, along with Jenny Odell, Cal Newport, and Johann Hari, and think about how it may resonate with you.

Ideas to Consider

The ubiquity of screens was celebrated as a landmark moment in education. Many districts raced to implement one-to-one initiatives, making sure that each student across K–12 was equipped with a device to support their academic needs in school and at home. Professional development was geared toward supporting, even encouraging, the ever-expanding daily use of devices. Teachers were prodded to make haste in digitizing course materials and instructional resources. As a result, students gained nearly constant access to their grades, assignments, and instructors, in addition to a wealth of digital resources designed to support and enhance their learning. Many of these developments have inarguably made our classrooms more engaging and efficient, and in this chapter, we in no way intend to contest these realities. Our intent here is to examine not *whether* technology has a place in the classroom, but instead *what role* it should play and when.

Technology overuse has become a reality of many a modern classroom, and indeed of modern life. Both long-standing and emerging research demonstrate that students' well-being, from their ability to think clearly and focus to their access to healthy identity development, is threatened by the dominance of screens in their everyday life (Beyers & Luyckx, 2016; Crone & Konijn, 2018; Dakanalis et al., 2015; Ehrenreich & Underwood, 2016; Eichhorn, 2019; Hale & Guan, 2015; Ra et al., 2018; Tamana et al., 2019). And *dominance* is no hyperbole. The American Academy of Child and Adolescent Psychiatry (AACAP, 2020) estimates that children aged eight to twelve years spend between four and six hours a day on screens; teenagers clock in at up to nine hours a day. Abroad, similar trends exist. In Australia, for example, children are spending at least three hours a day on screens by the age of twelve (Australian Institute of Family Studies, 2016). In Canada, children between five and seventeen years old are spending an average of at least three hours on screens each day (Statistics Canada, 2019). The impact of this overabundance of screen time amounts to no less than a public health crisis; virtually every aspect of a child's health is worsened by overuse of screens. The AACAP (2020) states that overuse can lead to issues with sleep, grades, mood, weight, self-image, body image, and a lack of relaxation. All these issues coalesce into attention problems, nervous system dysregulation, poor mental health, and compromised physical health. Tempting as it may be to place the onus solely on parents and caregivers, there is simply no way to separate these concerns from the work of the classroom—nor from the *screens in the classroom*.

In our shared enthusiasm to embrace the myriad ways technology has positively impacted schools, those of us who are educators have not had time to fully grapple with how technology use during the school day can feed our students' unhealthy relationships with screens. Ultimately, despite our best intentions, we are falling short of helping our students cultivate a habit that could not be more central to the work of learning: the ability to pay attention. William James (1918), often referred to as the father of American psychology, devotes much time to the issue of attention in his classic text, *The Principles of Psychology*:

> *Whether the attention come by grace of genius or by dint of will, the longer one does attend to a topic the more mastery of it one has. And the faculty of voluntarily bringing back a wandering attention, over and over again, is the very root of judgment, character, and will. No one is* compos sui *[master of oneself] if he have it not. An education which should improve this faculty would be* the *education par excellence. (emphasis in original; p. 424)*

Indeed, what we desire for every student is an education *par excellence*. But the present situation is dire; in our field's continued zeal for instructional technology, we have contributed to the short-circuiting of our students' ability to cultivate focus and attention (Beyers & Luyckx, 2016; Crone & Konijn, 2018; Dakanalis et al., 2015; Ehrenreich & Underwood, 2016; Eichhorn, 2019; Hale & Guan, 2015; Ra et al., 2018; Tamana et al., 2019).

In addition to harming students' focus and attention, further evidence of the negative effects of technology overuse on academic performance comes from a 2019 meta-analysis that used data from over ninety countries, including the U.S., Australia, and Canada. The comprehensive findings include the following (Bouygues, 2019).

- Research found "no increased learning outcomes with an increased investment in technology" (Bouygues, 2019, p. 27).

- Globally, students "appear to perform best on tests when they report a low-to-moderate use of school computers" (Bouygues, 2019, p. 27).

- Students with infrequent classroom computer use show better performance, but "when students report using these devices every day and for several hours during the school day, performance lowers dramatically" (Bouygues, 2019, p. 27). This is true in the U.S. regardless of students' backgrounds and whether the teacher is experienced in technology-based instruction.

- "A potentially negative relationship between technology and performance may be more apparent among early grade levels, such as when tablets are used for reading literacy among U.S. elementary school students. This fits with prior studies that show that reading on electronic devices is less likely to improve young students' reading ability" (Bouygues, 2019, p. 27).

This chapter is an invitation to think critically about technology use in your classroom and teaching practice. We (Beth and Katie) know that students are spending anywhere from four to nine hours on screens a day, and we know from experience in our own classrooms and knowledge of our colleagues' practices that students are often asked to use their devices on *most* days—and, based on our experience at the secondary level, in *most* classes. Therefore, it is easy to see how technology overuse cannot merely be a problem limited to the sphere of a student's home life. The applications that we and our students are immersed in, in our private lives and increasingly in our school and work lives, are designed by corporations that have a very basic business model. That business model can be summed up this way: the longer the users are engaged, the more money the corporations make from advertisers. As such, this technology is necessarily addictive, because addictive technology leads to more user engagement, whether that user is seven or seventy (Andersson, 2018; Levounis & Sherer, 2022; Montag, Lachmann, Herrlich, & Zweig, 2019).

In this chapter, we explore how addictive technology of the digital world negatively impacts people's time, attention, bodies, and minds. Then, we explore the implications for our pedagogy and practice and offer strategies for making changes that maximize students' ability to pay attention to their learning and their world. As educators, we are powerfully positioned to help reverse the tide of technology overuse. We can help our students reclaim their brains and attention from the distractions that abound in the digital sphere and the corporations that would gladly continue to profit from their attention.

While this chapter focuses exclusively on balancing technology use, you will find that the ideas intersect with others throughout the book as we strive to cultivate more self-awareness in our teaching and balance in our classrooms. In chapter 1 (page 9), for example, we discuss how to strengthen our own and our students' emotional intelligence, balancing a focus on academic skills with this other goal. In chapter 3 (page 79), you find the theme of balance emerging in our discussion of how to cultivate practices that help our students sow the seeds of a more civil society.

Jenny Odell on Addictive Technology, Attention, and Culture

What has addictive technology done to our collective ability to pay attention? To our bodies and minds? How has it impacted our ability to gain a nuanced understanding of the unique challenges of our time, and to summon the forces necessary to address these challenges? How does the attention economy demand ever more of our time, in the process disconnecting us from our physical selves, our place in the natural world, and one another? And how does the monetization of our attention by technology corporations hold us back as individuals and communities as we strive toward wellness and justice?

These are just a few of the questions that Jenny Odell (2019), artist and Stanford University professor of art and design, explores in her groundbreaking, widely acclaimed book, *How to Do Nothing: Resisting the Attention Economy.* The questions she asks are relevant to every area of our lives, and to the direction we choose to move toward as a culture. She notes the following:

> Patterns of attention—what we choose to notice and what we do not—
> are how we render reality for ourselves, and thus have a direct bearing
> on what we feel is possible at any given time. These aspects, taken
> together, suggest to me, the revolutionary potential of taking back our
> attention. (Odell, 2019, p. xxiii)

What does Odell mean, exactly, by the attention economy from which we must *take back our attention*? As this chapter has established, the business model of technology corporations is to capture our attention and sell it to advertisers. In short, *attention economy* is Odell's name for this economy, one that treats our attention as currency—not metaphorical currency, but an actual commodity to be translated into actual dollars and cents. To those who may fear that Odell (2019) is simply teetering into Luddite territory, opposing technology as a whole, she offers an important clarification:

> I am not anti-technology. . . . Rather, I am opposed to the way that cor-
> porate platforms buy and sell our attention. . . . I am concerned about
> the effects of current social media on expression—including the right
> to not express oneself—and its deliberately addictive features. But the
> villain here is not necessarily the Internet, or even the idea of social
> media; it is the invasive logic of commercial social media and its finan-
> cial incentive to keep us in a profitable state of anxiety, envy, and dis-
> traction. (p. xii)

In response to these conditions, Odell offers mindsets that can empower us to take back our precious time, energy, and ability to attend to the things in our lives that matter. First, we will examine her observations about reclaiming a physical sense of oneself and one's environment by grounding oneself in time and place. Then, we will review her recommendations for practicing resistance in the form of what she calls *refusal in place* (Odell, 2019).

Grounding Oneself in Time and Place

Odell (2019) observes that one of the most pernicious features of addictive technology is its ability, by design, to render irrelevant the features of time and place in which we physically exist. This may sound ideal to some—who does not enjoy the ability of technology to ease the monotony of some features of daily life? But our sense of time and place is our way of orienting ourselves to one another and the world. It is how we make sense, actual *sensory* sense, of our lives. And when we are swept away from these physical realities too often, we lose touch with our own needs, our relationships, and our surroundings, to the detriment of our physical and mental health (Brigham and Women's Hospital, 2014; Odell, 2019).

Further, Odell argues that when we are entrenched in the world of addictive technology, we don't just lose track of our physical time and place. We also become convinced that there is some vision of perfection we can meet (and that others have surely achieved it). We experience a "placelessness of an optimized life spent online" (Odell, 2019, p. xviii). When we start to spend too much time in the digital sphere, we begin to imagine that we are just one step away from the optimal *everything*: relationship, home, gadget, career, physique.

As an alternative and a salve to the way addictive technology yanks us out of place and time and convinces us that we can have the shiny life it advertises, Odell offers us the practice of *doing nothing*. She doesn't actually mean *doing nothing*—except she kind of does. Doing nothing translates into any leisure activity (or lack of activity) that you find pleasurable, meaningful, restful, or restorative. If our addictive technology implores us to ignore our bodily selves, doing nothing urges us to tap into them, to be aware, and to find the space we need for resting and reenergizing. Doing nothing can range from daydreaming in your bed or observing the natural world through your window to taking a walk outside or talking with a friend. The idea is to intentionally create habits that help you begin to resist the attention economy— habits that remind you of ways of engaging with your physical self instead of the digital world, and everything those ways have to offer you.

Doing nothing does not just help you reclaim your sense of time and place. It is a philosophical parting with the lifestyle addictive tech wants to sell us. Odell (2019) writes:

The practice of doing nothing has something broader to offer us. . . .
What I'm suggesting is that we take a protective stance toward our-
selves [and] each other . . . that we protect our spaces and our time for
non-instrumental, noncommercial activity and thought for maintenance,
for care, for conviviality. And I'm suggesting that we fiercely protect our
human animality against all technologies that actively ignore and disdain
the body, the bodies of other beings, and the body of the landscape that
we inhabit. (pp. 25, 28–29)

If you question whether Odell is overstating the degree to which the attention economy can draw us out of place and time and absorb great swaths of our time, pause to count the number of apps or websites you have consulted or visited in the last twenty-four hours. With the tally in mind (we, Beth and Katie, quickly found ourselves in the double digits), you can begin to perceive what Odell means by *place-lessness*—the power of immersive, addictive technology to fracture our time, pull us out of our physical circumstances, and keep our minds trained on the infinite alerts, notifications, updates, content, replies, likes, comments, data summaries, and tallies our digital world encompasses. This operating model forces our brains to feel like we must always be following up on some digital piece of information, keeping one metaphorical foot out the door of the actual time and place in which we find ourselves.

Perhaps most importantly, these experiences crowd our awareness, hampering our ability to regulate our bodies, including everything from being ready for sleep to paying attention to more complex signals about stress and anxiety (Brigham and Women's Hospital, 2014; Lissak, 2018). If you question whether *this* is true, consider how many times you have realized how badly you needed to use the bathroom or get a bite to eat just as soon as you finished a video call or stopped scrolling on your favorite social media site. Further, it stands to reason that this digital immersion taxes the cognitive bandwidth we might otherwise possess to attend to the messages and needs of those around us. Often, our children and partners need to remind us (or we must remind them) to put down our devices in order to be fully present and offer the time and attention we all deserve.

We only have so much attention to give, so much energy to tend to the particularities of daily life. Absorption in our devices cuts us off from another important facet of being a human—socializing with other humans in our environment.

Trying Refusal in Place

As a means of resisting the attention economy and reclaiming our sense of time and place, Jenny Odell (2019) offers an elegant solution she terms *refusal in place*. The concept of refusing in place is one that sounds more aggressive than, in practice, it truly is. Odell is not suggesting that we act confrontationally or that we adopt a smug, elitist approach to technology in which we simply drop out or go off the grid. Rather, the act of refusal she advocates is wiser: reasoned and informed, grounded in convictions, values, and beliefs. *Refusing in place* is the practice of "refusing the frame of reference" (Odell, 2019, p. xvi)—of remaining in your current circumstances, whatever they may be, while steadfastly refusing to engage in some practice of the common experience because you take issue with the underlying assumptions of that practice. For example, in our lives, this might look like having a social media account but refusing to engage in endless scrolling on social media, or using text messaging to communicate with friends and family but refusing to feel pressure to immediately respond to texts. It might look like downloading the behavior management app that your child's elementary school uses but refusing to engage in the so-called *applaud* feature that recognizes digital points assigned to your child throughout the day.

We can also think about this in terms of Odell's (2019) *third space*, a term she employs very differently from its use in the domain of sociology. For Odell, it is a space in which we are neither acquiescing nor rejecting, but deciding for ourselves the premise on which we will make decisions: an "exit to another frame of reference . . . the third space can provide an important if unexpected harbor" (p. 69). In this space, we can be *in* the circumstances but not *of* them, ever aware of them, and able to clearly articulate the ideas or practices with which we take issue.

In order to demonstrate these concepts more clearly and help us operationalize them, Odell traces how refusal in place and the third space have been embodied by real and fictional persons throughout history. One example she provides is found in the character of Bartleby, the scrivener from the classic Herman Melville short story of the same name. Melville's fictional Bartleby is a clerk at a law office whose main task is to copy text with great accuracy and speed. Though he performs this job exceptionally well, his employer, the narrator, is vexed by his continuously aloof manner.

One day, Bartleby's employer asks him to check his copy of an important document against the original for accuracy. Bartleby refuses with the simple phrase, "I would prefer not to" (Melville, 1856, p. 21). Confused, the employer repeatedly makes the request and is met each time with either silence or the same reply. The employer makes other requests—that Bartleby run to the post office, help with tying up a package, tell the employer anything at all about his life—but Bartleby remains steadfast: "I prefer not to . . . at present, I prefer to give no answer" (Melville, 1856, p. 40). He continues to baffle his employer to the very end, eventually refusing to vacate the office entirely.

Though clearly the events of this short story reach the bounds of the absurd, it nonetheless serves as a useful study in refusing in place and finding a third space. Odell (2019) notes how Bartleby's verbiage of refusal is enlightening. He does not offer any variation of no—not *I will not*, *I cannot*, or *I refuse*. Instead, he employs *I prefer not to* and *I prefer to give no answer*. These are not merely variations on refusal. They demonstrate the power of finding a third space by refusing to conform to the conventional set of options we associate with any given situation. Bartleby refuses to provide a *yes* or a *no*. In doing so, he successfully undermines the question, "Will you do this?" by indeed answering a *different* question or set of questions altogether, starting with, "Would I prefer to do this?"

Undermining the terms of the question is of no small consequence. When we feel strongly, we can easily become wrapped up in purely reacting to a situation with which we disagree. It is more difficult to pause and consider what is actually being posited, asked, or offered. When we do, we can fine-tune our response so that it is commensurate with the issue at hand as *we* see it, not as it is presented. Like Bartleby, we can challenge the premise of the question itself.

This small shift has major implications for how we think about our own agency in the digital world, one that is very accustomed to our passive consent. (When was the last time you perused the terms of use before your phone updated? Your answer might be *never*.) In practice, this might mean replacing the question of whether you want to use a platform, whether you find it appealing or attractive or fun, with questions that examine the degree to which your online activity can withstand the addition of another app without tipping into unhealthy, addictive use patterns. When you answer *that* question, you reject the terms of the first and change your relationship to it altogether. You remove yourself from the role of the consumer of addictive technology, and instead empower yourself to consider the boundaries you want to uphold or revise according to your needs. Hence, you occupy a third space—one outside the confines of simply accepting or rejecting what is offered.

Like Bartleby, when we are able to match our refusal with firm conviction, we begin to occupy that third space Odell draws out and better resist the negative impacts of a life consumed by the digital sphere.

There are many paths to undoing our collective sense of placelessness and learning to practice refusal in place. To support our efforts toward each, we will now turn to Cal Newport's (2019) *Digital Minimalism: Choosing a Focused Life in a Noisy World*, a text that offers insights (explored in the next section) and approaches (explored later in this chapter) that can aid us in deciding which digital tools we *will* refuse to engage with outright, and which we may choose to use through inhabiting a third space.

Cal Newport on Addictive Technology, Attention, and the Individual

In addition to the ways addictive technology has impacted our cultures and societies, computer science professor Cal Newport's (2019) *Digital Minimalism* offers readers the opportunity to reflect on their individual relationships with digital tech tools and to become aware of the role immersive technology is playing in their lives. Newport helps readers understand the powerful forces that have shaped their addiction to digital technology tools and offers ideas for creating a healthier balance. He looks at built-in social networks and prioritizing conversation over connection.

Our Built-In Social Network

Losing oneself in thought, whether while commuting home (*How am I already in my driveway?*), reading a book (*Oops, let me flip back a page . . . or three*), or even meditating (*And I lost track of my breath when exactly?*), is a universal human experience. Perhaps just as universal at times are feelings of self-admonishment or disappointment in our failure to summon the focus and fortitude needed to stay engaged with the task at hand and not be led astray by a constant stream of thought. If you begin to reflect on these experiences as they occur, you will likely become aware that an outsize percentage of the thoughts in which you find yourself entangled concern your relationships to other humans—parents, children, family, friends, and colleagues.

Cal Newport (2019) traces the evolution of scientific understanding of how thoughts about our social world are indeed central to the human mind. He explains that in the late 1990s, the usefulness of the positron emission tomography (PET) scanner, a technology once limited in scope to medical diagnosis, was realized in the field of neuroscience. Initially, scans of brain activity created more questions than answers as researchers observed that when people were not busy with cognitive tasks, a mysterious network, originally referred to as the *task-induced deactivation network* (Newport, 2019), took over their brain activity. During tasks requiring participants to use cognitive processes (to think about something specific required by the experiment), the network was *deactivated*, and the areas of the brain associated with the task at hand lit up. But anytime test subjects were given a break during experiments, the task-induced deactivation network activated—lit right up again—on the PET scanner.

Still puzzled, researchers came to call this phenomenon of brain activity the *default network* (Newport, 2019). This network was activated even during breaks as short as three seconds. This exceedingly brief window of time is helpful for understanding how the word *default* applies: because three seconds is "a duration too short for [subjects] to decide to start thinking about something else," it is clear that the network activated without subjects exercising any will to make it happen (Newport, 2019, p. 134).

What could this network be? What could it be *doing* without any active attempt on our part to make it do anything at all? In time, the mystery was elucidated. Drawing on the work of neuroscientist Matthew D. Lieberman (2013), Newport (2019) explains how, once the default network was mapped and the use of PET scanners for neuroscience research became more extensive, scientists were eventually able to match the map to a "virtually identical" network map observed in other experiments: the network for social cognition. So, our default network—one over which we have no control, over which we can exercise no conscious will—is our network for social cognition. This network helps us process information about other people, our interactions with them, and our broader social world.

How can we know that the default network is, in fact, *default*—switching on without our conscious control? After all, Newport (2019) notes, it is only natural that we take a deep interest in our social lives. But further evidence of the default nature of this network is derived from observation of its automatic activation in humans regardless of age. In one study, even newborns' networks lit up during downtime. Newport (2019) quotes Lieberman (2013) when he explains the importance of this finding: "They 'clearly haven't cultivated an interest in the social world yet [and] cannot even focus their eyes.' This behavior must therefore be instinctual" (pp. 133–134).

When we confront the existence of a network dedicated to social cognition that our brains automatically switch on during our downtime, we can come to understand much more clearly the mass appeal and addictive qualities of social media and other connective digital tools that promise social connection. If we are hardwired to practice social thinking as a means to connection and survival, any tool that purports to facilitate this socializing and immerses us in an unending stream of social thinking will attract users. The creators of such tools are quite simply tapping into one of the most powerful built-in instincts humans possess. At their core, these tech tools have exploited a quintessential aspect of our humanity and have successfully convinced our brains that the digital social worlds they draw us into are as real and deserving of our time and attention as the analog ones that have engaged our species for hundreds of thousands of years.

The question then becomes, Are they as real? Do these social media and technology tools *actually* make our social lives richer and more connected? Next, we'll examine Cal Newport's perspective on this complex question.

Conversation Over Connection

Newport's (2019) *Digital Minimalism* argues there is nothing about the digital social media world that can or should serve as a substitute for the in-person social lives we have evolved to experience. After all, "our brains evolved during a period when the *only* communication was offline and face-to-face . . . [requiring] our brains to process large amounts of information about subtle analog cues such as body language, facial expressions, and voice tone" (p. 142). Social media may be quicker, more convenient, and, ultimately, addictive, but none of these qualities approaches the qualifications that we would name as important to developing and maintaining strong relationships.

Newport (2019) surveys a bevy of research that demonstrates the effects of social media. Studies that evidence positive impacts (many funded by social media giants themselves) look at the impact of "*specific behaviors* of social media users," such as liking a relative's photo or posting more often, while those that find negative effects focus on how the "*overall use* of these services" (p. 140) impacts users. These studies, at best, find mixed results on whether social media makes individuals feel happier and more connected to others. At worst, they find social media significantly increases social isolation and feelings of loneliness and depression. This amounts to a bit of a paradox that Newport (2019) resolves by noting if something positive is gained from specific social media behaviors, it is far outweighed by the negative effects observed as the degree of someone's overall use increases.

We are very good at convincing ourselves that the positive impacts of quick, feel-good hits on social media, like a distant cousin's comment on our child's photo or a nostalgic post from someone in an alma mater group, outweigh the potential negatives. Yet, it is just these quick, feel-good moments that teach us to continue seeking out dopamine hits more and more often from these sites, increasing the likelihood that we will trade in more of our offline lives to immerse ourselves in these platforms. It's a simple equation: as our use increases, we are robbed of the "real-world socializing that's massively more valuable. As the negative studies imply, the more you use social media, the less time you tend to devote to offline interaction, and therefore the worse this value deficit becomes" (Newport, 2019, p. 141). Because we are social creatures, the negative impact of social media on the individual is necessarily linked to a negative impact on that person's familial and social relationships. And these relationships are what make or break our overall sense of well-being.

To further explore the degree to which social media and other connective technology tools fail to replace face-to-face social worlds, Newport turns to the work of Massachusetts Institute of Technology (MIT) professor Sherry Turkle. Turkle's research focuses on how humans experience technology, and Newport draws on ideas she surfaces in her 2015 book, *Reclaiming Conversation: The Power of Talk in a Digital Age*. She notes a trend that she refers to as a *flight from conversation* (Turkle, 2015) and details the harm and havoc this reality is wreaking on our relationships and well-being at all ages, from students to professionals:

> *Turkle, for example, introduces her readers to middle school students who struggle with empathy, as they lack the practice of reading facial cues that comes from conversation. . . . Turning her attention to the workplace, Turkle finds young employees who retreat to email because the thought of an unstructured conversation terrifies them, and unnecessary office tensions that fester when communication shifts from nuanced conversation to ambiguous connection. (Newport, 2019, p. 145)*

The nuances of facial cues and tone that we can pick up from face-to-face conversations are, of course, completely obliterated by digital communications. As educators, we know this all too well. We have received written communications from caregivers and students that confound and sometimes even frustrate us with their ambiguity, causing us to project our own ideas about tone onto them. (*Is this parent being rude, or are they just in a hurry? Doesn't this student remember that I retaught this lesson in an optional small group? Why are they demanding materials now?*)

Turkle encourages us to create more opportunities for conversation in our lives and to prioritize *conversation* over *connection*. Newport lauds Turkle's goal but goes a step further, asserting that digital communication tools, in all their allure and convenience, can easily make the aim of incorporating more conversation into our lives just one more failed resolution. Instead, he insists that "the shift in behavior will need to be more fundamental" (Newport, 2019, p. 146). He questions our contemporary conception that both connection (quick digital exchanges of information) and conversation (analog communication with people we care about) are elements we need in conjunction to support healthy social lives. He suggests we must break with the myth that we can, essentially, have it all—that we can maintain true relationships through both occasional, or perhaps even rare, actual conversations and quotidian use of social media functions such as the like, heart, or comment. Instead, he puts forth a philosophy and accompanying practices that he refers to as *conversation-centric communication*:

> The philosophy of conversation-centric communication takes a harder stance. It argues that conversation is the only form of interaction that in some sense counts toward maintaining a relationship. . . . Anything textual or non-interactive—basically, all social media, email, text, and instant messaging—doesn't count as conversation and should instead be categorized as mere connection. (p. 147)

Newport (2019) redefines connection, then, as a means to an end. You might use a text or email to schedule a visit or a phone or video call with a friend, or to ask a logistical question you need a quick answer to. But "connection is no longer an alternative to conversation; it's instead its supporter" (p. 148).

This shift away from connection and toward conversation necessitates that we confront the false sense of sociality we may believe we already have in our lives. After all, if we are prioritizing real conversation, we will simply have less time to maintain weak relationships via social media, less energy for the scroll and like. But this feeling of loss is entirely necessary for us to feel more connected in our actual relationships. It is also illusory:

> Conversation is the good stuff; it's what we crave as humans and what provides us with the sense of community and belonging necessary to thrive. . . . The richness of these analog interactions will far outweigh what you're leaving behind. . . . You cannot expect an app dreamed up in a dorm room . . . to successfully replace the types of rich interactions

to which we've painstakingly adapted over millennia. Our sociality is simply too complex to be outsourced to a social network or reduced to instant messages and emojis. (Newport, 2019, pp. 150–151)

Ultimately, it is hard to argue with the assertion that social media and other connective tech tools have robbed us of many elements of genuine relationships. Many of us feel so caught up in the matrix of social media that it seems inextricable from our social lives. But Newport shows us that another path is possible, and that we can take steps toward focusing on the relationships that matter most to our lives. As we consider this alternate path, we must also understand the systemic forces at play that are working against us, as outlined by journalist Johann Hari.

Johann Hari on the Business of Big Tech, Attention, and Society

Journalist Johann Hari is known for his ability to take on the complexities of understanding seemingly all-encompassing social and political problems (and to deftly explain them to the rest of us). In his past works, he has delved into the details of the war on drugs and its disastrous effects on communities and explored the roots of widespread depression in Western societies. In his work *Stolen Focus: Why You Can't Pay Attention—And How to Think Deeply Again*, Hari (2022) examines forces much larger than the individual and the cultural to understand how the attention span of entire societies has been ravaged by social media. He provides a thorough examination of the business model that social media corporations are based on: the model of *surveillance capitalism*, a term first coined by Shoshana Zuboff (2019) in her book *The Age of Surveillance Capitalism: The Fight for a Human Future at the New Frontier of Power.*

In a 2019 interview with *The Harvard Gazette*, Zuboff describes the process by which big tech corporations collect all the data they can about you and then use the data themselves or sell them to advertisers to target your potential interests, wants, and needs and sell you stuff (Zuboff's term is essentially synonymous with Odell's *attention economy*; Laidler, 2019). You've likely noticed that after searching online for new shoes, only moments later, you get ads for shoes on your social media feed and embedded in articles. Because this is *the* business model of tech corporations, Hari (2022) explains, their goal always must be to increase user engagement. That's it. The more we give over our attention to immersive tech corporations, the more they can ize it. All arguments about ethics, what is good or healthy for humans, and what responsibility tech corporations have to the rest of us cannot matter to tech companies as much as their bottom line, and their bottom line is user engagement. As such, the employees at these corporations are tasked with constantly redesigning their products to capture ever-increasing amounts of our attention.

To understand the complexity of this issue more deeply, Hari learned from Silicon Valley whistleblower Tristan Harris, with whom you may be familiar if you have seen the Netflix documentary *The Social Dilemma* (Rhodes & Orlowski-Yang, 2020), released in 2020. Harris helped Hari see through reductive debates about what to do about technology and social media, leading Hari (2022) to see how, as Odell notes, the business model is what needs examining, not technology itself:

> *Tristan taught me that the phones we have, and the programs that run on them, were deliberately designed by the smartest people in the world to maximally grab and maximally hold our attention. He wants us to understand that this design is not inevitable. . . [The way our tech works now to corrode our attention was and remains a choice . . . You could have all this technology, Tristan told me, but not design it to be maximally distracting. In fact, you could design it with the opposite goal. . . . Seeing this as a debate between whether you are pro-tech or anti-tech is bogus and lets the people who stole your attention off the hook. The real debate is: What tech, designed for what purposes, in whose interests? (pp. 128–129)*

What are the implications of this choice that Silicon Valley has made to corrode our attention in service to their business model? Let's turn, first, to the impact of surveillance capitalism on our ability to persevere toward task completion and achieve flow states.

Speed and Attention

In an attempt to escape the havoc addictive technologies were wreaking on his attention and sense of well-being, Johann Hari did something that he notes is very difficult for most people to do: he unplugged from all technology by leaving his devices behind and going to live in Cape Cod, Massachusetts, for an extended period. He says a notable effect of his time away from his devices was his regained ability to slow down, to read and think deeply, and, after a period of adjustment, to discover calm within himself. Leaving behind his two devices, he felt like he had "spent years holding two screaming, colicky babies, and now the babies had been handed over to a babysitter, and their yelling and vomiting had vanished from view" (Hari, 2022, p. 28). But after his time on Cape Cod ended, Hari eventually returned fully to the attention-destroying habits of a typical life spent on devices. In trying to understand what brought him such ease and focus during his days on Cape Cod, and what sent him right back to his unhealthy digital habits after his sojourn, Hari set out to map the relationship between the way our technology works and our capacity for attention.

If you are a regular user of social media and other immersive technologies, chances are that you can empathize with the feeling of not being able to harness the attention you once had. This is not, Hari came to understand, an individual problem. Hari (2022) spoke with Sune Lehmann, a professor of applied mathematics and computer science at the Technical University of Denmark who, after feeling like he had lost control of his own ability to pay attention and use the internet responsibly, "launched the largest scientific study yet conducted to answer a key question—is our collective attention span really shrinking?" (p. 30).

Lehmann and his colleagues discovered that, between the years 2013 and 2016 alone, the length of time people spent talking about a topic on Twitter, measured by data markers such as hashtags, dropped from 17.5 to 11.9 hours—a difference of 5.6 hours, a decrease in time on any given subject of almost 33 percent (Hari, 2022). They branched out to investigate whether the same phenomenon held elsewhere and found similar trends throughout other immersive technologies. Researching further, the team discovered that while the speed of information had been increasing even before digital technologies, it has been happening far more rapidly in the digital age. We tend to think of this as an overwhelmingly positive thing.

We have all the information we could ever need right at our fingertips. Yet, more information is not leading us to increased enlightenment. In fact, it is creating the exact opposite effect. Hari (2022) writes:

> We told ourselves we could have a massive expansion in the amount of information we are exposed to, and the speed at which it hits us, with no costs. This is a delusion: "It becomes exhausting." More importantly, Sune said, "what we are sacrificing is depth in all sorts of dimensions. . . . Depth takes time. And depth takes reflection. If you have to keep up with everything and send emails all the time, there's no time to reach depth." . . . There was a phrase in Sune's scientific paper, summarizing his findings, that kept rattling around in my head. It said that we are, collectively, experiencing "a more rapid exhaustion of attention resources." (p. 33)

With our systems completely flooded with instant information and individuals experiencing a rapid exhaustion of attention resources, it comes as no surprise that we cannot think as deeply or focus as we once could. But the difficulties don't end there. Amid this manufactured information overload, we have become convinced that we can, and should, manage it ourselves with the resources we have on hand. One of those resources we delude ourselves into believing in is our ability to multitask.

The Myth of Multitasking

Johann Hari exposes the untruth we have sold ourselves to help us manage the feeling of being adrift in a sea of information: the idea that we can think about many things at once, making this overload of information entirely manageable and within the scope of our cognitive abilities. To explore this faulty concept, he interviewed Earl Miller, an award-winning neuroscientist and professor at MIT:

> Your brain can only produce one or two thoughts in your conscious mind at once. That's it. . . . But rather than acknowledge this . . . we invented a myth. The myth is that we can actually think about three, five, ten things at the same time. (Hari, 2022, p. 37)

In order to justify this myth, we stole a concept that actually arose in the computer science world to describe how a machine can work when equipped with more than one processor: *multitasking*. But we are not machines. Our dogged belief in the myth of multitasking has clouded our understanding of what is really happening at the cognitive level—we're just switching between tasks quickly.

Miller notes three main ways that this switching negatively impacts our focus. The first has to do with the lag time our brains experience when we switch tasks. It's called the switch cost effect. When we switch back to a task after abandoning it for something else, we must first remember what we were doing and where our train of thought was going. This process takes time, and our performance suffers (Hari, 2022).

This negative effect would apply anytime we are drawn into the world of immersive technology, even for seconds, to check a social media notification, read a text, or refresh email. Our brains need time to refocus and reorient after each of these checks, even if we are not consciously aware of the lag.

In addition to the time needed to refocus, the second cost of constant task switching is it makes us far more error prone. The reason for this is intuitive: when you

must continually refocus and reorient yourself to your task, the likelihood th.
won't do it well increases.

It's easy to see how this instinct to constantly switch tasks, perpetuated by addictive designs dreamed up by tech corporations, is interfering with our everyday life, attention, and performance. The impact, Hari (2022) explains, is much higher than we might imagine. One study Hari considers demonstrates that distracting or interrupting workers with emails and phone calls hampers their IQs by an average of ten full points as compared to the uninterrupted group. This "suggests, in terms of being able to get your work done, you'd be better off getting stoned at your desk than checking your texts or Facebook messages a lot" (Hari, 2022, p. 39).

While it's simple to see how the first two negative effects of constant switching have outsize implications for students' academic success, the third really drives the matter home. Continuous scattering of our attention leads to "creativity drain" (Hari, 2022, p. 39). Because information overload and our attendant habit of constant switching leave no space for cognitive downtime (no *doing nothing*, as Odell describes it), creative thought has no opportunity to flourish. Miller explains to Hari (2022) that new thoughts and innovation "come from your brain shaping new connections out of what you've seen and heard and learned. Your mind, given free undistracted time, will automatically think back over everything it absorbed, and it will start to draw links between them in new ways" (p. 40). If we want creativity to flourish, we need to carve out time that is free of distractions.

The Decrease of Flow States

what could this look like in class?

Just as creative ideas emerge when we have the time and space to make new connections unencumbered by constant cognitive switching, carrying out creative *work* requires its own set of uninterrupted circumstances. To understand how our inability to focus is harming our ability to do deep, meaningful work, Johann Hari met with the legendary psychologist Mihaly Robert Csikszentmihalyi. Csikszentmihalyi's lifetime of research focused on defining and exploring the concept of *flow states*. In studying people deeply engaged in the work they love, such as artists creating a work, athletes performing in their sport, and chess players engaged in matches, Csikszentmihalyi was struck by what he observed and how these people talked about what they were doing. Hari (2022) explains:

> [Csikszentmihalyi] began to wonder if these people were in fact describing a fundamental human instinct that had not been studied by scientists before. He called it a "flow state." This is when you are so absorbed in

what you are doing that you lose all sense of yourself, and time seems to fall away, and you are flowing into the experience itself. It is the deepest form of focus and attention that we know of. . . . It didn't matter if they got there by performing brain surgery or strumming the guitar or making great bagels—they described their flow states with wonder. . . . He was discovering that if human beings drill down in the right way, we can hit a gusher of focus inside ourselves—a long surge of attention that will flow forth and carry us through difficult tasks in a way that feels painless, and in fact pleasurable. (p. 55)

When you read that description, what comes to mind? What activity immerses you in your own flow state? We (Beth and Katie) experience flow when we are engaged in the work that has come to define our professional lives as much as our personal ones: reading, writing, and immersing ourselves in the world of ideas. As positive and pleasurable as the feelings associated with flow states may be, flow is not achieved through relaxation, nor through a passive state. Csikszentmihalyi (1990) identifies three requirements for entering flow. First, you must choose a clearly defined goal, figure out how to pursue it, and set aside other goals while you focus on the one at hand: "Flow can only come when you are monotasking—when you choose to set aside everything else and do one thing" (p. 56). Next, you must do something that is personally meaningful. And last, flow will come more readily if the goal you have chosen is something that challenges your abilities while not being out of reach.

Csikszentmihalyi's discovery of flow as a natural human state of attention and motivator is remarkable for many reasons, but one that Hari highlights that stands out for educators is Csikszentmihalyi had to completely depart from the psychology of his day in order to define it. When Csikszentmihalyi embarked on his research, Hari explains, the world of psychology was all but defined by psychologist B. F. Skinner's work on behaviorism, grounded in the idea that punishments and rewards account for the full scope of human motivation. To Csikszentmihalyi, "this seemed like a bleak and limited view of human psychology. . . . He believed it was missing most of what it means to be human" (Hari, 2022, p. 53). Hari (2022) points out that Csikszentmihalyi's departure from the manipulation-focused world of behavioral psychology seems "to lay the groundwork for one of the defining conflicts in the world today" (p. 57), and describes it this way:

We now live in a world dominated by technologies based on B. F. Skinner's vision of how the human mind works. His insight— that you can train living creatures to desperately crave arbitrary rewards—has come to dominate our environment. . . . Obsessively posting selfies to Instagram [starts] to look to me like Skinner's pigeons. . . . [Csikszentmihalyi's] deeper insight has been forgotten: that we have within us a force that makes it possible to focus for long stretches and enjoy it, and it will make us happier and healthier, if only we create the right circumstances to let it flow. . . . We know, at some level, that when we are not focusing, we are not using one of our greatest capacities. Starved of flow, we become stumps of ourselves, sensing somewhere what we might have been. (pp. 57–58)

We know this sense of loss, whether we have experienced it ourselves or observed it in friends, family members, or students. When we are constantly switching between tasks in the digital world, it is simply impossible to become engaged in a flow state. Consider how many people, once avid readers, lament not being able to really read anymore, not being up to the task of taking on a weighty text. (Hari is among this group, he writes.) Weary from the weight of the information overload we are bearing, we have little left to give back to ourselves. We're giving all our attention away.

Bleak as this all may sound, Hari, Odell, and Newport offer us hope that we can operate differently as individuals, as cultures, and as a society. The answers are neither quick nor easy. But we have faced seemingly insurmountable societal challenges in the past and emerged triumphant. Let's think more about what this means for us, as educators, and for the work of the classroom: what we're up against, how teaching and learning can chip away at the present circumstances, and how we can empower our students to create a new vision for our relationships to technology and one another.

Implications for the Classroom

A deeper understanding of how addictive tech tools affect our students' health necessitates that we rethink and redesign the ways we implement technology in the classroom. In the education world's enthusiasm to rush into the digital age with one-to-one devices, learning management software, and instantaneous access to course-work, resources, grades, and feedback, educators were unable to fully anticipate the ways this immersion would pose significant challenges to our students' academic success and well-being. They were faced with a novel conflict. What other tool or practice, when used or overused in schools in the name of supporting learning, has the potential to adversely affect students outside of school? We don't need to worry that too much time with woodworking tools will turn our students into carpentry addicts, or that too much science will disrupt the balance of their lives outside of school. Never have we had to contend with a fear that too many books might jeopardize our students' free time or their ability to think clearly. But the same just cannot be said of technology.

We know well how successful the attention economy has been in capturing our students' attention during the school day; we see them huddled, hunched over, desperately sneaking glances at their own devices in classrooms, hallways, lunchrooms . . . . Let's be honest, they're even desperate enough to take their devices into the bathrooms, clicking and scrolling like teenagers huddled with their cigarettes in a 1950s movie. In rethinking how and when we use technology in our classrooms and considering how to guide students toward ways to disconnect from their devices, we must recognize that students' immersion in their personal technology throughout the school day and beyond is compounded by the compulsory use of digital tools for learning. The role of technology use during the seven- to eight-hour school day necessarily impacts the overall role technology plays in students' lives, and there is much at stake. When we begin to reconsider the degree to which we rely on screens for learning and assessment in our classrooms, we are not just supporting students to focus their attention toward learning and real social connection. We are also offering them an alternative to the ongoing stimulation, fragmentation of their attention and time, and feelings of pressure and overwhelm that are inherent to their constant use of screens.

While reading this section, notice feelings of resistance that may be coming up for you in the form of questions such as, *Isn't it our job to teach students how to use this tool? Aren't I neglecting my duties if I do not immerse them in the digital world regularly?* Of course, it is only natural to want to prepare students for the world they will enter, but our work does not fit tidily into the box of preparing students for the world *as it is.* Instead, we are called on to equip students with the skills, knowledge, and dispositions to create a healthier, more just world in which they can thrive as individuals and in communities. This involves disrupting the status quo. In rethinking not *whether* but *how* we use technology in our classrooms, we can support our students in envisioning what a new world could look like—how it could bring people closer to themselves and to one another.

Reconsidering the Digitized Classroom

At the time of this writing, many school districts have just returned to full in-person learning following the pandemic closures from 2020 to 2022. It is only natural that instructors and students alike have become accustomed to the housing of lesson materials and resources solely on learning management software. Now is a good time to rethink the extent of this practice in your classroom. Even if your school was not impacted by closures and distance learning, you should consider the degree to which you have digitized your course materials. This digitization practice can be an efficient, effective way to provide materials to students when circumstances deviate from the norm—for example, when students are absent for extended periods of time—or to provide necessary accommodations for individual students. However, we need to equally consider how these fully digitized materials have the capacity to create a sense of placelessness for students.

Toward the goal of decreasing our overreliance on the digital world, we can do a thorough audit of all the digital tools we use in a day in our teaching lives, holding each digital tool up for careful inspection and considering whether its benefits outweigh the risk of exposing students to the overstimulation and time fragmentation (Newport, 2019). We can also reflect on the total number of tools we are using and consider how often we are requiring students to access them. If you find that you are asking students to access digital tools for sustained periods of time on most days, you can begin to consider ways to strike a healthier balance.

In addition to issues of overstimulation and time fragmentation, requiring students to access materials online most of the time also requires them to engage in the constant task switching Hari (2022) speaks to—the precise thing that harms their ability to focus, complete tasks with accuracy, and enter flow states. Each time students open their school devices, they must shoulder the burden of navigating a great deal more than just the school's learning management software. When logging in, they must make a series of decisions and summon a tremendous amount of willpower to execute the task at hand as they are forced to sidestep various distractions created by tech corporations before even beginning what you have asked them to do. They must choose to ignore their school email account, likely full of notifications (and mountains of unread emails). Depending on their age, the chat function may be enabled. This constitutes another distraction to avoid. They must navigate to a specific course in their learning management software, avoiding feedback and notifications they may have about grades or due dates for work in other classes. They must resist the temptation to access literally anything else on the World Wide Web, including game sites that they have adeptly learned to access by navigating past firewalls and other restrictions. And then, they have to actually open the resources needed at the moment without giving in to the temptation to constantly switch to any of the aforementioned items. If you are asking students to read something online, another set of temptations and distractions are introduced, from ads to hyperlinks and more. And the research is now clear: reading digitally results in lower comprehension and engagement with the text (Clinton, 2019; Delgado, Vargas, Ackerman, & Salmerón, 2018; Singer & Alexander, 2017). Conversely, this level of willpower is simply not required to stay engaged in the analog world, where distractions exist but are not designed to manipulate and monopolize students' attention.

In avoiding the obstacles that myriad digital diversions present and coping with constant task switching, students are left feeling adrift in the broad sea of the internet, even if they are only accessing what they need for their classes. At the start of the 2021–2022 school year, Katie was speaking with a student about their experiences with distance learning during the COVID-19 pandemic, and they related feeling unmoored by the abundant internet use required. The student described a sense of not being able to locate where to *be* on their device. They were not having trouble with navigating to their learning management software, nor with understanding the ins and outs of websites, applications, or necessary access tools. They also were not held in thrall by gaming websites. Their complaint was nebulous yet entirely palpable: it was all just *too much.* The tabs, the classes, the notifications—all of it was just *there* for viewing, for checking, and for being up to date on all the time. This sensory overload created a serious case of decision fatigue for the student; prioritizing not just homework but also classwork tasks became difficult. Sadly, the student reported that their experience with technology had not changed much since returning to in-person learning. When we reconsider the degree to which we have digitized our classrooms, there is much we can do to carve out spaces in our classrooms that deliberately anchor students back in place and time.

Creating Classrooms That Anchor Students in Place and Time

We can begin to help students anchor themselves in the physical time and place of our classes by considering what elements could be carrying them away from it. First, we can start to recalculate the amount of time we ask them to spend on tasks in the digital world. This does not mean that learning management software should play no role in instruction, nor that students do not need the skills of researching, writing, and reading in the digital world. But, to the degree that you are reasonably able, offer students the opportunity to work with physical materials and eliminate the distractions inherent in having to navigate digitally so often, as this will ameliorate the sense of placelessness and time fragmentation created by the digital world.

Second, we can create and uphold regular routines in the environments of our classrooms that our students can expect and rely on so they can more easily move to our classes' rhythms. Routines that build in movement breaks and movement to different spaces in the room for lesson components are wonderfully helpful not just in helping our students stay focused on the present but in keeping their thinking fresh and creative (Carlson et al., 2015; Howie, Beets, & Pate, 2014).

We can also consider the physical environments of our classrooms and how they can support students' comfort with going offline. Flexible seating, designated workstations using the desks or furniture you have, and elements such as plants, rocks, or other items from nature can reconnect our students with their bodies and remind them of the larger world. This alternative seating can give your students back some bodily autonomy. Your room does not need to be Pinterest-worthy to do this work. You do not need to spend a fortune or scour giveaway groups online or surf the local garage sales. In fact, you don't even have to do this cognitive work alone—partner with your students to design a space that they find supportive and inviting.

We can work with our students to set and hold firm boundaries and norms on the use of tech in our classrooms and inform this process by engaging the students in inquiry and conversation about why this issue is critical to address. If you feel hesitant to limit personal device use in the classroom because you are uncomfortable managing students' personal property, partnering with students and offering them a designated space in the classroom where they can stow and charge the devices is one answer. If your hesitation lies in a suspicion that nothing can really be done to break the addiction young people have to their devices, do not despair. Our students' academic progress and overall well-being are at stake, and collectively, we can find solutions, as educators always do in the best interest of their students.

Prioritizing Conversation Over Digital Communication

So much of our students' communication has shifted to the digital sphere. This was unavoidable during school closures, but when we are engaging in in-person instruction, it's important to evaluate the usefulness of the digital communication tools we used for that time since students are once again present in living color.

Our students have been conditioned to interact on social media and via other addictive technologies in ways that do not suit the purposes of the classroom. The communications they have in these spaces are largely about image and ego: students are constantly forming and reforming the identities they wish to communicate to the world through their posts, comments, likes, and other social media behavior. And although it is the work of all adolescents to engage in the ongoing process of identity formation, never before has this process been so public and so high stakes.

In fact, 45 percent of teens report feeling "overwhelmed because of all of the drama" on social media, 43 percent report feeling "pressure to only post content that makes them look good to others," and 37 percent report feeling "pressure to post content that will get lots of likes or comments" (Anderson & Jiang, 2018). As such, when we ask students to communicate and engage in tasks via digital tools, they can't help but bring the emotional baggage they carry from their other digital worlds into the classroom.

In addition to this reality, let's take a moment to reflect on the digital communication we have witnessed in the spheres of our personal lives. How many times have you seen a productive and healthy conversation thread on Facebook or Twitter? When the parties involved agree, how often does a nuanced, thoughtful discussion occur instead of mere validation that they think the same? When the parties disagree, how often do they arrive at some kind of peaceable, respectful understanding about the opposing side, which you feel could inform their perspectives in the future? Chances are these experiences will account for a small percentage of what you have observed.

When we invite our students to communicate in the digital world (whether it's via a digital wall for sharing and viewing posts and responses, a text-based threaded discussion, or even a back-channel chat) instead of face-to-face, we are defaulting to a mode that necessarily limits their abilities to learn to have genuine conversations, think deeply, and arrive at a complex understanding of other human beings and their ideas. Students will likely be thinking about many items completely unrelated to the prompt to which they are responding. They might be thinking about whether their digital representation (in text, video, or some other medium) adequately represents the image they have been tending, whether their ideas adequately reflect the beliefs of their social groups, and whether their response to classmates will raise their social capital. It's impossible to count the ways that students will map their experience with the tools created by the attention economy onto the task of communicating digitally in the classroom.

Instead of using digital communication tools so often, we can start to take advantage of the built-in social network Cal Newport (2019) describes; we can empower students to work with it in the way it deserves and has evolved to be used. We can help students harness their intrinsic instincts by presenting them with regular opportunities to engage in discussions about issues that matter—to our content and curriculum and to the world—with their classmates. In doing so, we can help them learn to relate to one another more naturally. Through more regular opportunities to talk together and reflect on their experiences with in-person conversation, we can chip away at the problem Turkle describes with young people failing to understand social cues and shying away from true conversation in fear that they will be misinterpreted or misinterpret in turn.

In prioritizing more in-person over digital communication and in helping our students become self-aware and open about their communication quirks, we can help bring students out of the haze of online discussion and its many emotionally fraught trapdoors and build the skills they need to feel confident having real conversations.

Spotlight On: Co-Creating Tech-Free Norms

Co-create classroom norms with students to create agreed-on moments when devices are stowed away. Some suggestions follow.

We will stow away our personal and school devices during the following times.

- Individual and small-group conversations
- Independent reading time
- Teacher direct instruction
- Student presentations

Introspective Exercises for Teachers

Engage in the following exercises to examine how the ideas in this chapter could impact and inspire your teaching practice and inform your instructional decisions.

Introspective Exercise One: Redesigning Instructional Practices, Procedures, and Classroom Environments to Anchor Students in Time and Place

Use figure 2.1 (page 68) to reflect on different practices and areas of your classroom environment that you can reimagine in order to help students feel more present and grounded when learning in your room. Then, consider alternative ideas and the desired impacts of these ideas. If you are unsure of where to start, consider asking students for their feedback and input. (See Classroom Strategy One, page 71, for help starting this conversation.) You can also use the figure to track outcomes and redesign your approaches if needed. Examples in the first two rows of the chart help get you thinking.

Current Practice or Aspect of the Environment	Alternative Idea	Desired Impact	Outcome	Redesign Plan (If needed)
Example: Students read and annotate articles on an ed tech website.	*Example:* Print articles for students. Provide a digital copy after class for absent students and easy reference.	*Example:* Students will be able to interact with the text with more attention to the details and less distraction. Students will still have access to a digital copy if they need it later.	*Example:* Students' annotations were squished into the corners of the papers. They did not have enough room to record their ideas.	*Example:* Copy and paste the article (and source info) into a document, remove unnecessary images, and increase the margins. Provide an optional graphic organizer for students who would rather record the page and paragraph and their ideas there.
Example: Desks are in rows, but I share a room with another teacher who wants them that way.	*Example:* Decide on a new small-group desk arrangement that can be made quickly and moved back before the end of class.	*Example:* Students will be able to talk to one another more easily, and without having to constantly turn and talk across rows.	*Example:* Two small groups of volunteers are helping at the start and end of each class. It's going great!	*Example:* (Not needed)

FIGURE 2.1: Chart for redesigning instructional practices, procedures, and classroom environments to anchor students in time and place.

Visit go.SolutionTree.com/teacherefficacy for a free reproducible version of this figure.

Introspective Exercise Two: Evaluating Tech Tools and Avoiding Duplication

Cal Newport (2019) suggests auditing all the tech tools we use in a day to consider what each adds to our lives and whether there are overlaps. (There is no need to learn new tools that accomplish the same tasks as others we already know and like.) The exercise in figure 2.2 applies this concept to tech tools used in the classroom.

Follow these three steps.

1. Use the following chart to reflect on each tech tool you are currently using in your instruction and to understand the full scope of the digital interactions happening in your classroom.
2. Evaluate each tool, one by one, for its usefulness and for any duplication of another tool that works just as well.
3. Decide how often you want to use this tool and when. There's an example in the first row to get you thinking.

Tool	Specific Functions	Defense of Use	Frequency of Use
	Are these novel or duplicative?	*What makes this tool worth using? Does that justify an additional tech tool? Why or why not?*	*How often do I use this tool now in my classes? What would feel like the optimal amount of usage for this tool?*
Example: Google Docs	*Example:* This tool is novel because students do not have access to another word processor on their school devices.	*Example:* This tool is important for assigning work, offering feedback, and having students create their own work. It does not have any notifications, nor social media functions. It is easy for students to share their work with me via Google Docs or in Google Classroom.	*Example:* I use this tool almost every day in my classes right now. This is too often, because it tethers my students to screens most days. I will start to print more assigned work for students, and also provide students with the opportunity to handwrite their own work when applicable.

FIGURE 2.2: Chart for evaluating tech tools and avoiding duplication.

*Visit **go.SolutionTree.com/teacherefficacy** for a free reproducible version of this figure.*

Introspective Exercise Three: Planning How to Refuse in Place

Refusing in place is such a difficult skill to put into practice. But Jenny Odell (2019) reminds us that grounding our reticence in a principled stance (similar to Bartleby), as opposed to simply offering a yes or a no, can help us know how to respond to requests to which we might otherwise just immediately say no. She also encourages us to carve out a *third space*, an alternative to yes or no, which allows us to remain in community while upholding our own values. We can use her ideas (as in figure 2.3) to help us consider what to do when we meet with a practice our colleague, department, supervisor, school, principal, or district puts in place. There are no easy answers to navigating practices or procedures related to technology that we may take issue with—sometimes, we can do nothing but comply.

What is the practice I take issue with?	What is the root of my issue with this practice?	What can I say or do to refuse in place or practice finding a third space with this practice?
Example: My team is using the Google Classroom calendar for all student assignments.	*Example:* Posting assignment due dates and reminders here makes it harder for students to practice autonomy over their own work, and it puts many of them in the habit of consulting another digital tool every day when they could achieve organization through alternative ways.	*Example:* I respect my colleagues, so I'll keep using the calendar this year. However, I'll carve out a specific time at the start of every class to review homework and upcoming projects with students, keep this information on my board, and have students write this information in an agenda. Before next school year, I'll notify my team about my concerns more directly so we can agree on a system.

FIGURE 2.3: Chart for planning how to refuse in place.

*Visit **go.SolutionTree.com/teacherefficacy** for a free reproducible version of this figure.*

Classroom Strategies

These strategies are inspired by the ideas in this chapter and designed for immediate classroom use. Use these strategies with your students to increase their awareness of how they can balance their use of technology in order to prioritize real conversation and connection.

Classroom Strategy One: Creating a Classroom Environment That Prioritizes Presence and Connection

To help students feel more present in your classroom, more grounded in time and place, and more supported in having genuine conversations with their peers, use the questions in figure 2.4 to collect ideas from them and work together to design a comfortable, engaging space. You may find that it makes sense to inform students that you will be designing the classroom environment together, but to hold off on asking them these questions until they have had a few weeks together in the space.

What is something about the way our classroom is currently organized that helps you be comfortable and present in the space?

What ideas do you have about how we could rearrange the furniture in our classroom to make the space more collaborative and inviting?

What ideas do you have for making the walls in our classroom reflective of the people who make up our classroom community and the work we do together?

What elements of nature do you find most inspirational? Which of these could feasibly be brought into our classroom environment?

What ideas do you have for minimizing tech distractions in our classroom? These ideas can be about both the physical space we share and routines we could put in place.

What materials from home can you create or bring in to add to our classroom environment so we can make your ideas a reality?

FIGURE 2.4: Chart for creating a classroom environment together.

Visit go.SolutionTree.com/teacherefficacy for a free reproducible version of this figure.

Classroom Strategy Two: Fostering Better Conversations by Identifying Conversation Quirks

Use the prompts in figure 2.5 to help students get to know themselves and one another by reflecting on their personal conversation quirks and what they want others to know about them as communicators. Because we evolve as communicators, it can be helpful to have students complete the prompts in figure 2.5 early on in the year and share with their partners or groups at the start of any conversation. Later in the year, you can use the prompts in figure 2.6 to help students reflect on their progress and set new conversation goals.

Initial Reflection: Use these prompts early in the year.

Example for Students:

My Conversation Quirks

In a conversation with me, you might notice that I interrupt without noticing sometimes.

The reason I do this is because I get so excited about the ideas we are discussing!

When I talk with someone else, it helps me when the other person is patient but kindly reminds me of the point they were making.

This is helpful for me because it helps me remember to leave space for others' ideas.

Your Turn:

My Conversation Quirks

In a conversation with me, you might notice that I . . .

The reason I do this is because . . .

When I talk with someone else, it helps me when they . . .

This is helpful for me because . . .

FIGURE 2.5: My conversation quirks.

*Visit **go.SolutionTree.com/teacherefficacy** for a free reproducible version of this figure.*

Continued Reflection: Use these prompts throughout later parts of the year.
Now that I am more practiced at conversation, I have noticed that . . .
When in discussion with a peer or group, I can now . . .
One habit I want to keep working on is . . .
One thing I've noticed about how I communicate differently in person and on the computer is . . .

FIGURE 2.6: Ways my conversation style has changed.

*Visit **go.SolutionTree.com/teacherefficacy** for a free reproducible version of this figure.*

Classroom Strategy Three: Learning About Addictive Technology Across Content Areas

None of us can change what we do not understand. To understand the ways technology can evolve in order to better serve individuals, communities, and societies, students must have an understanding of the problems as they stand. Table 2.1 (page 74) lists ideas for engaging students in thinking about technology issues in different content areas.

TABLE 2.1: Learning About Surveillance Capitalism Across Content Areas

Content Area	Potential Avenue for Teaching and Learning
Science	Learn about how addictive technology changes our brain chemistry and keeps us checking our devices by delivering constant dopamine hits and hijacking our social instincts.
Mathematics	Track and graph the rise of social media apps, young people's use of addictive technology, corporations' use of surveillance and data collection, or other related issues.
English language arts	Read, listen to, or watch resources on concepts related to the rise and proliferation of addictive technology. Here are some suggestions. • The Netflix documentary *The Social Dilemma* (Rhodes & Orlowski-Yang, 2020) • Audio interviews with experts featured on the Stolen Focus (2021) website (https://stolenfocusbook.com/audio)
Social studies	Explore how resistance movements have successfully overcome powerful corporate forces throughout history. Learn about Silicon Valley whistleblowers.
World language	Examine how social media disinformation campaigns have spread and negatively affected communities living in countries speaking the target language.
Health	Explore the impacts of tech addiction on young people's mental health.
Design and engineering	Ideate and design technology that does not rely on addictive features and instead promotes ways to feel more fulfilled and less lonely in the real world.

*Visit **go.SolutionTree.com/teacherefficacy** for a free reproducible version of this table.*

Questions for Reflection and Discussion

In this section, you will find three different types of questions: questions for individual reflection, questions for conversation, and jigsaw questions across chapters. Each offers you a specific way to think through additional questions about concepts from the chapter.

Questions for Individual Reflection

Consider the following questions.

▪ In what ways did this chapter shift your thinking about the role technology corporations play in our students' habits and their ability to focus in and out of the classroom?

- Despite the hold addictive technologies have on our students, there are practices we can implement to help students cultivate attention and focus. Which strategies or ideas discussed in this chapter feel the most relevant or hold the most promise for your practice?

- Johann Hari (2022) insists that the negative effects of surveillance capitalism's addictive technologies on our focus and attention are social, not individual, issues. Jenny Odell (2019) points out that the attention economy lays waste to our ability to think clearly about important social problems of our day. How can you begin to help your students see the connections between our collective attention resources and our ability to work toward a more just and inclusive society?

Questions for Conversation

Consider the following questions to converse about the ideas in this chapter and to leverage these insights toward improving your school.

- Jenny Odell (2019) proposes that we begin to practice ways of being that stand in stark contrast to a life spent online. Discuss the degree to which you are currently able to *do nothing* in your life—making time for leisure activities that you find pleasurable, meaningful, restful, and restorative. What does doing nothing look and feel like for you? If you cannot think of many examples, reflect back on other parts of your life, and consider what doing nothing may have looked like for you in the past.

- Cal Newport (2019) offers ideas for transforming our individual relationships to technology and one another, asserting a truly zero-sum game: the more we give over our time and attention to addictive technologies, the less we have for the people and relationships we care about. Discuss your experience with navigating the balance between addictive technologies and your life outside of them. How has this balance shifted during different times in your life and in the development of these technologies? In what ways do you want this balance to shift now?

- Johann Hari (2022) explores the impact of addictive technologies on our collective ability to think clearly, focus, and find flow states.

Discuss the extent to which you have noticed this design of addictive technologies affecting your students. Try to be specific about the behaviors you have noticed, and then discuss what ideas from the chapter you think may help ameliorate these specific behaviors.

Jigsaw Questions Across Chapters

Consider the following questions for conversation with individuals who read a different chapter. Share insights and discover how the intersection of these ideas might spark creative solutions to both impact student learning and improve your experiences as educators.

- Can you summarize an inspiring idea from this chapter in your own words? In what way did this idea cause you to think differently about your practice? How might this idea offer insight to you personally?

- What word or quote from this chapter resonates with you?

- What voices and perspectives are not represented in this text?

- What idea, introspective exercise, or strategy from the chapter holds the most promise for you, and why and how would you implement it in your classroom?

- What is one takeaway from this chapter that you'd like to share with students, colleagues, or your team?

- What additional readings can you bring to the conversation? What other texts or articles could further advance everyone's thinking on this topic?

Conclusion

Peering through the lenses offered in this chapter, it is clear that technology overuse poses a serious threat to our students' brains and bodies. With a fuller understanding, we can make more informed, intentional decisions about how and when we will use technology to enhance learning in our classrooms. We encourage you to build your knowledge base in this area in order to effect change. To do so, consider accessing one of the resources referenced in Classroom Strategy Three: Learning About Addictive Technology Across Content Areas (page 73): watch the Netflix documentary *The Social Dilemma* or visit https://stolenfocusbook.com /audio and listen to some of the audio interviews with experts featured in Johann Hari's (2022) book, *Stolen Focus*. We also encourage you to reflect on the issue of technology overuse and engage your colleagues and administrators in conversation to examine the degree to which your team, department, or school may be able to create lasting changes in the culture of technology use for both students and staff.

CHAPTER 3

FOSTERING CIVIL CLASSROOMS FOR A MORE CIVIL SOCIETY

Estimated Read Time:
58 Minutes

Remember: The other people you're talking to are as complicated as you are.

—Loretta Ross

Throughout our careers, we (Beth and Katie) have been committed to justice and equity, both in our work and in our personal lives. We have felt deep joy witnessing social movements gain wider support in the late 2010s and early 2020s. At the same time, we have been dismayed at how easily genuine commitment to justice and equity can become twisted into rhetoric and sound bites, whether on social media, on cable news, or in our own communities. We have witnessed the ways this rhetoric—and the rhetoric that ostensibly represents a wide range of positions or opinions—hampers true communication, doing far more to divide people than to create any lasting change.

It is clear that these divisions are growing. For example, the Pew Research Center (2014) finds that over the years 1994–2014 in the United States:

> *Partisan animosity has increased substantially . . . . In each party, the*
> *share with a highly negative view of the opposing party has* more than

doubled *since 1994. Most of these intense partisans believe the opposing party's policies "are so misguided that they threaten the nation's
well-being." (emphasis added)*

Adding to this increasing negativity is a retreat to what the Pew Research Center (2014) refers to as *ideological silos*, a habit of associating only with those with whom we agree.

This trend is not limited to the United States. Polarization is on the rise globally as well. Thomas Carothers, with Andrew O'Donohue (2019b), notes that for editing the book *Democracies Divided: The Global Challenge of Political Polarization*, "We focused on nine diverse countries grappling with the problem [of polarization]: Bangladesh, Brazil, Colombia, India, Indonesia, Kenya, Poland, Turkey, and the United States . . . [and] the degree of similarity we found across countries was startling." Carothers goes on to describe the effects of polarization on not just democratic institutions but the fabric of societies:

> Polarization also reverberates throughout the society as a whole, poisoning everyday interactions and relationships [and] Partisan conflict takes a heavy toll on civil society as well, often leading to the demonization of activists and human rights defenders. More seriously still, divisions can contribute to a spike in hate crimes and political violence: India, Poland, and the United States have all seen such increases in recent years. (Carothers & O'Donohue, 2019b)

This state of increasing polarization pains us as educators and as people, and we deeply believe that educators have a serious responsibility to empower students to embark on a path toward healing the social fractures that divide people. Educators are well positioned to do so, and this chapter offers a few of the thinkers who have helped us consider how to do this work on ourselves, in our classrooms, and in our wider spheres of influence. We invite you to join us in exploring this topic, along with Ezra Klein, adrienne maree brown, and Frances Kissling, and think about how it may resonate with you.

As a complement to those ideas, we suggest checking out chapter 1 (page 9). Strengthening your own and your students' emotional intelligence is a necessary component of engaging more civilly with one another—a process that requires that you understand your own perspective and those of others in a more nuanced way.

You might also consider the ideas in chapter 4 (page 113), including the larger ideas on teacher leadership and the more specific discussion of overcoming reactivity and increasing self-awareness. They can bolster your ability to increase civil conversation in your spheres of influence.

Ideas to Consider

As society experiences growing divides between people with divergent beliefs, we have noticed that our students' ability to engage in civil discourse is suffering. What's more, divisiveness decreases our students' ability to have prosocial relationships with people who differ from them and even harms their ability to live well-adjusted lives (Taylor et al., 2014).

We cannot predict whether this trend will continue or wane, but we do know that a more civil society begins with preparing young people to meaningfully engage with others across their differences. We thus endeavor to teach students ways of participating in challenging, academic thinking and conversations that expand and refine their thinking, and to support them in working toward mutually beneficial solutions with those from whom they differ. We also see great promise in highlighting more firmly for our students the fact that, despite rhetoric that might portray the opposite, most Americans find themselves in agreement on a host of issues (Carr Center for Human Rights Policy, 2022; Clifton, 2018; Schaeffer, 2022).

We've been reading, listening, and thinking deeply about how we can support our students to learn to understand one another and disagree in democratic and civil ways that honor our shared humanity. We believe we can create the conditions for transformational educational communities that do not shy away from having necessary conflicts or difficult conversations, but instead embrace the goal of doing so civilly, empowering learners to play active roles in the creation of a more just and inclusive society.

In this chapter, we explore a journalist's hypothesis about why people may struggle to communicate across differences, and activists' ideas and strategies for communicating with those with whom you may profoundly disagree. We think these approaches can provide inspiration for how educators can work within their classrooms and schools to promote and facilitate social healing, which holds the promise to restore people, communities, and nations.

Ezra Klein on Barriers to Civil Discourse

Ezra Klein is an author and journalist who is a cofounder and former editor-at-large of the news and opinion website Vox and the host of the podcast *The Ezra Klein Show*. In his work, Klein considers deeply how people relate to each other in their personal and professional lives, and seeks to understand why people struggle to engage with, actively listen to, and willingly work toward solutions with others who have differing beliefs. His work has implications for how educators might foster civil discussions in their classrooms so students can become community members and world citizens who know how to work, live, and love across differences toward more peaceful and equitable societies.

While Klein's research examines why people may struggle with civil discourse, he doesn't offer many solutions. We feel it's important to consider some of his arguments because many may resonate with what you're seeing in your classroom and inspire you to focus on solutions. Klein's perspective has propelled us to action, and led us to find some of our own solutions as well as draw from other thought leaders who offer strategies to facilitate civility.

Klein's analysis of why people struggle to communicate civilly across differences is multifaceted, and it is based on history, political theory, and his experience as a journalist and a citizen. For our purposes, we are going to focus on three of the pivotal reasons he proposes in his 2020 book, *Why We're Polarized*: (1) like-minded groups, (2) identity politics, and (3) newsmaking in the social media era (Klein, 2020).

Like-Minded Groups

To begin, Klein explains our inclination as human beings to organize into like-minded groups. He offers numerous examples, ranging from political activists to sports fanatics, in an attempt to persuade the reader that humans have an inherent tendency to cleave to those with similar characteristics and viewpoints, and then unite in opposition to the group they have deemed the *other*. Klein (2020) writes that "the mechanism is evolutionary; our brains know we need our groups to survive. . . . Our brains don't always know the difference between the life-and-death stakes that group fortunes once held and the milder consequences they typically carry today" (pp. 58–59).

Klein believes that this primal instinct to organize ourselves into groups and thus view each other with skepticism and distrust seems to be inhibiting our ability to work together toward the collective good. Further, this evolutionary survival technique is inhibiting our ability to recognize our common humanity so we can work together and devise solutions for critical policy issues and fundamental human rights issues that have the capacity to increase well-being for us all.

Identity Politics

The second factor Klein (2020) cites as a barrier to civil discourse is what some call *identity politics*. He simply defines this factor as the conflation of our identities with our political positions to the degree that if someone disagrees with us on a political stance, it feels like an attack on who we are. And thus, when someone challenges our political beliefs, which we consider the very foundation of who we are, we will dig further into our position and also fight back with a vehemence and a vitriol that are disproportionate to the issue at hand. Klein (2020) describes what he refers to as *mega-identities*, by which he means developed senses of ourselves based on our race, religion, gender identity, politics, personal beliefs, and social status rather than our morals, values, core beliefs, and intuition.

Stacking these identity markers, and aligning ourselves with those who are similar, can divide us from those who don't share these same traits. As Klein (2020) writes, "As our many identities merge into single political mega-identities, those visceral, emotional stakes are rising—and with them, our willingness to do anything to make sure our side wins" (p. 74). In a 2020 interview, Klein (Commonwealth Club of California, 2020) says more about how our identities activate under threat (de Hoog, 2013); since our identities are so tied up with our political affiliations, we will react to any attack on our groups, even if we are unfamiliar with the issue at hand. Klein explains that the problem is "we know who we are more than we know what we believe about each policy or moment" (Commonwealth Club of California, 2020). In our quest to protect our identities, we have become more focused on ensuring that the other side loses than on having our side emerge triumphant when debating a particular issue or policy.

Newsmaking in the Social Media Era

Last, Klein maintains that there are forces at work capitalizing on and fanning the flames of groupthink and identity politics, including, most notably, news media. Media institutions decide what is newsworthy, and these decisions are often *not* based on increasing public awareness about important issues. Instead, these decisions are about what will attract the most clicks and likes, and what has the greatest potential to go viral. Media is not a nonprofit public service; it is a business:

> *The news is supposed to be a mirror held up to the world, but the world is far too vast to fit in our mirror. The fundamental thing the media does all day, every day, is decide what to cover—decide, that is, what is newsworthy. . . . In the modern era, a shortcut to newsworthiness is social media virality; if people are already talking about a story or a tweet, that makes it newsworthy almost by definition. (Klein, 2020, pp. 164, 167)*

This explanation clarifies the problematic nature of modern-day news media. Although we may want to believe that the news we are inundated with still has a whiff of impartiality, Klein (2020) questions this notion by offering an analogy from Chris Hayes, who anchors MSNBC:

> *"At some level . . . we're wedding DJs. And the wedding DJ's job is to get you on the floor." The point is not that this leaves no room for serious journalism. As Hayes says, there are good wedding DJs, and bad wedding DJs, and the work of being a cable news host is making sure you're one of the good ones. But this is the business context in which cable news decisions are made. (pp. 151–152)*

If the media have questionable motivations in determining what is newsworthy, it is incumbent on us, as educators and citizens, to understand that we need to think critically about the news we consume and how we form our opinions. The business of news making in the social media era is contributing to widening social divides as it inhibits our ability to find news that is impartial. When we are continually swayed by the portrayal of issues and unknowingly participate in not just confirmation bias but vilification of the other side, it increases the difficulty of uniting based on our true selves, who we are, and what we believe in. A system that operates and thrives on uniting people based on their mutual abhorrence for the other side creates a society that simply can't engage in civil conversations across differences, focus on shared values, or work toward the collective good. In his interview with the Commonwealth Club of California (2020), Klein says, "It's very, very, very hard to know what to do with a conversation that you can't actually have."

Klein's insights raise many questions in terms of how we, as educators, build the capacity to create civil classrooms that can lead to a more civil society: How can we help our students forge stronger senses of their identities in terms of their values, morals, and ethics rather than their politics or those of their family? In what ways can we prepare our students to avoid becoming ensnared by mega-identities and learn to engage in civil conversations toward mutually beneficial solutions? The work of social healing facilitators and human rights advocates can help us find some inspiration for reimagining civil classrooms that can begin to forge a path toward a more civil society.

adrienne maree brown on Turning Toward Interdependence

Writer, activist, and facilitator adrienne maree brown has worked within the worlds of human rights, social justice movements, and social healing facilitation for many years. She cofounded the League of Young Voters in the early 2000s, and in 2006 became the executive director of the Ruckus Society, a nonprofit that provides nonviolent activism training for organizers. In addition to publishing three books since 2017, she founded, in 2019, the Emergent Strategy Ideation Institute, a collective of facilitators working with organizations dedicated to human rights and social justice. Her work focuses on improving facilitation skills that enable groups to work together effectively in order to imagine new possibilities for a more just, inclusive society. This work is informed by the influence of her mentor, the philosopher, social activist, and feminist Grace Lee Boggs, along with the works of science fiction author Octavia E. Butler. In order to examine the promise brown's (2017) remarkable and expansive work holds for creating more civil and engaged classroom communities, this section will focus on ideas derived from her first book, *Emergent Strategy: Shaping Change, Changing Worlds*.

Emergent strategy is a broad term brown uses to identify a way of being that rejects competition as the main mode of survival and values instead the importance of connection toward making lasting change. Such strategies "let us practice, in every possible way, the world we want to see . . . plans of action, personal practices, and collective organizing tools that account for constant change and rely on the strength of relationship for adaptation" (brown, 2017, p. 23). Emergent strategy as a human act is also patterned after nature and what we know from the sciences of biomimicry and permaculture (brown, 2017).

An element of emergent strategy that holds the power of transformation for our classrooms and schools is the element of interdependence. brown (2017) explains:

Interdependence is mutual dependence between things. If you study biology, you'll discover that there is a great deal of interdependence between plants and animals. "Inter-" means "between," so interdependence is dependence between things, the quality or condition of being interdependent, or mutually reliant, on each other. (p. 83)

Indeed, we see interdependence throughout nature. brown (2017) highlights how species from geese to ants, oak trees, and mushroom mycelia rely on behaviors such as sharing resources, providing care to the sick, and growing together, not apart, to strengthen their species.

To the contrary, it is no secret that independence is a value, perhaps *the* value, people in the United States cherish, in concert with a reverence for freedom. And globally, the embrace of individualism is on the rise (Santos, Varnum, & Grossman, 2017). A belief in their rights to independence, freedom, and individualism shapes so many of the choices Americans make for themselves from a young age and, eventually, colors the way they view the decisions they make for their careers and on behalf of their families. And it affects their interpretations of others' decisions as well. Certainly, these are worthwhile values. It is honorable to want to decide for oneself, to provide for oneself, and to respect the rights of others to do the same.

Yet, it is equally important to examine how an allegiance to independence sometimes clouds one's ability to grasp the deep importance of *interdependence*. brown (2017) explains:

Most [Americans] are socialized toward independence—pulling ourselves up by our bootstraps, working on our own to develop, to survive, to win at life. Competition is the way we hone our skill and comfort with the opposite of mutual reliance—we learn to feel proud about how much we achieve as individuals, and sometimes, to actively work to bring others down in order to get ahead. . . . Humans are unique because we compete when it isn't necessary. We could reason our way to more sustainable processes, but we use our intelligence to outsmart each other. We compete for fun, for ego. The idea of interdependence is that we can meet each other's needs in a variety of ways, that we can truly lean on others and they can lean on us. It means we have to decentralize our idea of where solutions and decisions happen, where ideas come from. (pp. 87–89)

This makes it is easy to see how a too-narrow focus on independence can feed into the polarization we see across peoples and communities. When we "use our intelligence to outsmart each other" and "compete for fun, for ego," we are rejecting the possibility of moving forward by drawing on our collective strengths and building a vision for the future that includes mutual reliance, even when we disagree (brown, 2017, pp. 87–89). Paradoxically, allegiance to independence can lead to the very opposite of it. We become so trapped in our desire to assert our independence, to assert the superiority of our own ideas against the ideas of others, that we start to, as Ezra Klein (2020) notes, overidentify with and defend sociopolitical positions we may not even fully understand. This potentially aligns us with groups and movements that, in reality, demand conformity.

brown (2017) suggests cultivating interdependence two ways: (1) through being seen and (2) through being wrong.

Cultivating Interdependence Through Being Seen

brown (2017) offers practices for countering the allure of a too-heavy emphasis on independence by embracing interdependence. She notes that these practices are constituted by "a series of small repetitive motions" (p. 93) we must do again and again, reinforcing the idea that interdependence is a habit that must be cultivated, not one that comes easily for any of us.

The first practice she offers is the practice of allowing ourselves to *be seen*. This is a practice of being honest about our true selves: our needs, our capacity at any given moment, and our true feelings. It might mean asking for support when we are struggling to meet the demands in our lives, personally or professionally. It might also mean admitting that we aren't in a place to take on additional responsibilities at the moment—a sometimes difficult task for those working in schools. brown (2017) describes it in this way: "I show something I've been hiding, and hope I'm still lovable. This generally goes better than could be expected. . . . I can walk towards this 'being seen' and experience the beauty of releasing all that guard and protection" (p. 93).

brown's (2017) advice for implementing this practice of being seen includes the insistence that coming into interdependent relationships will inevitably require not just discomfort at first but even feelings of self-protectiveness, and a sense of releasing control. She notes we must be seen "initially with defensiveness" (p. 93) as though others just cannot understand who we are. (This practice is such a departure from how we might more conventionally conceive of vulnerability—even if we know it is difficult to be vulnerable with others, and to be honest and true, we often struggle to accept the initial defensiveness and seeming loss of agency that occur.

In accepting this fact, we can see that the first blush of *being seen* may not feel much like interdependence at all; it may feel more like a deepening of what Klein (2020) refers to as *polarization*, as we may initially feel judged and further isolated. But if we can accept that the process of being seen and building interdependence (which brown's work reminds us is never linear) must include these feelings, we can start to notice within ourselves, our students, and our colleagues the seeds of possibility where we might otherwise feel discouraged. We can then begin to recognize how strongly we hold to our self-conception, our *guard and protection*, and the narrative we each have of our independent self. We can also then accept that our own and others' defensiveness is not meant to further divide us; it is a necessary part of the process of coming together in a very beautiful and human way.

Cultivating Interdependence Through Being Wrong

The next practice brown suggests for moving toward interdependence is *being wrong*. This is another practice that presents, to thoroughly understate the case, considerable difficulty to most humans. If we recall brown's (2017) point that competition and independence have driven us to "use our intelligence to outsmart each other" and "compete for fun, for ego" (p. 87), we can see how being wrong can feel like a threat to our independence.

Yet in being wrong, we open ourselves up to sharing our common humanity, being in community with one another, and imagining new solutions to the problems we face:

> The easier "being wrong" is for you (the faster you can release your viewpoint), the quicker you can adapt to changing circumstances. Adapting allows you to . . . be in relationship in real time, as opposed to any cycle of wishing and/or resenting what others do or don't give you. Sometimes there isn't one definitive truth. (My favorite situations.) And sometimes there is one and you can't see it. (Least favorite. Least.) Just at least consider that the place where you are wrong might be the most fertile ground for connecting with and receiving others.

> *And in a beautiful twist, being soft in your rightness, as opposed to smashing people with your brilliance, can open others up to whatever wisdom you've accumulated. (brown, 2017, p. 94)*

The more we can practice bringing ourselves to conversations in a way that allows us to be wrong, the more easily we can move toward interdependence—toward looking to one another to help us grow, heal divides, and move forward toward more civil communities. Within brown's first practice, *being seen*, we can see the seed of *being wrong* when she mentions the power of showing something she's been hiding and hoping she's lovable anyway. As thought partners and friends who try to lean toward vulnerability and community, we (Beth and Katie) know there have been countless instances when we have turned to each other and held up a point of view or opinion that we weren't sure about—that we knew could just be wrong. In doing so, we are liberated from what brown (2017) calls *miracle distortions* of ourselves as having to be perfect and all-knowing, and instead are able to receive wisdom from each other or seek out resources to grow together. Accepting that we are wrong is not always easy, but we each ultimately appreciate the gentle corrective, and more importantly our ability to engage with greater accuracy and nuance moving forward.

Imagine the possibilities if the communities that exist in classrooms, teams, and schools were likewise willing to practice being wrong more often. Perhaps in cultivating interdependence, we might find that admitting we are sometimes wrong actually feels liberating. How might we, together, when we are open to inquiry and conversation, leverage our collective ideas to devise new solutions to long-standing problems? To explore these questions further, we will turn to Frances Kissling and her wise approach to communicating across divides.

Frances Kissling on Finding Good in the Position of the Other

Frances Kissling is the president of the Center for Health, Ethics and Social Policy and former president of Catholics for Choice. She has a decades-long history of activism in the realms of religion, women's rights, and reproductive rights. Kissling is widely regarded as uniquely skilled in her ability to talk, think, and write thoughtfully across issues of deep partisan divide. This section focuses on Kissling's advice for how we can find the good in the position of the other as a means for facilitating civil conversations, advice beautifully explored in her interview on Krista Tippett's (2011) podcast, *On Being*.

Frances Kissling has endeavored throughout her career to do the difficult work of maintaining that contradictory thoughts and beliefs are equally important for moral and ethical consideration in order to reach mutually agreeable solutions. The tools she offers the listeners of her 2011 *On Being* interview with Krista Tippett are applicable far beyond the debates surrounding reproductive rights. We can repurpose the tools to help us draw nearer to understanding one another in all our nuanced disagreements, and doing so in a way that honors the position of the other, especially when we are certain that we have no points of agreement and could never see things their way.

Recognizing the Folly of Seeking Common Ground

When we set out to decrease divisiveness, whether in our families, classrooms, schools, or communities, we are so often tempted to do so by finding something, *anything*, we can agree on. This is natural. It corresponds to our desire to decrease confrontation, finding similarity and thus moving toward the instinct Klein (2020) highlights to maintain like-minded groups. But Frances Kissling sees this as a chief mistake that we make when attempting to communicate across serious disagreements and divides (Kissling, as interviewed by Tippett, 2011). Kissling explains this perspective, referencing in the process two groups that hold very different opinions on the issue of abortion rights:

> I'm not a big believer in common ground. Let me be very frank about that. . . . I think that common ground can be found between people who do not have deep, deep differences. And in politics, you can find compromise. Politics is the art of the possible. But to think that you are going to take the National Conference of Catholic Bishops and the National Organization of Women and they are going to find common ground on abortion is not practical. It's not going to happen. . . . The pressure of coming to agreement works against really understanding each other, and we don't understand each other. (Tippett, 2011)

It's interesting that Kissling identifies what might feel like an instinct and even a basic civility—the act of seeking common ground—as, more essentially, a pressure, and not a social pressure that can be healthy and productive. Instead, she asserts

Rubric
outcomes?
↓
ideas for
Cameron/Gabe
coaching?

that this very pressure harms the likelihood of the outcome we should seek: mutual understanding. When we can let go of the pressure to find common ground, when we can admit that we do indeed disagree deeply on an issue, we can leave behind the understandable and unproductive habit of seeking common ground. And if we are honest with ourselves, it is likely that we will find relief in Kissling's suggestion that we release ourselves from the pressure of finding common ground.

How often do we make earnest attempts at finding common ground with family, friends, or colleagues only to end up feeling deflated, knowing the attempts only resulted in some combination of saying something we don't really believe, not saying what we really do believe, or merely placating our discussion partner for the sake of civility? But true civility in a time of deep polarization cannot result in placation; we cannot afford to be less than honest with one another or with ourselves. Uncomfortable as it may feel, if we wish to decrease the divisiveness that plagues our dialogues on small and large scales, we must find another way. Fortunately, Kissling offers us a way to begin in which we can maintain our integrity and loyalty to our own beliefs while at the same time drawing closer to each other's perspectives, regardless of how different they may seem.

Finding Good in Positions We Reject

In lieu of seeking common ground, Kissling proposes that a more productive approach is seeking not just to *understand* the positions of those with whom we disagree but to identify what in them rings good and true with us. In recounting her experiences speaking with those whose opinions lie across the divide, Kissling notes:

> I have changed my views . . . based upon having a deeper understanding of the values and concerns of people who disagree with me. And as a result, I have an interest in trying to find a way that I can honor some of their values without giving up mine. . . [Sidney Callahan . . . said that the hallmark of a civil debate is when you can acknowledge that which is good in the position of the person you disagree with. . . . What is it in your own position that gives you trouble? What is it in the position of the other that you are attracted to? Where do you have doubts? Because it is only, I think, if we are interested in understanding each other and if we are ultimately interested—and it's not a question of common ground— but if we are ultimately interested in [policy] that reflects what is good in the concerns of those who disagree, the only way we're going to get

any sense of what that is, is if we can acknowledge what is good in
the position of the other, acknowledge what troubles us about our own
position. (as interviewed in Tippett, 2011)

With so many contemporary issues feeling so very intransigent, this notion might seem like a tall task. But we simply cannot live our way into a more civil society by refusing to engage with those with whom we disagree or, if we do engage, seeking only to rebut and repel their perspectives. Mutual understanding requires us to genuinely grapple with the complexities of other human beings, their perspectives, and, more deeply, the values and morals that underpin them. And we must do the same with our own perspectives; we must hold them up for examination and determine where our own doubts lie. In the process, we will discover whether some of the opinions we have carried with us are truly our own or they spring instead from our devotion to a group identity. In brown's (2017) words, this begins with a willingness to be seen and admit where we might be wrong.

If this feels like work we are unwilling or unable to do as the flames of division are being stoked once again, Kissling's message feels more salient than ever:

What we've been doing hasn't been working. Now maybe some people
think it's been working, but I think that you become more willing to be
vulnerable at a moment when you recognize that what you have done
has not gotten you where you want to be. So there is that element of,
part of vulnerability is some modicum of helplessness. (Tippett, 2011)

During the writing of this book, we (Beth and Katie) can attest that Kissling's sentiments endure as we continue to face urgent controversial issues about which, as a society, we still can't have productive dialogue toward mutually beneficial solutions. Sadly we fear, as Klein clearly does, that this trend will only continue if we don't do something differently.

Along with this willingness to seek out good in the position of the other, Kissling explains how she has long rejected viewing one side as righteous and the other side as wrongheaded, noting that the "idea that there were extremists on [one] side . . . and rational people on the [other] side . . . never quite fit for me completely" (Tippett, 2011). She attributes this view to the many conversations she has had across the divide of abortion rights throughout her career, especially with those in religious organizations. These conversations showed her that while each side had its strongest hasis on one value (the rights of the fetus or the rights of the pregnant person), most people on both sides seriously engaged with deep and important questions the other side cared about even if they disagreed with the motivating value the other side held sacred.

Often when there is a profound difference of opinion, many of us have a tendency to get defensive and succumb to attitudes of *us* versus *them*. It is human nature to dig in our heels and resort to oversimplifications, but these tendencies stand squarely in the way of the more civil society we seek. And nothing will change until we are willing to re-examine ourselves and our actions with a readiness to transform the way we engage (or refuse to engage) with those whom we most vehemently disagree with. We must be willing to extend the same generosity of spirit that Kissling possesses—and that we very likely have for those in our like-minded groups—to those with whom we have deep disagreements if we truly seek a more civil society.

How can we find ways to help ourselves and our students overcome our instincts for cleaving to like-minded groups and thinking in simplistic either-or ways about those with whom we disagree? And how can we rethink our classroom practices and processes to equip students with the skills, dispositions, and habits of mind they'll need to engage in the civil conversations that are so critical to a peaceful, just, and inclusive society? We think our classrooms have the capacity to become the foundation on which we build a more civil society, one interaction at a time.

Implications for the Classroom

The thinkers throughout this chapter have emphasized the degree to which it is human nature to form strong, intractable opinions and stick to them. This instinct is at the heart of increasing polarization. Frances Kissling highlights how our habit of viewing our own side as rational, calm, and clear, while casting others as extreme and fundamentally wrongheaded, stands in the way of mutual understanding (Tippett, 2011). adrienne maree brown (2017) addresses the desire to be right as a condition that stands in the way of interdependence, and urges us to learn to be wrong in order to facilitate mutual understanding and community. And Ezra Klein (2020) explores how the formation of our mega-identities, so intimately bound up with the political group with which we identify, gives rise to "visceral, emotional stakes . . . and with them, our willingness to do anything to make sure our side wins" (p. 74).

together, these ideas help us understand the contemporary beliefs that one is entitled to their opinion, that one's opinion is sacrosanct, and that one does not need to reflect on, question, or (gasp) change their opinion. The thinkers explored in this chapter might make you wonder how you may be, unwittingly or even knowingly, perpetuating these messages in your classroom. We (Beth and Katie) fear that we have created opinion monsters—that we have contributed to our students' perceptions that they must always have opinions, they must seek chiefly to defend their opinions, and they are not expected to change their opinions even if presented with evidence to the contrary. How do we create opinion monsters, and how might we tame them?

Taming the Opinion Monster

We propose that we risk creating opinion monsters in our classrooms when we assume that our students have formed the same mega-identities that adults have, and thus cemented the attendant positions for their group on a host of issues. We compound this assumption when we place too much emphasis on soliciting students' opinions without providing them enough time to work out what they really think and why. For example, we might task students with writing an opinion piece in defense of an issue they feel strongly about. Generally, a student feeling passionate about an issue is sufficient for gathering research to argue in favor of their selected side. Of course, we may encourage students to include a rebuttal, but only one that they can quickly bury under a mountain of evidence to the contrary. We're wondering, when we guide students through this common writing task, if we ever begin by asking them not to defend a held position but to carefully examine a controversial issue, seeking to understand (which requires considerably more planned in-class time to accomplish). Do we ever challenge them, before they begin to write, to consider what morals and values underpin their fervent belief in their initial opinion? Do we ever ask them to think about the other side, why those on the other side believe what they do, what they might be afraid of, and what's important to them? Do we ever humanize the other side, or do we just encourage students to plow forward, asserting their side as powerfully and articulately as they can?

In hindsight, the first time we considered a more nuanced approach to student argument writing was after listening to Frances Kissling on the *On Being* podcast (Tippett, 2011). Just as we can cultivate opinion monsters, we can also guide our students to recognize the common humanity in the other toward mutual

Dream: 10 values of opp. view, then generate
Prompt solution that addresses/satisfies that value healing in a human way

understanding. As Klein notes (Commonwealth Club of California, 2020), we have become so accustomed to our mega-identities that "we know who we are more than we know what we believe about each policy or moment." But our students are *not* fully formed adults with fully formed perspectives. They do not yet have fully formed mega-identities, even if their families and community leaders do—even if they think *they* do. This understanding can be a powerful lever for cultivating more civil classrooms for a more civil society.

Educators are presented with an important opportunity to help students along a healthier path as they form their identities, to help them get some breathing room from the mega-identities of the adults in their lives and perhaps develop their identities along a different path. We can do so by asking them to reflect on their values, morals, and ethics more, and on their surface-level opinions less. This might look like a shift away from opinion-based questions, and a shift toward values-based ones that are perhaps more philosophical in nature. For example, instead of asking students their opinion on a proposed solution to address homelessness, we might ask students to examine what they believe about what responsibilities a society has to its most vulnerable citizens. Or we might ask students to analyze the ethics of a particular policy by researching and considering what harm and what good they see in its potential impacts.

By helping our students examine the values, morals, and ethics that underpin their sense of the way the world should work, we can help them bypass the reductive arguments they may have heard from social and news media on any number of partisan issues. This can free students to think critically and globally without the influence of the mega-identities of those around them that might make them feel that they have to think one way or another about an issue. Moreover, shifting focus to values, morals, and ethics helps students see themselves and their perspectives in a different light; it teaches them an alternative way of considering their opinions, a way that is more connected to their intuition and sense of self. This strikes us as an important way to help dim the appeal of the mega-identities they observe all around them. We must note that students are understandably drawn to the mega-identities of their family and community groups because this like-mindedness fortifies their sense of belonging. By challenging students to think differently, we are hoping to help students find real belonging and explore what is true in themselves so they can connect more authentically with both their personal groups and society as a whole.

Spotlight On: Taming the Opinion Monster

Encourage students to interrogate their firmly held opinions with the following stems.

- I developed this opinion based on . . .

- My position aligns with my morals, ethics, or values because . . .

- My understanding of the opposing argument is . . .

- One area I might learn more about to possibly expand, refine, or change my opinion is . . .

- The next person I will further examine my opinion with because this person has a different opinion is . . .

We can further tame the opinion monster by helping students become more fully informed on issues of great social, political, and cultural import before asking them their perspectives on these issues. In the interest of engagement and investment, we might invite students to share their opinions quickly, perhaps as part of a welcoming ritual or as a means for hooking students' interest in a new unit of study. If we're seeking opinions on trivial matters, such as students' favorite school lunch or character in a book, this practice is harmless. But when we employ it regarding large, important issues, we do so at great risk by encouraging students to immediately choose a side and by discounting the nuance inherent in these issues—both of which serve to hinder our students' ability to exercise civil discourse skills. Instead, if the opinions we seek on important issues really are central to students' engagement in a unit of study, they merit deeper exploration and support.

Before we even ask students to take a position, we must assess the degree—and quality—of experience they already possess about an issue. Then, it is incumbent on us to ensure that students are informed before they can truly express a position. Depending on the circumstances, this may mean providing resources and readings, both expository and editorial, that help students first understand the facts and then understand the spectrum of perspectives that stakeholders may hold. It may also mean providing students with resources to choose from or teaching skills of discernment and digital literacy and allowing students to research independently.

But it is a mistake to assume that students will, even with the best of intentions, arrive at a full understanding on their own. They often need more guidance than we anticipate, and we must be ready to step in to help tame the opinion monster

by helping students arrive at a thoughtful and comprehensive understanding o
issue at hand. This may seem like too time consuming an approach before students
are free to advance their opinion, but we firmly believe that our students' facility to
engage in civil discourse depends on this meaningful building of schema, or mental
concepts that help one understand how things work. However, if you want to have a
conversation with us about it, we are more than willing to listen and re-evaluate our
opinion as we seek to find what's good in the other.

Last, we must be willing to acknowledge that it is actually not possible nor
desirable to have an opinion on *all* things. Encouraging students to get comfortable
with ambiguity—and with the possibility that even upon becoming informed on
an issue, they may still be unsure of what they think—is another way to help reduce
divisiveness. Imagine how much more evolved public discourse would be if people were willing to admit that sometimes, they just don't know where they stand.
Teachers could even have a name for this stance in their classrooms. Right now,
we're considering perhaps saying something like, "Although I'm informed about the
issue, I'm decidedly undecided" or "Although I understand the different sides of this
issue, I feel like there is a *both/and* to be embraced." If you have other ideas for how
to cultivate this willingness to live in ambiguity in classroom communities, we'd
love to hear them.

human
barometer

Rethinking Rhetoric Toward Real Dialogue

The opinion monster takes another common form in the classroom when teachers
invite students to defend an opinion, particularly in debate formats. We, as educators, must think carefully about these practices, because they can serve as yet another
source for worsening polarization. Too often, what lies at the heart of our skill
instruction on defense of opinion is rhetoric. The art of rhetoric certainly includes
an important set of tools for students to possess, but that, as we see it, is the point
of rhetoric: to be used as a tool toward making oneself understood. The persuasion
of rhetoric is intended to make a good point in an effective way. It is a means to an
end. But too often, it is taught as an end in itself. Too often, we see rhetoric prized in
classrooms for its ability to help students crush their opponents, win arguments, and
shut down contrary perspectives. While some of this may be explained by our desire
as educators to get our students inspired and engaged, we frame the use of rhetoric
in this way at great peril to the goal of creating more civil classrooms.

We must think carefully about the ways rhetoric is practiced in our classrooms. We
should consider carefully both how we teach these skills and what the objective is

when we use them in practice. Debates can be fun and motivational, but also reductive and harmful to civil dialogue. Knowing how to argue is an important skill, but not when its sole purpose is to convincingly cut down the opposition rather than engage with it thoughtfully. We must parse these issues deliberately, educating students on the wonders and the risks of rhetoric-heavy arguments and engaging them in thinking about what kinds of writers, speakers, and thinkers they want to be. Polarization depends on cutting rhetoric to thrive. Students deserve to know that the same skills that can uplift a worthy argument can help a dubious, divisive one pass.

Facilitating Interdependence

Much of the work of creating more civil classrooms lies in undoing the competition frame so many students have operated in throughout their academic careers. You likely went through your years of schooling feeling, at least some of the time, pressured to compete with and outperform other students when putting forth your opinions. This pressure may not originate in our classrooms—families, communities, and wider school cultures can drive it. But there is no doubt that many of our students still feel it, and that it impacts our classroom communities and students' ability to civilly engage with one another.

adrienne maree brown's (2017) emphasis on interdependence can help us reduce competition in our classrooms and cultivate classroom communities where students are more naturally able to talk across differences and turn to one another for support. When we can see one another as resources and not opponents, we can begin the work of building a more civil society.

One path for encouraging interdependence is to build in regular opportunities for students to engage in study groups or learning groups. We often ask students to work together on group projects, but it is less often that they have the opportunity to work together to construct or repair and strengthen their knowledge. When we invite them to be in community in this way, they can start to see one another as learning resources and develop a sense of confidence in one another. brown (2017) notes additional benefits: "having community to learn with . . . means we learn to see ideas, not just through our own singular and limited perspectives, but to see how different experiences create different ways of thinking about things, of comprehending and applying ideas" (p. 248). Once students come to understand one another better, they can gain valuable perspective to help them challenge monolithic, mega-identity-based views that dominate representation in social and news media.

We can continue to cultivate greater interdependence in our classrooms by attending to adrienne maree brown's point that when students do begin to allow themselves to be seen by their peers and teacher, this may initially look like defensiveness. For example, when sharing in small or large groups about aspects of their identities, students may at first express something about themselves in opposition to other identity markers. These attempts may trend toward the too general or even the stereotypical. Imagine you have invited students to share about themselves at the start of the year and a student describes himself as "a man's man, not into sharing feelings, like a girl." Your first instinct may be to worry about the impact of what he has said—that his reply will alienate other students. Though the language may feel forced, the student may simply be feeling the initial defensiveness inherent in allowing himself to be seen, resulting in a desire to overgeneralize aspects of his personality in order to self-protect (Levine & Heller, 2012) and avoid any possibility of confusion regarding how he self-identifies. We can see this as a sign of productive work toward helping our students feel seen, as opposed to a warning sign that our efforts to create more interdependence are fruitless.

Instead of worrying in situations like this, we can get curious. We can use this information as a springboard for better understanding this student and his values, morals, and ethics as the year goes on. And we can feel assured that we have provided an opportunity for our students to be seen, and that this student has gladly accepted the invitation. Three words that can help you manage these potentially awkward moments are, "Tell me more." These words serve to both give you a chance to contemplate your response and offer a student a chance to clarify what they are actually trying to express.

As we move away from the polarizing habits and ways of being that we witness in the spectacle of public political debate and false binaries, we can do right by our students, and our society, by preparing them to forge another path. The exercises that follow provide ways to reflect and act to continue making this vision a reality.

Introspective Exercises for Teachers

Engage in the following exercises to examine how the ideas in this chapter could impact and inspire your teaching practice and inform your instructional decisions toward cultivating a more civil classroom.

Introspective Exercise One: Valuing Our Beliefs *and* the Other

Frances Kissling (Tippett, 2011) offers us an invaluable tool for carefully considering both our own positions and the positions of those whom we believe to be on the opposite end of the spectrum. When we are willing to hold our beliefs up for interrogation in the way she suggests and truly consider the merit in the beliefs of others, we come to know ourselves better and forge a space between our mega-identities and our true selves. This makes communication with those who differ from us clearer, more effective, and more respectful and civil.

Using figure 3.1, think about a strongly held belief or position of yours, and work through Kissling's questions. Perhaps your introspection will bring you into even firmer conviction about your belief or position. But it will likely also help you begin to recognize what in the position of another is worthy, good, and honorable.

My strongly held belief or position: I believe that it's important to involve young people in decisions that impact them.		
Question	**Sample Response**	**Your Response**
1. What is it in your own position that gives you trouble?	*I know that sometimes leaders, whether of families, classrooms, or schools, must make decisions that they feel are best without gaining the input of all stakeholders.*	
2. What is it in the position of the other that you are attracted to?	*I am attracted to the point that young people often do not have enough life experience to have needed perspective on important decisions.*	

3. Where do you have doubts?	*I do worry that we underestimate the degree to which young people can think about complex matters, and in turn cut them out of decision-making processes entirely.*	

Source: Adapted from Kissling, as interviewed in Tippett, 2011.

FIGURE 3.1: Chart for valuing our beliefs and the other.

*Visit **go.SolutionTree.com/teacherefficacy** for a free reproducible version of this figure.*

Introspective Exercise Two: Unpacking Our Mega-Identities

If we are to truly become a more civil society, we must start with both our students and ourselves. One way to reflect on our own communication habits and patterns that may feed into social polarization is to consider how we have conversations across differences with those in our own lives—family, friends, and colleagues. Likely, in these conversations, we are often speaking from our mega-identities or espousing the beliefs of the groups we belong to instead of looking more closely at the values, morals, and ethics that underpin our beliefs.

Esther Perel, psychotherapist, relationship expert, and *New York Times* best-selling author, offers a protocol of sorts to help facilitate these challenging conversations. Though this protocol was developed for people in relationships (Perel & Miller, n.d.), in 2022 she broadened its application:

> *Like couples who are polarized in conflict, what we fight about as a society is often beyond the particular issue in the center of the conflict. . . . Both sides exhaust themselves fighting to maintain their point of view and bring the other person to their side. Neither is able to give ground, because that yielding threatens their world view. (Perel, 2022)*

..begin changing this familiar dynamic, Perel's (2022) protocol helps guide dialogue toward the context of our beliefs and the deeper ideas that underpin them, including what we fear and what we value in a more perfect world. Try the following conversation sequence with some willing participants in your life. Practicing framing conversations this way will help you internalize the steps and build automaticity. You can also use the following questions to reflect individually on beliefs you hold (Perel & Miller, n.d.).

1. **Ask questions:** Ask your conversation partner, "How did you come to think this way?"

2. **Listen for the underlying fears:** What does your conversation partner seem afraid of? Why do you think this is personal for them?

3. **Share with your conversation partner your own fears:** Tell them how you came to think this way, what you are afraid to lose, and why this is personal for you.

4. **Ask each other these questions:** Ask, "What is your vision for a just and safe world? Can we disagree on this issue and still respect each other? Can we disagree on this issue and still find a way to realize your ideal vision of the world?"

Classroom Strategies

These strategies are inspired by the ideas in this chapter and designed for immediate classroom use. Use these strategies with your students to create the conditions for more civil classroom communications, conversations, and relationships.

Classroom Strategy One: Developing Baseline Assumptions and Norms

One way to cultivate more civil conversations in the classroom is to work together as a classroom community to create expectations and boundaries around these conversations ahead of time. Katie and her colleague and friend Justin Dolcimascolo-Garrett have thought carefully about how these structures can be established in a way that prioritizes collaboration and a sense of mutual understanding and respect. What they have found is that many classrooms have norms in place, such as having only one speaker at a time or using agreed-on language or sentence starters to navigate discussions. For instance, we might maintain a classroom norm that we will use language like the following if we get confused during a conversation: *I think when you said that . . . you meant this, but I'm not sure. Can you please clarify?* This language gives a speaker the chance to explain their point of view so we do not misinterpret their meaning.

But classrooms often feature another necessary element that, when in place before norm formation, contextualizes the norms for the instructor and students alike. Some organizers and facilitators have referred to this additional element as a set of *community assumptions*, but we (Katie and Justin) prefer the term *baseline assumptions*. Whereas norms guide behavior in the classroom, helping everyone understand what is acceptable and unacceptable and providing a road map for navigating the practice of civil conversation in real time, baseline assumptions are what individuals agree to be true ahead of time. Baseline assumptions are foundational to all discussions, as they set down agreed-on values, beliefs, and non-negotiables that are co-created as a class and set boundaries around what people are and are not willing to debate. The baseline assumptions may center on beliefs about rights and responsibilities in the classroom, or about rights and responsibilities of individuals and societies. For example, you may set a baseline assumption that all humans deserve access to basic human rights, including food, water, and shelter. This baseline assumption then serves to guide conversations in real time, helping students remember that this belief is assumed to be true and so is not up for debate, and thus placing boundaries on the conversation that keep it on track. Whereas norms guide the *how*, baseline assumptions work to guide the *what*.

Baseline assumptions are not simple or quick to form and maintain, and they may require revision over time as students arrive at increasingly nuanced thinking. Like most worthwhile endeavors, the work is necessarily cyclical and never really over. But baseline assumptions are valuable, and the need for them perhaps makes itself clearest if you consider what could (and often does) go wrong without them. When students do not have a firm sense of what is and is not off-limits in conversation, it's possible for them to make observations that could do real harm. If you have strong discussion norms in place but no class-determined baseline assumption (to help students understand, for instance, that everyone agrees it is wrong to discriminate against others because of their race or gender), you could employ all the skills in your norms toolbox to clarify, empathize, and assume best intent, and still end up with a conversation in which a student, knowingly or unknowingly, raises a hateful or harmful point.

We suggest establishing these baseline assumptions with your class. We also suggest thinking carefully about whether there are any baseline assumptions you, as the lead learner and facilitator in the room, would like to put into place ahead of the collaborative process. As you co-create baseline assumptions and norms, consider doing the following.

- Have students peruse several mentor text sets of norms and baseline assumptions before coming together to work collaboratively so they can suggest or rework some for classroom use.

- Make the work of brainstorming assumptions and norms both verbal and written, thereby providing options for students who may feel more comfortable with one modality or the other and making the process more responsive to all students' needs.

Figure 3.2 has questions for creating baseline assumptions and norms and examples of each.

Questions for Creating Baseline Assumptions

- How do we want everyone to feel in our classroom community?
- What would you like classmates to assume about you when we enter into class discussions?
- What are our responsibilities to one another within this classroom community?
- What are our responsibilities to one another within our society?
- What rights do all people deserve?
- How can we ensure that we are able to discuss ideas without attacking one another?

Sample Baseline Assumptions

- Every person deserves access to basic human rights, including food, water, and shelter.
- Everyone in this room matters and deserves to be treated with dignity.
- We can disagree with ideas, but we must always keep everyone's humanity in mind.
- The way we speak to one another impacts the quality of connection we have.
- People are allowed to change their minds.

Questions for Creating Norms

- How can we make sure that everybody can participate and that their voices are heard?
- What do we do when someone says something that concerns us or may violate a norm? How can we act in supportive ways to repair the situation?
- How can we all take responsibility for our classroom and our classroom discussions?
- How can we encourage one another to think critically?

Sample Norms

- Practice and model respectful curiosity (On Being Project, 2022).
- Express yourself if a thought or idea feels hurtful, and then explain why.
- Recognize that everyone is coming to the conversation with different amounts and types of knowledge and experience (Cornell University Center for Teaching Innovation, n.d.).
- Be OK with being wrong.

FIGURE 3.2: Chart for developing baseline assumptions and norms.

*Visit **go.SolutionTree.com/teacherefficacy** for a free reproducible version of this figure.*

Once you have set some baseline assumptions and norms, we suggest making them highly visible and accessible in both physical and digital spaces and continually revisiting them (especially before class discussions) to create a foundation that becomes a habit of mind.

Additional resources and mentor texts for norms and baseline assumptions follow to help you and your students begin building your own.

- Black Lives Matter at School (https://bit.ly/3HYnQHk)
- The Center for Teaching Innovation (https://bit.ly/3zFM6dy)
- The National Equity Project (https://bit.ly/3K8Yppv)
- The On Being Project (https://bit.ly/3E4BK9J)

Classroom Strategy Two: Distributing Classroom Leadership With a Who Can Help? Chart

adrienne maree brown (2017) sees increasing interdependence as paramount to healing social fractures and building a healthier, less polarized future. When we can turn to one another, across our differences, for help, support, and a genuine sense of belonging rooted in who we truly are, we can communicate more confidently and problem solve more effectively. One way toward cultivating interdependence in the classroom community is to decentralize the authority in the room. When students know they can turn to one another for support and even expertise just as they can turn to the instructor, they develop stronger trust and confidence in one another and themselves. This, in turn, helps them communicate more clearly and decreases their need to self-protect and hold firmly to their not-fully-formed beliefs. We can help students communicate in this way by facilitating opportunities to both provide and seek support.

Figure 3.3 is intended to be flexible in its use. You might employ it for an entire unit of study, or just for a specific set of lessons. You might find it useful during a review portion of a unit. We suggest you schedule in some dedicated in-class time for students to meet, but they can also look to team time, study hall, lunch, or other less-structured times that you may have within your school schedule to autonomously schedule time with one another. Use this chart to help students both volunteer to provide help or support and seek it out.

Our class will use this resource in two important ways.		
1. If you want or need additional support to understand a concept or skill we learned and you would like to seek this support from a peer, you can find willing classmates here.		
2. If you feel you understand a topic really well and are willing to be a resource for your classmates, add your name to the I Can Help column. It's OK if there are multiple names for any given concept or skill! You can also feel free to sign up to provide support for more than one!		
Here is the concept or skill we learned.	**I can help.** (Name and email)	**Outside of class, these are the best times to help.**

FIGURE 3.3: Who Can Help? chart.

*Visit **go.SolutionTree.com/teacherefficacy** for a free reproducible version of this figure.*

Classroom Strategy Three: Recognizing the Position of the Other

Because our students are often asked to assert and evaluate opinions without the opportunity to explore them deeply, they have become quick to defend (and argue against) positions they may not have completely thought through. To help them be less polarized in their thinking, we can give them opportunities to analyze positions or opinions from the perspective of the underlying values they are built on.

Figure 3.4 is intended to be used with any text that demonstrates an opinion or position.

Stimulus (Reading, Transcript, or Link)	Questions
	What are the values that seem to underpin the position being argued or defended? (Note: you may want to refer to the values list in figure 3.5, page 108; James Clear's list at https://jamesclear.com /core-values; or Brené Brown's list at https://bit.ly/3lzARIR.)
	In what ways do you see these values as important and worthy of defense?
	Now that you understand the speaker or writer's values more clearly, consider the following questions. What is it in your own position that gives you trouble? What is it in the position of the other that you are attracted to? Where do you have doubts?

FIGURE 3.4: Chart for recognizing the position of the other.

*Visit **go.SolutionTree.com/teacherefficacy** for a free reproducible version of this figure.*

These texts can be print or digital readings, speeches, or videos—any medium that expresses a nuanced opinion you'd like students to critically read and think about. The questions in the right column help students dig beneath the rhetoric and surface-level points (advanced to uphold and defend an option or position); students think through Kissling's questions in order to discover the good in the position regardless of whether they agree or disagree. Figure 3.5 offers a list of values as examples for your students to reference as they work through the chart.

The following list has examples of values: qualities of action that make life meaningful for some people. Which qualities are especially important to you?

Active	Enthusiastic	Intentional	Reasonable
Adventurous	Expressive	Kind	Resourceful
Ambitious	Fair	Knowledgeable	Respectful
Authentic	Flexible	Loyal	Responsible
Bold	Generous	Modest	Reverent
Careful	Graceful	Open-minded	Serious
Compassionate	Grateful	Organized	Skillful
Considerate	Honest	Patient	Spiritual
Cooperative	Honorable	Peaceful	Steady
Courageous	Hopeful	Perceptive	Supportive
Creative	Humble	Persistent	Thorough
Curious	Humorous	Playful	Traditional
Decisive	Imaginative	Practical	Trustworthy
Diligent	Inclusive	Precise	Warm
Efficient	Independent	Productive	Wise

Source: Porosoff & Weinstein, 2023.

FIGURE 3.5: Examples of values.

Visit go.SolutionTree.com/teacherefficacy for a free reproducible version of this figure.

Questions for Reflection and Discussion

In this section, you will find three different types of questions: questions for individual reflection, questions for conversation, and jigsaw questions across chapters. Each offers you a specific way to think through additional questions about concepts from the chapter.

Questions for Individual Reflection

Consider the following questions.

- How did this chapter help you imagine how you can cultivate a more civil classroom for a more civil society?

- The thought leaders in this chapter offer ideas for how we can help our students to resist the temptation of forming mega-identities and to create more nuanced opinions. Which strategies or ideas discussed here feel the most relevant or hold the most promise for your practice?

- Upon reflection, which of your current classroom practices potentially serve to create opinion monsters by encouraging students to take sides, valuing rhetoric over thoughtful contemplation, or in some other way fostering polarization instead of civility? What changes can you make this school year to reverse these practices?

Questions for Conversation

Consider the following questions to converse about the ideas in this chapter and to leverage these insights toward improving your school.

- Ezra Klein (2020) argues the divisiveness that exists in society is deeply rooted, and he doesn't foresee it changing in the near future. In what ways do you agree with his assessment? In what ways do you feel more hopeful? How can we use our roles as educators to help bridge this divide toward creating a more civil society?

- adrienne maree brown (2017) emphasizes the importance of interdependence to society's ability to move forward into a healthier and more whole future. How can we cultivate a greater sense of interdependence in our classrooms, enabling our students to trust one another more deeply and in turn communicate more authentically and work together more productively?

- Frances Kissling challenges us to resist our temptation to seek common ground with those who have opposing views, and instead find what's "good in the other" in order to have greater compassion so we can engage in civil conversation (Tippett, 2011). How do you envision cultivating this kind of approach in your classroom to help your students develop the skills and dispositions for having productive conversations regardless of what seem like irreconcilable, polarizing viewpoints?

- How have the strategies and ideas explored in this chapter inspired you to make changes in your classroom as we work together to create the foundation for a more civil society?

Jigsaw Questions Across Chapters

Consider the following questions for conversation with individuals who read a different chapter. Share insights and discover how the intersection of these ideas might spark creative solutions to both impact student learning and improve your experiences as educators.

- Can you summarize an inspiring idea from this chapter in your own words? In what way did this idea cause you to think differently about your practice? How might this idea offer insight to you personally?

- What word or quote from this chapter resonates with you?

- What voices and perspectives are not represented in this text?

- What idea, introspective exercise, or strategy from the chapter holds the most promise for you, and why and how would you implement it in your classroom?

- What is one takeaway from this chapter that you'd like to share with students, colleagues, or your team?

- What additional readings can you bring to the conversation? What other texts or articles could further advance everyone's thinking on this topic?

Conclusion

We hope reading this chapter has convinced you of educators' responsibility to structure their schools and classrooms in ways that support students in creating a more civil society. Small changes to the way you conduct discussions and invite your students to learn about polarizing issues can yield substantial changes in the ways your students communicate across differences and position themselves in relationship to one another. And relationships are at the heart of the healing we believe needs to occur to mitigate polarization. If you are interested in exploring relationships further, we suggest following Esther Perel (@estherperelofficial) on Instagram and visiting www.gottman.com to subscribe to one of the Gottman Institute's email newsletters. Although both resources are primarily focused on spousal and partner relationships, the advice and tools they provide are almost always applicable to other types of relationships. Use these resources to continue exploring how you can work against the ways polarization divides people in both your personal life and your school or district.

CHAPTER 4

SUPPORTING STUDENT GROWTH AND MASTERY THROUGH TEACHER LEADERSHIP

Estimated Read Time:

40 Minutes

You do not rise to the level of your goals. You fall
to the level of your systems.

—James Clear

The importance of cultivating teacher leadership has been a throughline for both
of us, Beth and Katie, in our paths as educators and as instructional coaches.
We are interested in growing as leaders so we can best serve our colleagues and support teachers in connecting to their own agency and becoming leaders themselves
who inspire their students and colleagues to flourish. For us, the work of learning
and growing as leaders requires that we look not only to mentors who inspire us
within our field but also to lessons of those beyond the silo of education. This chapter includes a few of the organizational leaders who have inspired and informed
our work, from figuring out how to manage our own professional lives to creating
boundaries between our home lives and our work lives, and deciding how we show
up for our students and colleagues. We invite you to join us in exploring this topic,
along with Brené Brown, Melinda Gates, and James Clear, and think about how it
may resonate with you.

Ideas to Consider

Some of the world's most successful leaders draw on research from the fields of neuroscience, psychology, sociology, and the like to see beyond their own areas of expertise and develop innovative strategies and solutions grounded in what is known about human behavior. The secrets behind organizational success, which is generally measured in profits, prestige, and longevity, often have implications beyond the business world. Therefore, it's no surprise that in books about organizational success written by effective leaders, you'll sometimes find a few paragraphs or pages suggesting that these ideas also have the potential to impact schools.

The ideas are often compelling but not fully developed because authors from fields outside education cannot clearly envision or measure *how* these practices might affect what matters most in education—including student learning, a sense of belonging for students and staff, teacher expertise, and positive relationships. The authors know their topic, and they know it could work in schools, but they don't know *how* it works there. Their experience of the classroom was many years ago, and it was usually from the perspective of their much younger self, sitting behind a desk. But as educators, when we read these books, we *do* know it is nearly impossible to read and learn about these ideas and not imagine how they might positively impact our schools, classrooms, and student learning. And that is what we want to offer you in this chapter: an opportunity to consider a few ideas and strategies from effective leaders who have thought deeply about how truths about human behavior and hallmarks of responsive leadership can impact successful outcomes so we can apply these toward cultivating a classroom culture that supports student growth and mastery.

These ideas intersect with many others across this book either serving as prerequisites to the outcomes we desire or working together to create a synergy that promises greater success. As explored in chapter 1 (page 9), developing emotional literacy toward increased self-awareness is critical to developing effective leadership skills. As we grow as leaders, not only can we better support our students academically, but we can better support their increased personal freedom, which is explored in chapter 6 (page 173).

Brené Brown on Daring to Lead

Brené Brown, an author, organizational leader, podcast host, and research professor at the University of Houston's Graduate School of Social Work, has brought to the forefront conversations about courage, vulnerability, shame, and empathy and how these impact relationships in every sphere of people's lives. Brown's (2018) advice to leaders advances the idea that for leaders to be successful, the first and most important step is a willingness to be vulnerable. This advice is perhaps not the kind many people in leadership positions are looking for, but Brown makes a compelling case that vulnerability is the breeding ground for trust, curiosity, creativity, and innovation, all of which are necessary for companies to thrive. She defines *vulnerability* as "the emotion that we experience during times of uncertainty, risk, and emotional exposure. . . . It's having the courage to show up when you can't control the outcome" (Brown, 2018, pp. 19–20). According to Brown, vulnerability is necessary in order to stay present and engage in hard conversations, such as listening to uncomfortable feedback about how others are experiencing our efforts, or trying to stay curious amid conflicting opinions about the best action to reach a desired outcome. Brown (2018) insists that to be more inclusive and truly make decisions based on collective intelligence, we need to stay vulnerable and engage even when it's hard. She says, "The big shift here is from wanting to 'be right' to wanting to 'get it right'" (p. 92).

Fortunately, this willingness to be vulnerable, according to Brown (2018), is bolstered by boundaries and guided by a person's value system. This suggests that we can embrace vulnerability—a foundational quality to becoming an effective leader—while still maintaining our personal safety. Organizations can create language and norms designed to prioritize and respect everyone's emotional bandwidth and resilience; no one, then, is expected to share beyond what they feel is comfortable and appropriate. Brown identifies key tenets that leaders need to cultivate in order to build a strong foundation for successful outcomes that have clear implications for the classroom. She delves into how establishing boundaries based on our values, building feelings of psychological safety, and creating a sense of belonging are the hallmarks of successful leadership.

Establishing Our Boundaries and Core Values

For those of us who might balk at the idea of vulnerability as some kind of prerequisite for successful outcomes, Brown (2018) stresses the importance of boundaries. She clarifies, "Vulnerability minus boundaries is not vulnerability. It's confession, manipulation, desperation, or shock and awe, but it's not vulnerability" (p. 39). Brown teaches, as inspired by her friend, artist Kelly Rae Roberts, that "setting boundaries is making clear what's okay and what's not okay, and why" (p. 39). For example, some teacher leaders might be comfortable sharing personal anecdotes or struggles with their students to demonstrate an understanding that everyone has challenges that may impact their outlook or performance on a particular day. But teachers don't need to share anything beyond what they feel comfortable with or find appropriate in order to model vulnerability. It is sufficiently vulnerable to indicate that you sometimes struggle with difficult issues but don't feel comfortable sharing the details. To further set boundaries about sharing, you could perhaps indicate that you value privacy and ask that students not take a change of affect personally, as you do not take theirs personally. This kind of communication demonstrates vulnerability, normalizes the uncertainties we all face, and builds connections.

When we embrace vulnerability and sufficiently protect ourselves with boundaries, it actually brings us closer to one another. On her podcast, *Unlocking Us*, Brown (2021) cites writer and educator Prentis Hemphill's (2021) eloquent description of boundaries: "Boundaries are the distance at which I can love you and me simultaneously." If leaders are clear about their boundaries, they can open themselves to the vulnerability that is required for engaging in inquiry, solving problems, and embracing uncertainty and risk within parameters that ensure their personal safety. Boundaries enable educators to model vulnerability for their students (and colleagues) and reveal enough of themselves to forge connections with their students, while being very clear about how much they're willing to share.

With appropriate boundaries in place, leaders also need to ensure that their decisions are aligned with their values and anchored in their most fundamental beliefs. Brown (2018) writes, "Leaders need the grounded confidence to stay tethered to their values, respond rather than react emotionally, and operate from self-awareness, not self-protection" (p. 168). The interesting thing about values is that, according to Brown (2018), "we have only one set of values" (p. 187). The good news here is that we only have to do the hard work of identifying and naming our values one time, because they will be true for us in both our personal and professional lives.

Brown advocates identifying two central values and then leaning on those values to guide you through all your decisions. When teacher leaders are clear on their values, they work to ensure that their words, actions, policies, and norms are in alignment, allowing them to co-create a healthy, consistent classroom environment for their students. For example, if you value relationships, this would be evident as you compassionately offer feedback to students when their performance isn't meeting standards. If you value learning above everything else, then you wouldn't hesitate to reteach a lesson or exempt an assessment grade if the entire class didn't adequately demonstrate understanding, and you would value success in student growth and mastery, not test scores.

Operating in alignment with our values not only creates a classroom environment that reflects who we are but, as explored in chapter 5 (page 143), eases our ability to make tough decisions. It also helps us connect to why we became a teacher in the first place by creating a space that tells a truer story about ourselves, as explored in chapter 6 (page 173). On her website, Brown offers a reflective exercise and a list of values that can help individuals and organizations identify their top-two core values. (Visit https://bit.ly/3xzLiWO to find her list.) She then recommends that leaders and organizations operationalize their values so everyone can understand what they look like in practice, as this explicit mutual understanding is the breeding ground for successful outcomes.

Building Psychological Safety

If teacher leaders want their students to feel confident enough to take risks, share their ideas, try, fail, and try again, they need to create a space in which everyone can freely exchange ideas without fear that their teacher or their peers will judge their worth in the process. Hence, there needs to be a sense of *psychological safety*, a term coined by Harvard Business School professor Amy C. Edmondson. In her book *Teaming: How Organizations Learn, Innovate, and Compete in the Knowledge Economy*, Edmondson (2012) writes:

> *Simply put, psychological safety makes it possible to give tough feedback and have difficult conversations without the need to tiptoe around the truth. In psychologically safe environments, people believe that if they make a mistake others will not penalize or think less of them. (p. 36)*

Psychological safety is necessary for members of an organization to explore and share curiosities and bold ideas that can lead to innovation and success. As Brown (2018) states, "curiosity is uncomfortable because it involves uncertainty and vulnerability [yet it is essential because] researchers are finding evidence that curiosity is correlated with creativity, intelligence, improved learning and memory, and problem solving" (p. 171). Psychological safety is a prerequisite to student growth. Students need to feel safe enough in school to try, make mistakes, and try again and to experiment with new ideas and creative solutions.

Creating a Sense of Belonging

According to Abraham Maslow's (1943) hierarchy of needs, our need for belonging is third only to our physiological and safety needs. Brown (2018) defines *true belonging* as the "spiritual practice of believing in and belonging to yourself so deeply that you can share your most authentic self with the world" (p. 107). In an environment that fosters a sense of belonging, people can show up and feel accepted for who they are and connected to each other through shared values and a common mission. As discussed in chapter 1 (page 9), when people feel a sense of belonging, it creates an environment where they can forge more meaningful and, in Shawn Ginwright's (2022) words, *transformative* relationships that support mutual growth and personal freedom. As humans are a social species, Brown (2021) writes, "finding a sense of belonging in close social relationships and with our community is essential to well-being" (p. 154).

Further, when people feel like an integral part of the larger whole, they can collaborate and rise together. Brown (2018) writes:

> Only when diverse perspectives are included, respected, and valued can we start to get a full picture of the world: who we serve, what they need, and how to successfully meet people where they are. Daring leaders fight for the inclusion of all people, opinions, and perspectives because that makes us all better and stronger. (pp. 107–108)

When students feel assured that they belong, it can liberate them to be fully themselves and participate in the messy work of sharing their best ideas in order to nurture their own intelligence and amplify the collective intelligence of the class. A sense of belonging in school is particularly critical because as students are still developing their sense of self, they need to know that they matter beyond their last test grade or trophy earned (Allen, Kern, Vella-Brodrick, Hattie, & Waters, 2018). It also motivates them to more actively engage in school—an essential condition for their growth and mastery (Singh, Srivastava, & Singh, 2015).

Melinda Gates on Responsive Leadership

Through her work as a philanthropist and cochair of the Bill and Melinda Gates Foundation, Melinda Gates (2019) began to understand that even leaders' very best ideas need what she calls a *moment of lift*. She also learned that, regardless of whether she was working to reduce rates of infant mortality, deliver vaccines to impoverished communities, or provide access to contraceptives, the way to achieve successful outcomes is by applying the same principles: focus on delivery systems and work in connection with others and the people you serve. When her work was grounded in these foundational principles, Gates was able to create changes that improved relationships, empowered people to become more independent, and saved lives.

Delivery Systems

Although a primary focus of the Bill and Melinda Gates Foundation has been product development, which Gates (2019) describes as "scientific research to develop life-saving breakthroughs" (p. 42), she has learned during her work that other factors result in successful outcomes that are just as important as the science, if not more so. Gates (2019) writes, "You have to understand human needs in order to effectively deliver service and solutions to people" (p. 42). She calls these factors *delivery systems*. Gates explains (2019):

> What do I mean by a "delivery system"? Getting tools to people who need them in ways that encourage people to use them—that *is a delivery system. It is crucial, and it is often complex. It can require getting around barriers of poverty, distance, ignorance, doubt, stigma, and religious and gender bias.* [It means listening to people, learning what they want, what they're doing, what they believe, and what barriers they face.] It means paying attention to how people live their lives. That's what you need to do if you have a life-saving tool or technique you want to deliver to people. (pp. 42–43)

To illustrate this point, Gates (2019) shares how the people of Uttar Pradesh, a state in northern India that had extraordinarily high rates of maternal and infant mortality at the time, came to understand and adopt the practice of skin-to-skin contact to warm newborns after childbirth once they learned the story of Ruchi. Ruchi was a trained community health worker from a high-caste family who went to a poor, rural village to see a mother who had just delivered a baby. When she arrived, the mother was unconscious and the child was cold. Ruchi knew she had little choice if she wanted to save the baby's life; despite caste rules and the fact that this was an unknown practice in the community, she placed the newborn against her skin. Gates (2019) writes, "Every woman there leaned in and watched as the baby's temperature rose. A few minutes later, the baby started to move; then he came alive; then he started to cry" (p. 41). This story spread like wildfire through the village and nearby villages—an area that constituted the "global epicenter of newborn and maternal deaths" (p. 39).

By breaking with social norms to save a newborn's life amid a group of women from a lower caste, Ruchi was able to gain the community's trust, demonstrate her expertise, and deliver this life-saving practice to the community she was serving. Overnight, "women went from saying 'We're not sure about this practice' to 'I want to do this for my baby'" (p. 42). Gates therefore concludes "you don't get behavior change unless a new practice is transparent, works well, and gets people talking" (p. 42). Whether with regard to adopting a new practice, causing a shift in thinking, or inspiring people to take action, effective delivery systems matter.

You may be left with lingering questions, such as, "What are my current delivery systems in my classroom, and how can I make them more effective to serve my students' needs?" If we want our students to actively engage in the tasks we offer to support their growth and mastery, then we need to be mindful of our delivery systems. To ensure student buy-in, consider asking yourself these questions: "What knowledge and skills do I want students to gain from this assignment? Why do I care about the assignment and why should they? How can I involve them in my thought process so they can engage with and partner with me to shape these ideas?" In a language arts class, this could look like having students write about issues that matter to them for an authentic audience, offering them the option to brainstorm and choose what they're most passionate about. It could sound like sharing with them how formulating an effective argument can be a powerful way to effect change, and showing them examples from beyond the classroom of how people raise their voices in speech, writing, and collective action to create the kind of world they want to live in. Ask them what would make an assignment more meaningful for them, and include their ideas. Explaining to our students *why* they are doing what they are doing (Gaspard et al., 2015) and offering them choice and voice in the process (Levine & Patrick, 2019) are some of the most effective ways to support their growth and mastery.

Connection

Ultimately, Gates (2019) believes that the only way a true moment of lift can occur is by working with one another. The most effective of her philanthropic efforts were informed and supported by heads of state, experts, and activists. More importantly, the services and resources offered were primarily welcomed by the people they served not only because the need was so dire (and it was), but also because Gates and her collaborators listened and learned about the cultures and communities of the people with whom they partnered.

In more than one instance, when the Gates Foundation was working toward creating more equitable conditions for women and listening to the women at the center of issues, they learned that they were proposing a misaligned strategy or that they were trying to solve the wrong problem altogether (Gates, 2019). How often might we, as educators, do this in our classrooms? How might our best intentions often fall short or fail to cause learning because we are adhering to unresponsive practices rather than adapting strategies so that they are relevant and engaging to the students in front of us? How might we be bypassing root causes and instead attempting to solve surface-level problems?

Gates (2019) offers the example of when the Gates Foundation launched an HIV prevention program in India. After women who were forced into sex work were beaten for asking customers to wear contraceptives, Gates came to understand that, instead of HIV prevention, violence prevention was the most urgent concern. Only when violence was identified as the root cause of the spread of HIV was the foundation able to implement measures to ensure the women's safety—the first and most essential step to stop the spread of HIV.

In the classroom, we might seek to solve a problem yet apply the wrong solution because we made the decision in isolation and not in concert with the students we serve. Perhaps our solution for an apathetic or reticent class is to implement more engaging activities. Yet, perhaps a better solution is to seek anonymous feedback from students about their experiences in the class so we can make wiser, more informed decisions in response to students' needs.

Interestingly, Gates's observations about the effectiveness of building connections and tapping into the intelligence and understanding of those within a community to catalyze change dovetail with the work of Liz Wiseman, a researcher and executive adviser. Wiseman's work with organizations across the globe focuses on the idea that as leaders, we need to believe in the inherent worth, intelligence, and capabilities of the people we serve, and that when we do, we can collectively flourish. Wiseman (2017) calls leaders who abide by this philosophy *multipliers*, and she writes these leaders "see intelligence as continually developing" and ask questions like, "In what way is this person smart?" and "What could be done to develop and grow these capabilities?" (p. 19). When Gates listened to the women she sought to help in India, it was the women themselves who provided the solutions that would improve their conditions. When leaders work in connection with the people they serve, they can amplify the intelligence of each individual and create stronger, more resourceful solutions. Gates (2019) writes, "When we come together, we rise. . . . We see ourselves in others. We see ourselves as others. That is the moment of lift" (p. 264).

James Clear on Building Lasting Habits

James Clear (2018) is an organizational leader and the author of *Atomic Habits: An Easy and Proven Way to Build Good Habits and Break Bad Ones*, which spent over a year on the *New York Times* bestseller list and was the number-one best-selling book on Amazon in 2021. Clear primarily works with organizations to build better habits toward continuous improvement and successful outcomes. His work has implications for how teachers, as classroom leaders, can support students as they develop habits that support their learning and overall well-being. Clear asserts we often become so focused on our goals that we don't pay proper attention to our habits. Our habits create the systems that will help us achieve our goals, and even changes to very small but important habits can contribute to our overall well-being:

> An atomic habit refers to a tiny change, a marginal gain, a 1 percent improvement. But atomic habits are not just any old habits, however small. They are little habits that are part of a larger system. Just as atoms are the building blocks of molecules, atomic habits are the building blocks of remarkable results. . . . They are both small and mighty. This is the meaning of the phrase atomic habits—a regular practice or routine that is not only small and easy to do, but also the source of incredible power; a component of the system of compound growth. (Clear, 2018, p. 27)

According to Clear, our atomic habits do not just help us achieve our goals; they have the power to infuse happiness and purpose into our daily lives when we are able to build effective systems in pursuit of these goals. Clear suggests three ideas for doing exactly this: (1) employing what he calls a *systems approach*, (2) building enduring habits, and (3) linking our habits to desired identity changes.

A Systems Approach

Clear (2018) offers this clarification between goals and systems: "Goals are about the results you want to achieve. Systems are about the processes that lead to those results" (p. 23). Clear (2018) believes that we focus too much on our goals and instead need to think about systems, and writes, "A systems-first mentality provides the antidote. When you fall in love with the process rather than the product, you don't have to wait to give yourself permission to be happy. You can be satisfied anytime your system is running" (p. 26).

He offers the examples of losing weight and running a marathon. In each case, the ultimate goal is at a distant point in the future, so it is easier to sustain your motivation if you can find joy in the habits that lead toward the successful outcome. For example, if you are trying to lose weight, you might give yourself license to spend a little more money in your grocery budget to try out a new nutritious food or two each week to replace something you're phasing out. If you want to enjoy more home-cooked meals with your family, you might fortify the time spent grocery shopping and cooking by simultaneously listening to music, a podcast, or an audiobook. Students who want to master a concept or earn a particular grade might build in rewards to sustain the habits of additional study time and iterative practice. Although the reinforcement of each individual habit may seem inconsequential, the repetition and consistency of good habits over time have the capacity to transform your life. Clear (2018) explains, "If you can get 1 percent better each day for one year, you'll end up thirty-seven times better by the time you're done" (p. 15). When we can adopt and sustain habits designed to support us as we develop into the people we want to be, we are able to ultimately achieve what success means to us.

Enduring Habits

Clear (2018) offers a framework for how to create habits, which he calls the Four Laws of Behavior Change. Table 4.1 (page 124) details that framework.

TABLE 4.1: Clear's (2018) Four Laws of Behavior Change

Law	Explanation	Example
1. Make it obvious.	*Time* and *location* are the most common cues that support habits.	I will [*behavior*] at [*time*] in [*location*]. I will take my vitamins every morning when I make my coffee. (The vitamins are next to the coffeepot.)
2. Make it attractive or appealing.	Link an action you *want* to do with an action you *need* to do.	I will watch my favorite shows when I'm on my treadmill.
3. Make it easy or convenient.	Habits require practice. Repetition and frequency lead to automaticity.	I will scale down any desired habit to a five-minute version to get started. ("Read before bed each night" becomes "Read one page before bed each night.")
4. Make it satisfying.	Offer yourself short-term rewards for the successful completion of a habit.	I will use some of the money I'm saving from not eating out to buy some new clothes or housewares.

Source: Adapted from Clear, 2018.

As we think about creating better habits, it is important to consider how our environment shapes our behavior. Clear (2018) explains:

> *Our behavior is not defined by the objects in the environment but by our relationship to them. In fact, this is a useful way to think about the influence of the environment on your behavior. . . . Think in terms of how you interact with the spaces around you. (p. 87)*

Clear offers examples such as how we may associate a certain spot on the couch with eating ice cream in front of the television, and how, if we work from home, we may have difficulty creating boundaries between work time and personal time as we are using the same physical space for both.

Since your environment provides cues to your behavior, Clear (2018) uses the mantra, "One space, one use" (p. 89). He feels this mantra can be followed even if you reside in a small space because the relationship you form to the objects in your environment is what matters, not the size of your space. Clear (2018) explains,

"If your space is limited, divide your room into activity zones: a chair for reading, a desk for writing, a table for eating" (p. 90). We (Beth and Katie) follow this mantra to manage our technology use. We have both, at times, deleted social media accounts from our phones so we could limit our social media engagement. We also read on e-readers or paper books because trying to read on phones does not sustain our attention and there are too many distractions.

Adapting your environmental cues also simplifies the number of decisions you must negotiate, which is explored further in chapter 5 (page 143). Ideas about how technology can impact your ability to sustain your attention and focus are in chapter 2 (page 41).

Habits and Identity

Clear (2018) suggests that instead of focusing on a desired outcome in order to form new habits, we anchor our habits with a focus on who we want to become, calling this an *identity-based approach*:

> *Your habits are how you embody your identity. When you make your bed each day, you embody the identity of an organized person. When you write each day, you embody the identity of a creative person. When you train each day, you embody the identity of an athletic person. The more you repeat a behavior, the more you reinforce the identity associated with that behavior. (pp. 36–37)*

According to Clear, the reason we have difficulty maintaining good habits is because they often are not aligned with who we are. We have a colleague who uses an assessment tool that reduces grading time, but we identify it as too untraditional to fit in with our own teacher identities. We buy home exercise equipment when the motivation we really need to get moving is the social aspect of attending a gym. We decide to change our eating habits, but we choose a program that doesn't honor our fundamental belief that prepackaged meals and short-term solutions are not healthy choices. Clear (2018) maintains, "Behavior that is incongruent with the self will not last" (p. 32). It is very likely that many of us have failed diets and exercise routines that support his point.

It is helpful to think of each of our habits as part of a larger system that shapes our identity, not just in terms of the goals we want to accomplish. This shift requires us to think not about how we are going to change what we do, but about how our habits are going to reinforce our values and beliefs and bring us closer to who we are and want to be. As Clear (2018) so eloquently writes, "Every action you take is a vote for the type of person you wish to become" (p. 38).

Implications for the Classroom

When we (Beth and Katie) began contemplating this chapter, we imagined that what we would learn from thought leaders might be either successful strategies that dovetail with common best teaching practices or new strategies to adapt for classroom use. Yet, as demonstrated by the ideas in this chapter and the research cited by the thinkers we discuss, we now understand that successful outcomes are not the result of replicable, one-size-fits-all strategies—we can't hack our way into more effective teaching. Instead, successful outcomes are achieved when teachers embrace vulnerability and do the hard work required to build what are often considered *soft skills* in themselves and their students. These skills have the power to shape the cultures of classroom communities into ones that value individuals and their personal growth, prioritize relationships, and foster collaboration. Management guru Peter Drucker puts a fine point on it: "Culture eats strategy for breakfast" (as cited in Groysberg, Lee, Price, & Cheng, 2018).

For leaders and teachers alike, if we don't examine the deeper assumptions that underpin why we are doing what we are doing, we end up replicating old formulas and generating the same outcomes. If we apply some of this chapter's lessons from thought leaders about how to achieve successful outcomes, we can see that we must invest our time and attention in educational systems that are responsive to our own and our learners' needs in order to co-create environments that support students' growth and mastery.

Creating Classroom Environments That Support Good Habits

One question we can ask ourselves when we think about our classroom cultures is, "How does our classroom foster the kind of behavior we are looking to elicit from students?" In keeping with Clear's (2018) insight that "environment is the invisible hand that shapes human behavior" (p. 82), we can design our classrooms so students can gain a sense upon entering of what norms and routines they can expect to meet with.

Depending on your values and desired norms, this might inform what students will do every day when they arrive: Will they engage in a check-in or other welcoming ritual? A regular Do Now activity? During class, there might be audible cues that indicate transition and movement between activities, such as playing music or setting a timer. Visual cues such as anchor charts or regularly referenced slides that support discussion protocols or norms can bridge routines for partner and small-group work. Classroom spaces can be designed with specific areas for fostering collaboration and others for supporting independent work. Communicating early and often with your students about both the expectation (the what) and the underlying objective (the why) makes it apparent to students how these routines shape a culture that supports personal success.

If we help students understand Clear's (2018) insistence that goals are reached through habits that honor our identities and help us envision the people we want to be, we can arrive at co-created norms and routines that support behavior, participation, group discussion, and active listening toward a collective vision for an equitable and responsive classroom community.

In these ways, classroom design can support the formation of good habits by following Clear's (2018) Four Laws of Behavior Change—(1) make it obvious, (2) make it attractive, (3) make it easy, and (4) make it satisfying—and minimize undesirable ones by doing the inverse (make it invisible, make it unattractive, make it difficult, and make it unsatisfying). We intuitively follow this guidance all the time—phones and other items that distract students are tucked safely away, school-issued devices block particular websites, and schedules limit unsupervised time to minimize tempting choices that may detract from the learning environment.

But what if you follow these principles as you work to cultivate good habits? Perhaps when students arrive to your class, your welcoming activity is clearly displayed (obvious), engaging and relevant (attractive), and accessible to all learning levels (easy), and it yields a sense of accomplishment (satisfying). Creating environments that support students as they develop positive habits and avoid negative ones is a worthwhile endeavor; these environments amplify both academic achievement and students' overall well-being. As Clear (2018) writes, "The process of building habits is actually the process of becoming yourself" (p. 37).

Embracing Vulnerability to Lead and Learn

The vulnerability required for effective leadership in any organization applies to the work of leading in the classroom. Again, Brown (2018) defines *vulnerability* as "the emotion that we experience during times of uncertainty, risk, and emotional exposure" (p. 19). The very fact of being the only adult in a classroom of upwards of twenty students means that even with the most careful planning, the many personalities and social and emotional realities will make for some measure of unpredictability. This ongoing uncertainty is inherent in the work we do.

Teachers must navigate a myriad of paradoxes in their practice: They must consider how to foster student engagement and collaboration while managing a busy, productive, inquiry-based classroom. They must decide which student behaviors to address and which to ignore, when an incident simply necessitates a one-on-one conversation, and when it's time to contact parents or administration. They must make all these moment-to-moment decisions while continuing to deliver instruction, transition between activities, and make wise use of classroom time. During planning time, teachers must consider long-term curriculum goals and learning standards, and decide how best to break them down with daily lessons and activities that are meaningful and engaging for students. (If this particularly resonates with you, you may want to learn more about decision fatigue in chapter 5, page 143.)

When we are willing to allow ourselves to be vulnerable and embrace the complexities inherent in navigating unpredictability and paradox, we can be honest with ourselves about how challenging and important our work is. We can also be brave enough to wade into the deep waters of uncertainty to find our way through in lieu of constructing easy solutions. Making intentional, well-considered decisions amid uncertainty and being willing to share pieces of ourselves with our students with boundaries may be cognitively and emotionally challenging. However, these practices have the power to transform our practice and catalyze student learning.

It is not just teachers who need to embrace vulnerability to manage the uncertainty inherent in learning environments. Students, too, must lean into vulnerability, because, as Brown (2018) writes, "without vulnerability, there is no creativity or innovation. . . . Show me a culture in which vulnerability is framed as weakness and I'll show you a culture struggling to come up with fresh ideas and new perspectives" (p. 43). In order to encourage the kind of generative and creative thinking we want for our students, we need to help them embrace vulnerability as a precursor for learning.

Regardless of whether emotions and vulnerability make us uncomfortable, we must welcome them into our classrooms in service of learning. Brown (2018) quotes neuroscientist Antonio Damasio: "We are not necessarily thinking machines. We are feeling machines that think" (p. 43).

Listening to the People We Serve

Ultimately, to create a transformative culture in which people can perform their best, leaders must be responsive to the people they serve. Melinda Gates (2019) illustrates this point with her understanding that even the most effective life-saving techniques will not help anyone if the delivery system isn't based on an understanding of people's lives and culture. For people to contribute and thrive, they need to work in an environment built on a foundation of trust and connection where they are valued for who they are, not just the job they do.

When we listen to our students—whether by co-creating classroom norms, eliciting students' feedback about their experiences in our class, or responding to their feedback by implementing change—we can fine-tune our delivery systems. Perhaps as importantly, doing so demonstrates to our students that more than any curriculum guide, lesson plan, or set of preconceived expectations, their real-life experience and needs are what impact the decisions we make. Inviting students into this iterative process, indeed to be partners in their learning, empowers them and has the potential to change their relationship to school and learning.

It is equally true that by considering the needs of our most vulnerable students, we can more effectively meet the needs of all students, whether we are planning a unit, writing a lesson plan, welcoming a class, giving feedback, having a brave conversation, or building in scaffolds, supports, and resources to address their specific needs. All students benefit from differentiated instruction, multiple modalities, flexible seating, various ways to demonstrate their understanding, and many of the other delivery systems required for our most vulnerable learners.

Spotlight On: Co-Creating Discussion Norms

Co-create discussion norms with students to foster mutual respect and ensure all voices are heard. Here are some suggestions.

- Listen actively.
- Address one another respectfully.
- Base all opinions and comments on facts and textual evidence.
- Address comments to the group; have no side conversations.
- Take turns and do not interrupt others.
- Monitor talk time.
- Be courageous in presenting your own thoughts and reasoning.

- Be flexible and willing to change your mind in the face of new and compelling evidence.
- Assume goodwill and best intentions.

Leading Toward Mastery

We teachers are leaders who have a tremendous impact on the people we serve, and as we have the power to change students' lives, we need to leverage it wisely. According to the Thomas B. Fordham Institute (2021):

> In a healthy, supportive climate, students are engaged and take intellectual risks. They follow well-established rules and norms for behavior that their teachers and school leaders model and maintain. Such a community is characterized by positive relationships between teachers and students, a place where genuine respect is the norm, and where all students feel they belong.

Teacher leaders who prioritize and nurture their students' social and emotional well-being are creating an environment that supports students' growth and mastery. This outcome is further supported by data from the U.S. Department of Education's Readiness and Emergency Management for Schools Technical Assistance Center (n.d.): "When students feel safe, they are better able to focus on learning, which in turn leads to increased academic achievement" (p. 1).

This supports the lessons learned from Brené Brown, James Clear, and Melinda Gates that all point to how, as leaders, we have the greatest power to impact both students' learning and their overall well-being if we embed our teaching practice in what works to shape human behavior. An adherence to these philosophies can be a transformative way for any teacher leader to create a learning environment that equitably honors all students' identities. A strengths-based approach doesn't just make everyone feel good (though this effect does matter to academic success, too). When we help students surface the assets they bring to the table, and when we use those assets to the benefit of the learning community, we supercharge these strengths in the process and have the capacity to raise the collective intelligence of the entire class. And when we focus our efforts on cultivating a positive classroom culture built on the principles of trust, psychological safety, and belonging and designed to foster good habits, be responsive to the learners' needs, and communicate a belief in the limitless capacity of intelligence, we create an environment that holds the greatest promise for learning.

Brené Brown (2018) expresses in *Dare to Lead* that teachers are some of society's important leaders, and we concur. As educators, we have the power to change students' lives through not just what they learn in our classroom but who we enable them to become:

> What we are ethically called to do is create a space in our schools and classrooms where all students can walk in and, for that day or hour, take off the crushing weight of their armor, hang it on a rack, and open their heart to truly being seen. We must be guardians of a space that allows students to breathe and be curious and explore the world and be who they are without suffocation. . . . And what I know from the research is that we should never underestimate the benefit to a child of having a place to belong—even one—where they can take off their armor. It can and often does change the trajectory of their life. (Brown, 2018, p. 13)

If you take one lesson from leadership, know that what we do matters; it seems that *how* we do it matters more.

Introspective Exercises for Teachers

Engage in the following exercises to examine how the ideas in this chapter and your own values and beliefs can anchor and inform your instructional decisions.

Introspective Exercise One: Overcoming Reactivity and Building Self-Awareness

Brené Brown (2018) reminds us that "leaders need the grounded confidence to stay tethered to their values, respond rather than react emotionally, and operate from self-awareness, not self-protection" (p. 168). Building greater self-awareness, as explored in chapter 1 (page 9), is an invaluable tool for moving from *reacting* to *responding* in our work with students. We *all* have moments when we react rather than respond, and holding them up for examination can be challenging. When we are able to do so, we can cultivate the self-awareness needed to break the patterns that produce these reactions, granting us greater confidence and, ultimately, autonomy in our leadership.

Use figure 4.1 (page 132) to examine times in your practice when you were reacting, not responding, and consider ways you could have behaved differently. The first row is provided as an example.

At what times in my teaching career have I not been proud of my words or actions?	What was the precipitating event?	What is it *within me* that could have caused this reaction?	What is it about my reaction that troubles me?	What could I have done or said instead?
Example: I asked a student in front of the entire class, "What is the matter with you?"	*Example:* The student embarrassed another student in front of the class.	*Example:* Wher I repeatedly put a lot of time and energy into the same student, and they don't respond, I become frustrated and overwhelmed.	*Example:* I criticized the student instead of the behavior, and it was compounded by saying it in front of the class, which alienated the student and made them defensive.	*Example:* I could have taken a breath and not responded in that moment until I could decide what would be a more optimal time and manner to address the issue. I could have spoken one-on-one with the student.

FIGURE 4.1: Chart for overcoming reactivity and building self-awareness.

Visit go.SolutionTree.com/teacherefficacy for a free reproducible version of this figure.

If you want to continue working toward becoming less reactive and more responsive, check out Brené Brown's exercise "Living Into Our Values" (https://bit .ly/3ScktBv), which helps you explore how you can align your words and actions with your values. You can use the exercise to reflect on how your values show up in your teaching practice and consider how you can use these values to guide your decision making going forward. An awareness of our values can help us make more intentional decisions that will consistently align with who we are and what we believe, leaving us more confident and at ease, which benefits both our students and ourselves.

Introspective Exercise Two: Cultivating Trust

An environment built on mutual trust is essential for students to feel safe enough to share their ideas, try, fail, and try again. Brené Brown (2018) has created the acronym *BRAVING* to delineate these elements of trust: boundaries, reliability, accountability, vault, integrity, nonjudgment, and generosity. Use figure 4.2 to consider how you foster each of these elements, identify ways that these elements are explicit in your practice and evident to students, and reflect on which elements to strengthen and give greater attention.

Element of Trust (Brown, 2018)	Introspective Question	Evidence From My Teaching Practice
Boundaries	How do I define for and with students what is acceptable and what is off-limits in our classroom community?	
Reliability	Do I follow through with what I say I'll do? Am I careful to not take on too much so I can deliver on my commitments?	
Accountability	Do I admit when I'm wrong, apologize, and make changes going forward?	
Vault	Do I keep student information confidential, particularly when students share personal things with me?	

FIGURE 4.2: Chart for cultivating trust.   continued ▶

Element of Trust (Brown, 2018)	Introspective Question	Evidence From My Teaching Practice
Integrity	Do I choose what is right over the path of least resistance? Are my actions aligned with my values?	
Nonjudgment	Can students ask for what they need without fear of being criticized or judged?	
Generosity	Do I assume that everyone is doing the best they can in intentions, words, and actions?	
Elements of trust to make more explicit or cultivate more intentionally in my practice:		

*Visit **go.SolutionTree.com/teacherefficacy** for a free reproducible version of this figure.*

Introspective Exercise Three: Amplifying Student Genius

When teachers trust that students have an infinite capacity for intellectual growth, and express that belief through their words and actions, it creates an environment in which students can thrive. Use figure 4.3 to think more deeply about the ways you already possess what Liz Wiseman (2017) calls a *multiplier mindset*—a belief in the capacity of the people you serve to grow into and thrive as the highest versions of themselves given the space and support they need. Think about how Wiseman's habits of mind, listed down the leftmost column of figure 4.3, show up in your teaching. If you come across areas that bring up resistance, explore the nature of this resistance and consider how you can counter it in service of student learning. Experiment with adopting these assumptions about students, and reflect on how these small shifts positively impact your practice.

Multiplier Mindset (Wiseman, 2017)	How Does My Teaching Practice Explicitly Demonstrate This Mindset?	How Do Students Know?
Everyone is brilliant at something.		
Everyone can grow.		
By being small, others get a chance to be big. By being big less often, your own ideas will be more impactful.		
Mistakes are part of the natural learning and achievement process.		
People learn best from the natural consequences of their actions.		
People want to learn from those around them.		
People are capable of doing hard things.		
Involve people in the decision-making process. When people understand the logic, they know what to do.		
People operate at their best when they are in charge and held accountable for their work.		
People are smart and will figure it out.		

FIGURE 4.3: Chart for amplifying student genius.

*Visit **go.SolutionTree.com/teacherefficacy** for a free reproducible version of this figure.*

Classroom Strategies

These strategies are inspired by the ideas in this chapter and designed for immediate classroom use. Use these strategies with your students to cultivate qualities that empower them to gain greater self-awareness and lead their own learning.

Classroom Strategy One: Helping Students Identify Their Values and Set Atomic Habits

One of our roles as teachers and leaders is to offer students opportunities to be self-reflective in order to grow into who and what they want to become. Providing scaffolding for this type of self-exploration bolsters both students' academic progress and their overall social-emotional well-being. Students can use figure 4.4 to identify their values so they can build habits that align with their belief systems, and in the process forge their identities. Prior to sharing this exercise, you will want to help students build an understanding of what James Clear's (2018) atomic habits and Four Laws of Behavior Change are and how habits build the systems of people's lives.

Follow these steps to build enduring habits that align with your values and identity.

1. Examine the following table. On the left side, you will see a column with general categories. Each of these categories has three to five specific values.
2. Identify four or five of your current values from the list.

Category	Values (Peterson & Seligman, 2004)			
Transcendence	**Appreciation of Beauty and Excellence** Appreciating beauty, excellence, or skilled performance in various domains of life	**Spirituality** Having coherent beliefs about the higher purpose, the meaning of life, and the meaning of the universe	**Gratitude** Being aware of and thankful for the good things that happen; taking time to express thanks **Hope** Expecting the best in the future and working to achieve it	**Humor** Making other people smile or laugh; enjoying wit

Temperance	Forgiveness	Humility	Prudence	Self-Regulation
	Forgiving those who have done wrong; accepting the shortcomings of others; giving people a second chance; not being vengeful	Letting one's accomplishments speak for themselves; not regarding oneself as more special than one is	Being careful about one's choices; not taking undue risks; not saying or doing things that might later be regretted	Regulating what one feels and does; being disciplined; controlling one's appetites and emotions
Justice	Teamwork	Fairness	Leadership	
	Working well as a member of a group or team; being loyal to the group	Treating all people the same according to notions of fairness and justice; not letting personal feelings bias decisions about others	Encouraging a group of which one is a member to get things done and at the same time maintain good relations within the group	
Humanity	Love	Kindness	Social Intelligence	
	Valuing close relations with others, in particular those in which sharing and caring are reciprocated	Doing favors and good deeds for others	Being aware of the motives and feelings of other people and oneself	
Courage	Bravery	Persistence	Integrity	Vitality
	Not shrinking from threat, challenge, difficulty, or pain; acting on convictions even if unpopular	Finishing what one starts; persisting in a course of action in spite of obstacles	Presenting oneself in a genuine way; taking responsibility for one's feelings and actions; speaking the truth	Approaching life with excitement and energy; feeling alive and activated
Wisdom and Knowledge	Creativity	Curiosity	Open-Mindedness	Perspective
	Thinking of novel and productive ways to conceptualize to do things	Taking an interest in ongoing experiences for their own sake; exploring and discovering	Thinking things through and examining them from all sides; weighing all evidence fairly	Mastering new skills, topics, and bodies of knowledge, whether on one's own or formally

Source: Adapted from Peterson & Seligman, 2004.

FIGURE 4.4: Chart for identifying values and setting atomic habits. continued ▶

Choose two values. Think about how others might see this value show up in your behavior. Explain it to someone by completing this phrase for each of the two values: *I value* _____, *so you may notice that I* _____. (Example: *I value self-regulation, so you may notice that I sometimes turn down invitations to hang out because I need routine time by myself to recharge when I'm not at school or working on schoolwork.*)

Finally, answer these questions.

1. What atomic habit can you build to further live into this value? (Example: *I value self-regulation, so I journal for five minutes every day before I get ready for bed to reflect on my words and actions toward self-improvement.*)

2. How does this habit help you create your identity (who you are and who you want to be)? (Example: *This habit helps me stay regulated and self-aware so that I can make healthy decisions that I feel good about.*)

3. How can you follow the Four Laws of Behavior Change (make it obvious, make it attractive, make it easy, and make it satisfying) to ensure that this habit will become part of your life? (Example: *I can leave my journal on my nightstand with a favorite pen. A reminder on my phone prompts me to put on Do Not Disturb mode and begin my journal entry. I always feel better after I write.*)

Classroom Strategy Two: Helping Students Harness Their Individual Genius

We, as educators, are powerfully positioned to support students in the work of discovering and cultivating their individual genius and their identities as lifelong learners. This work is intrinsically motivating—when we are in touch with our strengths and passions, we can, and want to, harness them toward greater success. Use the activity in figure 4.5 with students, but don't stop there. Invite them to revisit these findings often throughout the school year so they can continually leverage these strengths to realize greater academic success.

Directions: Reflect on each of the following questions and answer with at least one example. You can include more examples if you have them. You may notice as you go that your answers overlap—that's OK! In fact, this will bring you closer to identifying your individual genius.

- What do you do better than anything else you do?
- What do you do better than everyone around you?
- What do you do well without much effort?
- What do you do without being asked?
- What would you readily do without being paid?
- What are you curious about? Think about what you love to learn—what sparks a flame inside you?
- What is something that you do that makes you completely lose track of time (besides scrolling on your phone)?
- What is something that people often rely on you for or come to you for advice on?
- What is something that you do that brings you peace and calm or makes you feel centered?
- What is something from your family or culture that brings you joy or makes you feel connected?
- Now ask your teacher, "What have you observed that I do especially well?"
- Now ask a classmate, "What have you observed that I do especially well?"
- Now ask a trusted family member or friend, "What have you observed that I do especially well?"
- Finally, consider this: Is the picture of you that emerged from your responses and those you received from others surprising, or is it what you expected to discover?
- Now that you have these data, what can you do with them in order to bring positive changes into your academic, social, emotional, and familial lives?

Source: Adapted from Wiseman, 2017.

FIGURE 4.5: Chart for harnessing individual genius.

*Visit **go.SolutionTree.com/teacherefficacy** for a free reproducible version of this figure.*

Questions for Reflection and Discussion

In this section, you will find three different types of questions: questions for individual reflection, questions for conversation, and jigsaw questions across chapters. Each offers you a specific way to think through additional questions about concepts from the chapter.

Questions for Individual Reflection

Consider the following questions.

- In what ways did this chapter shift your thinking about the concept of teachers as leaders?

- A leader's behavior has a direct impact on the outcomes of a community, organization, or classroom. Which leadership skills or competencies discussed here feel the most relevant or hold the most promise for your practice?

- Notice how the suggestion to be more vulnerable sits with you. Consider what factors—from your personal life, your experiences within your district, and your history in the classroom—might shape your response to this suggestion. What boundaries could you put in place that might make you feel more comfortable embracing vulnerability?

Questions for Conversation

Consider the following questions to converse about the ideas in this chapter and to leverage these insights toward improving your school.

- Brené Brown's (2018) text is titled *Dare to Lead*. In what ways does adopting a more expansive view of one's own leadership require some daring or some bravery?

- Melinda Gates's (2019) text *The Moment of Lift* highlights how essential it is to know the people you serve in order to best meet their needs. Share some approaches you presently use to get to know your students. In what ways might you incorporate these practices into your curriculum and instruction throughout the school year?

- In *Atomic Habits*, James Clear (2018) suggests pairing the building of new habits with consideration of the identity we desire to grow into. How can this approach support students in a different and more comprehensive way than other strategies, such as general goal setting or resolution making?

- Liz Wiseman (2017) urges us to be multipliers. Describe the impact of a multiplier you have seen in action. This person could be a former teacher, a mentor, a colleague, an administrator, or anyone else who embodies the qualities she outlines. Try to convey their impact on those around them. What specific actions do they take (or avoid)? Discuss some ways that you could emulate their leadership.

- In what ways do the leadership skills and competencies discussed in this chapter help cultivate more equitable learning environments?

Jigsaw Questions Across Chapters

Consider the following questions for conversation with individuals who read a different chapter. Share insights and discover how the intersection of these ideas might spark creative solutions to both impact student learning and improve your experiences as educators.

- Can you summarize an inspiring idea from this chapter in your own words? In what way did this idea cause you to think differently about your practice? How might this idea offer insight to you personally?

- What word or quote from this chapter resonates with you?

- What voices and perspectives are not represented in this text?

- What idea, introspective exercise, or strategy from the chapter holds the most promise for you, and why and how would you implement it in your classroom?

- What is one takeaway from this chapter that you'd like to share with students, colleagues, or your team?

- What additional readings can you bring to the conversation? What other texts or articles could further advance everyone's thinking on this topic?

Conclusion

The ideas in this chapter led us to believe even more deeply in teachers' capacity as classroom leaders to positively impact students' growth and mastery by creating the scaffolds and conditions to realize one's full potential. Brown inspired us to remember the importance of being appropriately vulnerable with our students in order to cultivate a sense of safety and trust. Gates reminded us to always listen to and be responsive to the people we serve. And from Clear, we learned strategies to build good habits for ourselves and create the supports to do the same for our students.

If you are interested in continuing your learning about how to be a stronger teacher leader who supports student growth and mastery, we recommend James Clear's weekly *3-2-1* newsletter of inspiring quotes (https://jamesclear.com /3-2-1). Also, each episode of Daniel H. Pink's biweekly *The Pinkcast* podcast (www .danpink.com/pinkcast) offers a short video that features research-based tips for improved living, along with a few ideas that he feels are worth sharing. And on his *Ten Percent Happier* podcast (www.tenpercent.com/podcast), Dan Harris interviews thought leaders from across disciplines who offer ideas for increased well-being and happier and more productive lives.

CHAPTER 5

REDUCING DECISION FATIGUE TO INCREASE EQUITY

Estimated Read Time:

45 Minutes

In a world of infinite choices, choosing one thing is the revolutionary act. Imposing that restriction is actually liberating.

—Priya Parker

I t's no secret that educator burnout is real. One of its many factors is the number of critical decisions educators have to make and the pace at which they have to make them. Both of us, Beth and Katie, have driven home after a long school day only to replay and subsequently doubt our words and actions from the day. The shame and regret that follow when you feel you may have mishandled an exchange with a student, a conversation with an administrator, or an email from a parent can plague you long after the moment has passed.

In our quest to discover how to free ourselves and our colleagues from this seemingly endless spiral, we've learned that a secret to becoming more effective and sure-footed decision makers lies in identifying and then abiding by principles that can guide us. In chapters 3 (page 79) and 4 (page 113), we explore the importance of understanding one's guiding values. In learning from the thinkers in this chapter, we've come to see that adopting guiding principles, as well as incorporating a few research-based strategies, can lead us to make decisions with greater ease, feel more confident in our subsequent decisions, and produce more equitable outcomes for students. We invite you to join us in exploring this topic, along with Daniel Kahneman, Emily Oster, and Barry Schwartz, and think about how it may resonate with you.

It's important to note that for this chapter, we have opted to focus on introspective exercises only; you will not find classroom strategies. After careful consideration, we felt the takeaways that emerged from this chapter's thinkers were ultimately most applicable to educators themselves, not their students, serving to support you in creating more predictable, informed structures for decision making in your practice.

Ideas to Consider

An educator's work requires near-constant decision making. Think about your first few years in the classroom. (If this is you right now, welcome! We are happy you are here.) Much of the cognitive and emotional labor that went into establishing your teaching practice likely centered on making decisions, and indeed on learning *how* to make them. Regardless of how structured or wide open a curricular document is, or how specific or general a school's policies are, planning your lessons, selecting your resources, and welcoming your class for the day are ultimately about you, your students, and your choices.

The sheer number of decisions educators must make in a given school day is mind boggling. Alyson Klein (2021), assistant editor for *Education Week*, examined the number of decisions that teachers make each day:

> When you Google that question, the first answer that pops up is "1,500." That number, which equates to about three decisions per minute in an 8-hour workday, is based on research that was conducted in the 1980s and 1990s, but is still widely cited in education circles today.

Similarly, educational researcher Deborah Loewenberg Ball, in her American Educational Research Association (AERA, 2018) presidential address, counts a towering twenty decisions in one and a half minutes of filmed instruction. Ball (AERA, 2018) deeply examines just one of these decisions to clarify how the choices educators make in micro-moments, which she calls *discretionary spaces*, can have a critical impact on students' access to equitable learning conditions in their classrooms. As Jill Barshay (2018), writing for *The Hechinger Report*, notes:

> Loewenberg Ball makes the argument that teacher training ought to address these constant judgment calls directly. "We need to scrutinize habits that we've come to assume are just neutral practices that aren't neutral at all. . . . The challenge for us . . . is not to leave to chance that teachers will exercise good discretion."

It's likely that without a focus on the quality of these decisions, without careful consideration of the power we have as educators in these discretionary spaces, some of our decisions will be inequitable. We may inadvertently apply a rule or norm inconsistently, confusing students. We may lose track of our guiding principles when we feel challenged by student behavior and respond in ways that communicate messages we do not intend or that alienate the students from learning. We may, in haste, use language that makes a student feel unseen or as if part of their identity has been erased. Indeed, with so many decisions to make each day, and with student learning at stake, we must consider how to make the required decisions effectively and equitably. This starts with addressing a main factor standing in the way of good decision making: decision fatigue.

Decision fatigue was coined by psychologists Roy F. Baumeister, Kathleen D. Vohs, and Dianne M. Tice (2007), who posit that all humans have a limited supply of willpower to exercise prudent decision making. Journalist John Tierney (2011) sums up the concept this way:

> *Decision fatigue helps explain why ordinarily sensible people get angry at colleagues and families, splurge on clothes, buy junk food at the supermarket and can't resist the dealer's offer to rustproof their new car. No matter how rational and high-minded you try to be, you can't make decision after decision without paying a biological price. It's different from ordinary physical fatigue—you're not consciously aware of being tired—but you're low on mental energy. The more choices you make throughout the day, the harder each one becomes for your brain. . . . The cumulative effect of these temptations and decisions isn't intuitively obvious. Virtually no one has a gut-level sense of just how tiring it is to decide. Big decisions, small decisions, they all add up.*

As we are all vulnerable to decision fatigue, it is critical that we work to mitigate its impact; the consequences of our decisions profoundly impact students. More effective decision making is an issue that resonates throughout this book. When we develop our emotional intelligence, discussed in chapter 1 (page 9) we are poised to make decisions with more confidence and greater self-awareness. In chapter 2 (page 41), we consider how the decisions we make about technology can protect our students' well-being. And in chapter 4 (page 113), we consider how strong leadership emerges from the decision to respond to the needs of those we lead.

In this chapter, we explore why even our most well-intentioned decisions can still result in less-than-optimal outcomes, and discuss the steps we can take to sharpen our decision-making skills toward increased effectiveness and equity.

Daniel Kahneman on Flaws in Decision Making

Daniel Kahneman is a psychologist, economist, and professor emeritus at Princeton University. In 2002, he and Vernon L. Smith, professor of economics and law at George Mason University, won the Nobel Prize in Economic Sciences for their insights into human judgment and decision making. In the 2021 book *Noise: A Flaw in Human Judgment*, which Kahneman coauthored with Olivier Sibony and Cass R. Sunstein (2021b), the authors explore the surprisingly wide variabilities in human judgment and decision making. These discrepancies are of particular concern in evidence-based professions such as medicine, forensic science, and the judicial system, in which consistency and accuracy are crucial. The authors also address how bias affects decision making, but as bias has been written about extensively, they focus more deeply on the concept of noise.

They define *noise* as the "unwanted variability in judgments that should ideally be identical, [that] can create rampant injustice, high economic costs, and errors of many kinds" (Kahneman et al., 2021b, p. 21). They offer numerous examples in the book to highlight these unfair inconsistencies in judgments, and offer actionable strategies for how to reduce this noise toward more equitable outcomes.

Kahneman and colleagues (2021a, 2021b) offer these research-based examples of *system noise* to illustrate decisions that should be the same, or at the very least close to one another.

- There is a variability of three and a half years in judicial decisions sentencing for the same crime.

- Insurance underwriters differ by as much as 55 percent in establishing premiums for the same risk.

- Radiologists disagree on their interpretations of images.

- Doctors differ in terms of diagnoses and treatment plans.

- Economic forecasts vary widely.

- Fingerprint experts disagree on what constitutes an exact match.

These variations often result from individual differences in temperament, mood, and fatigue, along with outside circumstances such as the time of day, the weather, and even, the researchers note, the loss of a local city's football team (Kahneman et al, 2021b). And the consequences of this noise are clear: these inconsistent decisions result in unfair treatment across systems with regard to time, money, health, and even personal freedom (Kahneman et al., 2021b).

This research has implications for educators, as teaching styles and classroom norms vary widely. One example of noise across schools and classrooms is the variability in judgments about course placement, leading to disproportional access to advanced coursework. Another is the inconsistent application of grading policies, which disadvantages equally-deserving students and affects their access to higher education, in time perpetuating income disparities (Kim, 2021). The education system could benefit from more consistent instruction, assessment, and placement decisions in pursuit of equitable outcomes for students while still honoring the autonomy and professional judgment of each teacher.

When it comes to considering how to silence this noise to move toward increased fairness across systems, it is important to first understand more about the types of decisions that are impacted by noise.

Making Two Kinds of Decisions

Much of our decision fatigue lies in the many moment-to-moment decisions we make to maintain an orderly classroom in which students can meaningfully engage and focus on their learning. In Kahneman's (2013) landmark book, *Thinking, Fast and Slow*, he refers to these types of decisions as *thinking fast*, in which we are largely unconscious that we are even engaged in decision making and thus respond with *automaticity* (automatically, without thinking consciously).

Sadly, for educators, the margin of error can be unusually high. Not only do we make hundreds and hundreds of these decisions in a school day, but our decisions are often compromised by any number of factors, from personal fatigue to external circumstances. Kahneman explains to Adam Grant (2021a) on his *Taken for Granted* podcast why there tends to be a large margin of error in these cases: "If you jump to conclusions too early or jump to decisions too early, then you're going to make avoidable mistakes." In a classroom, these mistakes are somewhat less avoidable due to the pace of the school day and the sheer volume of decisions, allowing little time for contemplation amid a roomful of students. We will, however, discuss later in the chapter a few strategies that can help when we're thinking fast.

Kahneman's work on noise also focuses on the more analytic decisions that professionals are tasked with, which fall into his category of *thinking slow*. For educators, these are the more long-term decisions involving curriculum, instruction, assessment, administrative tasks, and academic and behavioral interventions. Similar to other professions, even though these decisions involve greater contemplation, there is still a wide margin of inconsistency both between educators and within each educator's individual practice. Therefore, adopting strategies to quiet our own very noisy system has the capacity to result in more equitable conditions for students and families as well as increased confidence for teachers. Everyone can benefit from being part of a system that operates with increased consistency and accuracy and that serves everyone more fairly.

Making More Considered and Accurate Decisions

In his conversation with Adam Grant (2021a), Kahneman discusses the role of intuition in making better decisions:

> Our advice is not to do without intuition. It is to delay it. That is, it is not to decide prematurely and not to have intuitions very early. If you can delay your intuitions, I think that they are your best guide, probably about what you should be doing. . . . I don't think you can make decisions without their being endorsed by your intuitions. You have to feel conviction. You have to feel that there is some good reason to be doing what you're doing.

In *Noise*, Kahneman and colleagues (2021b) further explore how we can couple our intuition with wait time and specific strategies to make more informed decisions that have the capacity to reduce noise. The authors call these strategies *decision hygiene* and explain their use of the term this way:

> When you wash your hands, you may not know precisely which germ you are avoiding—you just know that handwashing is a good prevention for a variety of germs. . . . Similarly, following the principles of decision hygiene means that you adopt techniques that reduce noise without ever knowing which underlying errors you are helping to avoid. The analogy with handwashing is intentional. Hygiene measures can

be tedious. Their benefits are not directly visible; you might never know what problem they prevented from occurring. (Kahneman et al., 2021b, pp. 243–244)

Table 5.1 offers two strategies that can reduce noise, which Kahneman and colleagues (2021b) refer to as an *invisible enemy*, noting that "preventing the assault of an invisible enemy can yield only an invisible victory" (p. 244).

TABLE 5.1: Decision Hygiene

Strategy	Description	Example
Structuring Complex Judgments (Kahneman et al., 2021b, p. 307)	This strategy is defined by three principles. 1. **Decomposition:** Break down the decision into components, or *subjudgments*, to act as a road map to specify exactly what data are required for the decision-making process. 2. **Independence:** Require that each piece of information be collected and evaluated separately. 3. **Delayed holistic judgment:** Review all the data collected, their ratings, and other relevant information (including intuition) to make a final determination.	*Scenario: The Interview Process* 1. **Decomposition:** Create a list of the independent criteria required in order for a candidate to be considered for the position. 2. **Independence:** Assess each of these items independently. For example, conduct structured interviews with predefined questions, record the answers, and measure them independently on a rating scale. 3. **Delayed holistic judgment:** After all the data are objectively collected and scored, a committee reviews the ratings and makes a collaborative, holistic decision about whether to hire the candidate.
Sequencing (Kahneman et al., 2021b, p. 256)	Limit the amount of information provided to prevent being swayed by intuition or data that are irrelevant to the decision at hand, and document your judgment at each step.	*Scenario: A Forensics Laboratory* Withhold all the details of the case from the examiner so they can focus solely on the specific information they need in order to eliminate intuition and bias.

Each of these strategies involves the creation of policies and procedures that contain specific guidelines, checklists, or rubrics to mitigate flaws in human judgment and support better decision making. As we endeavor to decrease the variability in decisions across professions that have serious implications for people's lives, another strategy worth considering is how to connect our smaller, everyday decisions to our values and priorities.

Emily Oster on the Business of Decision Making

Emily Oster is an economist and the JJE Goldman Sachs University Professor in Economics at Brown University. But to many parents, she is more widely known as the best-selling author of the books *Cribsheet: A Data-Driven Guide to Better, More Relaxed Parenting, From Birth to Preschool* (2019) and *Expecting Better: Why the Conventional Pregnancy Wisdom Is Wrong—And What You Really Need to Know* (2021a). Through her work, Oster seeks to debunk conventional wisdom about pregnancy and parenting through educating her audience about using data to guide decision making. In *The Family Firm: A Data-Driven Guide to Better Decision Making in the Early School Years*, Oster (2021b) maintains allegiance to the form she established with her first two titles, providing loads of data and distilling them to help families understand the bottom line. Oster also adds a welcome element to the decision-making mix: a toolbox of approaches to making large, difficult, lasting decisions for one's family.

Oster's (2021b) toolbox is grounded in the practices of economists and the business world; she sees merit in examining how these worlds can be instructive for the process of decision making in the complex arena of family life:

> Making decisions—big and small—is something firms do all the time. When you enter business school, one of the primary things you are trying to learn is how to make good decisions. A key component of this is setting up good decision-making structures and approaches. Although it doesn't always work in this way, business decision making is ideally organized and deliberate. . . . When a choice comes up . . . do you have the processes in place to make it thoughtfully? (pp. 37–38)

In families, as in classrooms, we can easily become overwhelmed by the sheer volume of decisions to make. Oster (2021b) insists that the key to managing this overwhelm is to figure out "not *what to do*, but *how to decide*" (p. 37). In order to establish these processes and learn to make better decisions in service of the family firm, Oster (2021b) offers some structures to put in place. Though intended to support family life, her ideas have great potential to minimize decision fatigue for educators, arming us with tools to examine and refine how we make decisions that impact teaching and learning. Oster's approach holds the promise to create more equitable classrooms and a greater sense of confidence, ease, and joy for educators. In the following sections, learn why mission statements aren't enough and how the Big Picture can help you align values with details.

Why Mission Statements Aren't Enough

When operating within complex systems like companies or schools, we are generally aware of the values and beliefs that underlie these organizations, which are often expressed through mission statements. Oster (2021b) explains having a mission statement is important, as the aim of a mission statement is to ground a group in shared values and make sure that all stakeholders understand what really counts—the core focus and purpose of the group. With a mission statement securely in place, all subsequent decisions can then be aligned with and informed by this mission.

Oster sees great value in grounding all these groups, including families, in mission statements. But she notes that, in considering the family as a firm, broad values-based statements that express our desired vision are not enough. We must consider how day-to-day logistical details will correspond to our overall commitment in order for good decision making toward a clear mission to happen:

> The statement "Create a great search engine and don't be evil" is perhaps a good mission statement for Google, but it's not a recipe for how to run the firm. Just as "Prioritize family time and raise thoughtful kids" may be a good broad mission, but it doesn't tell you the right bedtime. These logistical details matter, because if you fail to think about the logistics holistically, you could find yourself almost accidentally in a very different place than you imagined. Each individual choice may seem inconsequential in the moment, but they add up. (Oster, 2021b, pp. 39–40)

Fortunately, Oster provides readers an answer with what she calls *defining the Big Picture*, which applies to families as well as to the work of educators.

The *Big Picture*: Where Values Meet Details

In order to establish a framework for effective decision making, Oster (2021b) suggests creating a Big Picture, which is a multistep process that begins with first crafting a mission that expresses family values and priorities. She then advocates being very intentional and specific about the day-to-day principles and responsibilities that would serve your decided-on mission. She notes, "When I talk about creating the family Big Picture, I'm talking about these overall principles, but I'm also talking about confronting 'What does Thursday night look like?'" (p. 39).

An added benefit of creating a Big Picture is that it protects us from the risk of making what economists call *decisions on the margin*, which are individual decisions that we make on the fly, without a framework to guide us (Oster, 2021b). Oster uses the example of children's birthday parties to demonstrate the concept. If parents don't have a framework for deciding how to approach the numerous birthday party invitations their children will receive throughout a school year (Oster estimates about sixty invites for a family with three children), family weekend life could quickly be consumed by a revolving door of birthday parties. Reaching a frustration point, a parent may decide to cut off parties altogether. But what about the next party, which happens to be for their child's best friend? Oster (2021b) demonstrates that in this scenario, parents are making decisions on the margin: "while adding each marginal birthday has a small effect, the aggregate may be, quite simply, not acceptable" (p. 40).

For educators, on-the-margin decisions might occur when providing opportunities for students to redo an assignment to earn a higher grade. Without a framework, we could end up making random decisions and causing students to feel that our grading systems are unfair and unpredictable. If we reflect on our own lives, personally and professionally, we can no doubt call to mind examples of on-the-margin, case-by-case decision making—our own or others'—that we have found frustrating and confusing. In order to eliminate this faulty decision-making approach, we must have a deliberate, thoughtful system in place. In addition to eliminating factors that increase variability in our decision making and implementing systems to make more well-informed, consistent decisions, one final challenge to healthy decision making is how to manage the overabundance of choices.

The following sections take you through the three steps.

1. Establish values and priorities.

2. Dig into the details in two main ways: (a) by focusing on schedules and (b) by focusing on principles.

3. Lay out some principles.

Step One of the Big Picture

Step one, establishing values and priorities, entails thinking about detail
the following (Oster, 2021b).

- What is my main goal for this group?
- What are three smaller goals that correspond to the main goal?
- What are three priorities that are essential to me—three things I
  must have time for as a leader of this group?
- What are three activities that are essential to weekdays?
- What are three activities that are essential to weekends?

While some of these questions are clearly more suited to family life (especially the
consideration of weekend time), it's easy to see how our answers can help us clarify
our priorities for the learning happening in our rooms. And most importantly, this
exercise "may also reveal things we care about . . . but that differ from what we are
doing now" (Oster, 2021b, p. 44).

When completing step one as an educator, you might use the last two bullets to
focus on how the Big Picture applies to your own professional life. Considering the
workload you shoulder each week, you can start to make some decisions about what
your weekdays—including prep time during and after the school day—need to look
like in contrast to your weekends. This exercise may lead you to consider when you
are most effectively able to provide feedback and grade summative assignments, and
when you are best poised to do the creative work of lesson and unit planning. It can
also help you identify and prioritize items from outside work that are essential to
your lifestyle, such as family time, exercise, recreation, and rest.

So often, as teachers, we maintain a vision of education and our role in it—perhaps
the one that compelled us to enter the work of the classroom in the first place. But
over time, our commitment to the vision can become compromised, and Oster's proposed framework can help us return to our most fundamental values and priorities.
Next, Oster explores how we can begin articulating the details of day-to-day life in
order to realize and operationalize our vision.

Step Two of the Big Picture

Step two of Oster's (2021b) Big Picture requires us to dig into the details in
two main ways: (1) by focusing on schedules and (2) by focusing on principles.
When scheduling, Oster suggests starting with a blank schedule and filling in the

details as you'd like them to look. These details should correspond to your Big Picture vision.

Because Oster is writing about families, her schedule template runs a full twenty-four hours. This is likely excessive for our purposes. However, including after-school hours in your schedule template may be useful, as some of your responses to the Big Picture questions will probably impact how you use this time, such as intentionally deciding *not* to work during your off-hours. To lead effectively, we need to take time away from the job so we can return to work with increased resources and internal reserves. For example, when Katie was teaching high school English, being prepared for every class, exercising, and eating healthy were her three essential priorities for weekdays. Adding these priorities to a schedule template clarified for her how much time she could realistically spend on a workout if she wanted to prepare materials for the next morning's first period beforehand and make it home in time to cook dinner after. With these time commitments in black and white, she might decide that during the weekdays, it was best to use the school gym instead of attempting to make it to her fitness club; prep materials for first period during her prep period instead; or grab some nourishing takeout once a week instead of cooking. You can ensure your three essential priorities are met in different ways, and working through a weekly schedule template enables you to make the decisions necessary to meet them.

Step Three of the Big Picture

For step three, Oster (2021b) suggests laying out some *principles*, which she defines as a set of rules or guidelines that are more specific than your mission, but not so specific that they can't address decisions that need to be made frequently. In the family world, these principles will likely be set by parents alone, and may govern issues related to sleep, health, and friends.

In the classroom, principles may apply to issues such as the type and frequency of homework you assign, the way you manage work deadlines, and your approach to behavioral expectations. For example, if one of your goals is to foster a love of reading, a corresponding principle may be choosing not to collect reading logs (which hamper student motivation and interest in recreational reading; Pak & Weseley, 2012), but to instead provide students with weekly book talks on high-interest texts to pique their curiosity.

Some principles, perhaps those regarding work deadlines and behavioral expecta-
may be most effective when they involve a mix of guidelines set by the teacher

individually and by the teacher and their colleagues as a team. (See chapter 3's [page 79] focus on identifying baseline assumptions and norms for more on working with students to develop behavioral expectations.) After all, "the goal of principles, really, is to translate the set of shared values into a set of shared 'rules'" (Oster, 2021b, p. 47). When we think about them this way, we can see how these principles deviate from rules, as the principles are informed by the values, ensuring that they are not arbitrary but based on a well-considered vision. These principles, in turn, help ease decision fatigue. Oster (2021b) notes that principles can be thought of as a triage system similar to an emergency room, enabling you to make decisions quickly based on the context because you've, in essence, already made them.

Barry Schwartz on Why More Is Less

Barry Schwartz is a psychologist whose work focuses on the intersection between morality, decision making, and behavioral science. His work explores how the abundance of choices available to us has resulted in reduced satisfaction and decreased happiness.

Recognizing the Downside of Choices

In his 2005 TED Talk, "The Paradox of Choice," Schwartz describes that the abundance of choices we face surprisingly has negative effects. He states, "One effect, paradoxically, is that it produces paralysis rather than liberation. With so many options to choose from, people find it very difficult to choose at all." Schwartz further indicates that even once we do make a choice, whether it's a minor decision about a type of salad dressing or a variety of cookie or a critical decision regarding a financial or medical issue, we tend to be less satisfied. There are three reasons for this dissatisfaction: (1) perceived missed opportunities, (2) imagined opportunity costs, and (3) sought optimal choices.

For one, we are always left wondering if we made the best decision as we leave so many alternatives behind. Schwartz (2005) explains:

> What happens is, this imagined alternative induces you to regret the decision you made, and this regret subtracts from the satisfaction you get out of the decision you made, even if it was a good decision. The more options there are, the easier it is to regret anything at all that is disappointing about the option that you chose.

Schwartz suggests that we may also perseverate on what economists call the *opportunity costs* of the option we did not choose, imagining all the benefits we might be missing from a different decision. The option could be the salad dressing we eschewed that had fewer calories or the medication we declined that promised decreased side effects. The plethora of choices we left behind can plague us with considerations of the benefits we might be missing as a result of our choice. As Schwartz (2005) says, "Opportunity costs subtract from the satisfaction that we get out of what we choose, even when what we choose is terrific."

Last, all these choices lead us down a path to perpetually seek the most optimal choice, which can be overwhelming. This weighing of multiple options often leads us to spend exponentially more time, energy, and resources than the task necessitates. We might find ourselves paralyzed by choices of streaming movies or paint colors. Often, we would feel much less overwhelmed if we had fewer choices and could choose with greater ease. And ultimately, with all these decisions, we feel we have no one to blame but ourselves if we become critical of or dissatisfied with our choices, as we are the final arbiters of which to choose.

Simplifying the Abundance of Choices

Certainly, having some choices can be liberating and can contribute to our overall well-being. The problems begin when there are too many options to choose from among the seemingly endless decisions we need to make. In his book *The Paradox of Choice: Why More Is Less*, Schwartz (2016) writes:

> Choice has negative features, and the negative features escalate as the number of choices increases. The benefits of having options are apparent with each particular decision we face, but the costs are subtle and cumulative. In other words, it isn't this or that particular choice that creates the problem; it's all the choices, taken together. (p. 226)

Fortunately, Schwartz offers ideas for how we can mitigate this arduous process of considering multiple options prior to making every decision, with the goal of becoming happier and more satisfied. First, he recommends reflecting on some of our recent decisions that involved considering multiple options. We can ask ourselves if the time, effort, and anxiety involved in the decision-making process actually resulted in exponentially better outcomes. In circumstances where it seems that this energy was unproductive, Schwartz (2016) recommends setting parameters for choosing, such as deciding in advance "how many options to consider, or how much time and energy to invest in choosing" (p. 227).

We have attempted to synthesize and consolidate Schwartz's specific recommendations by creating the following list. Consider this an invitation to think about how they apply to you personally, how they might ease some of your professional decisions, and also how they can provide guidance about how and when to structure choice for your students so they feel empowered and liberated.

- Establish guidelines and parameters for how to make decisions, particularly how many options to consider and how much time to dedicate to a decision task.

- Consult these three pieces of criteria for decision that matter to you: does it align with my values? Does it align with my goals? Does it align with my aspirations?

- Skip these criteria for less important decisions; prioritize efficiency.

- Aim for satisfaction, rather than optimization. In other words, as the saying often attributed to the philosopher Voltaire advises, "Don't let perfect be the enemy of good."

- Resist thinking further about the options you didn't choose, and if you need to, consider your decisions permanent once you have followed the established criteria.

- Practice gratitude for the decision you made.

- Remind yourself that any decision often begins with heightened expectations, and then the novelty will wear off.

- Avoid comparing yourself to others.

It is worth remembering that, in Schwartz's (2016) words, "as the number of choices we face increases, freedom of choice eventually becomes a tyranny of choice" (p. 239). For educators, this is a contributing factor to decision fatigue, and we (Beth and Katie) have been thinking a lot about ways to manage this more effectively to support both teachers and students.

Implications for the Classroom

Our initial inspiration for this chapter was our desire to figure out how to support educators to feel less overwhelmed and more confident in their decisions so they can focus their attention more toward amplifying the learning that's happening in their classrooms. We think that the ideas in this chapter hold the promise to increase consistency in decision making and reduce the number of choices required that result in decision fatigue. If noise can be successfully reduced in schools, it can create more equitable conditions for students and for teachers as well. Consider noise in education, the classroom firm, and the tyranny of choice.

Noise in Education

There is an enormous amount of variability in decision making among public schools, private schools, charter schools, and schools that are formed based on particular philosophies about how students learn best. However, we are primarily concerned about the inconsistency in classroom decisions made by individual teachers and the variability of decisions between teachers in the same school. This type of "noise" compounds decision fatigue and results in unfair conditions for students as teachers are plagued with uncertainty about the efficacy of their decisions and students don't know what to expect from day to day.

As a result of both external circumstances and dysregulation due to hunger, thirst, fatigue, or frustration, a teacher may react to student misbehavior and classroom disruptions, respond to inquiries, and enact policies in different ways. Late work may be acceptable from a certain student on a certain day, but not on another day; a violation of classroom norms may be ignored one day and addressed the next; and an onslaught of questions that might one day be answered generously with grace and finesse might another day be met with frustration and criticism. These varying teacher responses, although understandable to us, can be mystifying for students and create inequities. Students who feel uncertain about what they can expect from their teacher are less likely to ask questions and advocate for themselves, and they are hesitant to seek critical feedback that is essential for learning. Additionally, in our experience, these destabilizing conditions cause students to be more inhibited; troublingly, they may learn that remaining passive is not only the safest route but the desirable one in terms of pleasing the teacher. When a teacher's behavior is unpredictable, it affects a student's sense of safety in the classroom, which affects their ability to focus on their learning.

Clearly, reducing noise will benefit students and lead to more equitable classrooms. When students know what to expect from their teacher, it makes them feel more confident and gives them greater access to learning. When they don't have to navigate the bias and unfairness that can occur when teachers make decisions on the margin, they are able to focus on their social-emotional and academic needs. Reducing noise also benefits teachers, since more consistent decisions will result in increased teacher confidence and reduced teacher-student conflicts (as students will have a clear picture of what to expect and what is expected of them).

One strategy teachers can implement to ease decision fatigue is to limit the number of discrete decisions that need to be made. They can do this by applying some of the decision hygiene strategies in this chapter. We particularly like the idea of structuring complex judgments into *subjudgments*. Then, we can give ourselves time and space to consider each of the subjudgments, and additional time to reflect in order to "delay [our] holistic judgments" before acting on both the data and our intuition (Kahneman et al., 2021b, p. 309). For example, if you believe strongly that students can benefit from revising their work based on feedback and you want to incentivize this process by offering students the opportunity to raise their grade (a complex judgment), you can break down this judgment into subjudgments. Although this might seem like increasing the number of decisions, it actually supports you in making more purposeful, careful decisions that align with your values and that can then apply in other circumstances. That means fewer decisions overall.

Spotlight On: Subjudging Grading Policies and Procedures

What kinds of assignments should be available to revise for a higher grade, and why? Ask yourself the following questions

- "What can students learn from this process, and how will I know that they learned it?"
- "How much time should students have to complete their revision?"
- "What factors are considered in the recalculation of the grade?"
- "What can I do to ensure that this process is accessible to all students?"
- "What can I do to ensure that the process is equitable for all students?
- "How do I communicate these parameters to students for mutual clarity?"
- "Is there a way to include students in this decision-making process?"

Although this process can be time consuming, this kind of reflection and advanced decision making is worthwhile because it will ease the subsequent microdecisions during the year. As a result, it will reduce noise and create more equitable conditions for students; the policy will be clearly articulated and defined in advance so they will understand the parameters for when, how, and under what circumstances revisions are acceptable. All students will receive the same opportunities and realize the same consequences because the process has been thoroughly examined by the teacher and communicated to students.

This implementation of decision hygiene also has great promise to cultivate increasingly equitable conditions for students if departments, teams, or entire school buildings collaborate to create standards for common classroom decisions. Experiencing similar, clearly communicated routines from class to class, such as opening and closing rituals, late work policies, and procedures for remaining aware of homework and upcoming due dates, results in an increased sense of safety and fairness for students (Lester, Allanson, & Notar, 2017). Not all teachers necessarily need to enact policies and procedures in a lockstep fashion, but collaboration increases the likelihood that teachers will work in further alignment and with an awareness of students' experiences in other classes toward increased equity.

The Classroom Firm

Another way to address decision fatigue is to think of your classroom as an organization with a mission statement that identifies what you value in order to articulate a list of priorities. When we thought about how to apply this approach to our teaching practice, we realized that although we may not have had a name for it at the time, we were in many ways already doing this in our classrooms. For example, as former language arts teachers, part of our tacit mission included developing students into independent, purposeful, lifelong readers.

As we sought to achieve this goal, we knew we needed to prioritize students selecting independent reading books and time for sustained silent reading of these books. We also knew that students needed time to reflect on their reading, talk about their books with each other, and conference with us about their reading journeys. In thinking about our "classroom firm" (again, we didn't have this name for it at the time), we created schedules prior to the start of the school year to ensure that our students' reading growth remained a priority. Our schedules included elements such as regularly scheduled visits to the library and time to peruse classroom libraries, whole-class book talks and book passes for building to-read lists, and dedicated, in-class independent reading time, during which we conferenced with students about their reading and supported their text selection skills toward greater confidence and independence. We made time for students to discuss their independent reading books with peers, identify similarities and differences, and generate ideas for what to read next. These intentional decisions—made ahead of time and deliberately scheduled into weekly, monthly, and marking-period plans—allowed us to operationalize our values around supporting lifelong readers.

One of Katie's priorities in helping students grow as readers involved increasing their background knowledge. In order to achieve this goal, she drew inspiration from author and educator Kelly Gallagher's program to support literacy development called Article of the Week. Gallagher's (n.d.) website explains:

> *Kelly recognizes that part of the reason students struggle with reading is because they lack prior knowledge and background. They can decode the words, but the words remain meaningless without a foundation of knowledge. To help build his students' prior knowledge, he assigns them an Article of the Week every Monday morning.*

In her classroom each week, Katie assigned a short current events article curated for students to read, annotate, and reflect on. Since the assignment followed a predictable schedule, it became an automated system in her classroom, which, as a result, required few decisions on her part to maintain. In the same vein, one of Beth's priorities was to ensure that students always had a running list of books they were excited to read. In order to increase this likelihood, one school year, she had students sign up to do a quick book buzz every Monday to share a book they were excited about. They would bring the book to class; share the title, the author, and a short teaser; and read an excerpt. She had a sign-up sheet that covered the entire school year, which generally meant that each student shared twice during the year. In both cases, these initiatives aligned with a larger mission and became parts of the classroom environment that required little decision making, as once they began, they were systems that ran themselves.

Building in these larger systems can keep you purposely tethered to what you most value. Further, doing so protects your priorities from becoming derailed by changes in school schedules and units that go on longer than anticipated for any number of reasons. When your schedule serves your priorities, it can act as a guardrail to help you reach the goals you most want for your students. This schedule also reduces the number of decisions you need to make because many of the requisite decisions are made in advance.

Having a mission statement grounded in your values is also helpful in guiding many of your decisions, both big and small. Even the smallest decisions, if they're not grounded by a mission, can derail you from your priorities and leave you feeling unsuccessful. In addition to having some built-in schedules, regularly consulting your mission statement and corresponding priorities can inform decisions toward greater consistency, personal satisfaction, and equitable conditions for students. For example, if a normally flexible student requests to work alone on a group assignment, your first instinct might be to insist the student work with the group. And yet, if you consult your values and priorities, you may discover you are in greater alignment with them if you honor this student's needs today (and check in later that day to determine if something is wrong and how you can help), rather than emphasizing the importance of collaboration.

A clearly considered list of values and priorities can help ensure that all your decisions align with what you value most. It can also prevent you from getting caught by old narratives you may have once believed about teaching and learning, or being swayed by colleagues whose classrooms operate differently. When educators are consistent in their decisions and responses to students, it reduces their fatigue and makes students feel safe. This reduced cognitive load frees them to focus on learning.

The Tyranny of Choice

Educators have a great deal of autonomy when designing lessons, activities, and assessments. The challenge often inherent in this flexibility is the number of choices available along with the abundance of resources at your fingertips. The internet beckons with the lure of infinite ideas, you likely receive many different emails that promise to exponentially increase student engagement, and the colleague next door might be doing something you'd love to try. It may seem that the key to student success lies just beyond your classroom door, in the free offerings of the latest tech tool, somewhere in your social media feed, or, even worse, on a paid teacher site. This flood of different options coupled with your good intentions can cause you to flail around in the endless sea of resources. Inevitably, these feelings result in increased discord and an inability to make a choice. And as you get lost in the myriad of available options, the process often derails you from the most important piece of your instruction: your initial learning objectives. In order to combat what Barry Schwartz (2016) calls the *tyranny of choice*, it can be helpful to get clear on the types of resources you need, work on developing them yourself, and then only seek out specific resources to build on and enhance the work you are doing. No one knows better than you do what your students need to be successful.

We (Beth and Katie) feel strongly that an underlying problem here is teachers' urgent desire to be the best for their students while somehow, paradoxically, not trusting themselves or feeling that they're not enough. Instead of becoming paralyzed by the abundance of choices, they can strengthen their teaching by staying informed on research-based best practices, following their own intuition and creativity, and listening to their students—and what formative assessment data indicate the students most need. We also find that partnering with colleagues and pooling our collective resources and ideas yields far superior outcomes than any internet search. For us, our best ideas come from a little bit of outside inspiration, and a lot of work on it with each other or one of our like-minded colleagues. When we free ourselves from sifting through email subscription offerings and scrolling our social media feeds, we have more cognitive bandwidth to plan what is best for our students and for ourselves.

We admit that resisting the siren call of limitless resources requires diligence on our part, and we aren't always successful. We subscribe and we unsubscribe. We get lost on social media and then delete the apps from our phones to resist temptation. We endeavor to become proficient in a few tech tools that are suited to different purposes and let the other ones go, and we advise teachers to do the same. It is not easy; the reality of seemingly unlimited choices has become the norm, and yet we are continuing to learn that our freedom often lies in resistance to these choices.

If educators work to become more centered and focused on making professional decisions for their classrooms, they will realize that the next big thing is actually not beyond their reach; instead, it exists in them, their mentors, their colleagues, and their students. This commitment can both ease teacher decision fatigue and lead to increased equity for students by giving them back voice and agency over their own learning. When you are less compromised by decision fatigue, your students win as well. Then, you have more bandwidth to respond fairly and consistently to the moment-to-moment decisions, Loewenberg Ball's discretionary spaces, affirming equity for your students. Even further, by resisting the tyranny of choice, you are modeling for students that it is OK to reject a way of being that, although it has become normalized, is not healthy for anyone.

Introspective Exercises for Teachers

Engage in the following exercises to examine how the ideas in this chapter could impact and inspire your teaching practice and inform your instructional decisions.

Introspective Exercise One: Establishing Your Classroom Firm

In order to make wise decisions about your schedules and principles, you have to get clear on your vision, your values, and your priorities. You can begin this work by reflecting on why you became a teacher in the first place. What was your vision of education for your students? What kind of classroom were you inspired to create? What were your most deeply held values and priorities for your work?

Use the questions in figure 5.1 to reflect on your ideas, and return to them to help you make decisions about the rest of your Big Picture, including scheduling choices and principles. We also recommend returning to the questions listed in *The Big Picture*: Where Values Meet Details section (page 151) of this chapter.

1. One of my most deeply held values as an educator is . . .
2. One of my most important priorities for my students is . . .
3. One way I can incorporate each of these ideas into my Big Picture schedule and principles is . . .

FIGURE 5.1: Chart for establishing your classroom firm.

*Visit **go.SolutionTree.com/teacherefficacy** for a free reproducible version of this figure.*

Introspective Exercise Two: Implementing Decision Hygiene

When you practice decision hygiene, you eliminate factors that can influence you to make erratic or unfair decisions, and you bring more consistency to your work. Earlier in the chapter, we looked at two strategies, descriptions, and examples for practicing decision hygiene in the real world (see table 5.1, page 149). Now, take some time to reflect on how these two strategies might be useful to you in your teaching practice. Reflect on the examples provided in the left column of figure 5 the space in the right column to consider how to address decisions that you yourself making inconsistently or on the margin, which are causing decision fatigue.

Examples in Education	My Decision Hygiene
Strategy One: Structuring Complex Judgments	
Issue: Equitable Late Work Policy **Decomposition:** Break down the decision into components or subjudgments. 1. What is my intention in choosing to or choosing not to accept late work? 2. Does completing work after its due date still benefit students? 3. At what point in the marking period will it be impossible for me to handle late work flow? 4. Will I deduct points for late work? Why or why not? How many? 5. Does this practice align with the values and priorities established in my classroom firm Big Picture? **Independent assessment:** Require that each piece of information be collected and assessed separately. • Create a student survey to gather additional data to determine main root causes of late work. • Look for relevant research to inform any gaps in knowledge. • Reflect on past practice and the results it has yielded. **Delayed holistic judgment:** Review all the data collected and other relevant information, including intuition, to make a final determination.	Issue: Decomposition and subjudgments: Independent assessment: Delayed holistic judgment:

FIGURE 5.2: Chart for implementing decision hygiene.

continued ▶

Strategy Two: Sequencing	
Limit the amount of information provided to prevent being swayed by intuition or data that are irrelevant to the decision at hand.	
Issue One: Equitable Grading Practice	
Consider removing student names from papers before assessing them. Students can be assigned numbers (student IDs work well), or names can be physically covered by sticky notes.	
Issue Two: Equitable Recommendations Practice	
Before making decisions about placement recommendations for advanced coursework, consider exporting student grades to a spreadsheet and hiding the column that lists students' names. Then, review relevant grade information to inform your recommendations. Only reveal the column of names once you have made decisions. The same practice can be used during group processes in teams or within departments.	

*Visit **go.SolutionTree.com/teacherefficacy** for a free reproducible version of this figure.*

Introspective Exercise Three: Considering Contributors to Decision Fatigue

Now that you have a sense of how damaging decision fatigue can be to your ability to make good decisions, you can start to reflect on the factors that might contribute to individual feelings of decision fatigue at any given time. Use figure 5.3 to reflect on the different states that might increase your decision fatigue. Then, brainstorm ways you can regulate these states both proactively and in the moment to gather your resources in order to make more effective decisions. Additional space is provided for you to reflect on other states that might be affecting the degree of decision fatigue you encounter in your life.

State That Affects Decision Fatigue	Example Ideas	My Ideas to Regulate This State During and Outside of the School Day
Hunger or thirst	Bring a water bottle to work and leave snacks in your desk or school bag.	
Exhaustion	From time to time, take your lunch by yourself to restore your energy (listen to music or a meditation app, make a phone call, or enjoy the quiet time).	
Strong in-the-moment emotional reaction	Know your trigger points (or triggering students) and give yourself permission to delay your response.	
Stress (personal or professional)	Use your personal days when you need them. Use the time in the school day to take care of what you need so you can be more patient with and present for your students.	
Accumulation of decisions throughout the day	Reduce the number of decisions required by adhering to your predetermined principles and norms.	

FIGURE 5.3: Chart for considering contributors to decision fatigue.

*Visit **go.SolutionTree.com/teacherefficacy** for a free reproducible version of this figure.*

Introspective Exercise Four: Deciding Who Decides

When planning units of study, teachers spend so much time planning the *what*—sifting through resources, considering sequencing and timing, and deciding what content students need—that they sometimes neglect the *how*. Figure 5.4 is intended to help you think holistically about your school year and consider which decisions need to be made by you and which might be better made with your students or even by your students alone. This exercise can decrease the weight of decisions you face up front while also increasing student autonomy and choice. This is intended to be a continuum, not an exercise in binary thinking. Further, each design choice will not necessarily be applicable to every context.

Consider the following variables when working to reduce instructor decision fatigue and increase shared responsibility for decision making in your classroom. Determinations for each variable should be based on the learning outcomes, experience and needs of students, available resources, and feasibility.

Decided by Teacher	Codetermined (Teacher With Student) ◄————————————►	Decided by Student
	Process Choices	
	Norms: Who sets the norms for the classroom expectations and dialogue?	
	Environment: Where will students sit? When are students allowed to move? What areas of the room do students have access to?	
	Grouping: Who chooses who students' partners or groups are or whether they can work independently?	
	Feedback: Who provides feedback (the teacher, peers, oneself)? Who decides what feedback is needed and when? How is feedback provided (audio, written, student recorded)?	
	Scaffolds: Who decides when a student needs reteaching, conferencing, or support resources? When can the resources be accessed?	

	Content Choices	
	Content or topic: Who selects the content or topic students are working on (to what degree is it based on student interest)?	
	Texts and materials: Who selects texts or materials? Are multiple media offered (print or web, video, audio, visual)?	
	Content delivery: What are the modes of content delivery available (whole or small group, one-on-one conference, required or opt-in minilesson, synchronous or asynchronous)?	
	Product Choices	
	Criteria: Who develops the success criteria (constraints, rubric elements, checklists)?	
	Form: Who decides what form a product or summative assessment will take (written piece, presentation, video, podcast, student-generated option)? Who decides the intended audience?	
	Focus: Who decides the topic or direction of summative assessment?	

Source: © 2022 by Katie Cubano & Mark Wise. Adapted with permission.

FIGURE 5.4: Chart for deciding who decides.

*Visit **go.SolutionTree.com/teacherefficacy** for a free reproducible version of this figure.*

Questions for Reflection and Discussion

In this section, you will find three different types of questions: questions for individual reflection, questions for conversation, and jigsaw questions across chapters. Each offers you a specific way to think through additional questions about concepts from the chapter.

Questions for Individual Reflection

Consider the following questions.

- In what ways did this chapter shift your thinking about the concept or the consequences of decision fatigue in your teaching practice?

- Based on the reality that educators are inundated with choices that can lead to both noisy decisions and decision fatigue, what actionable strategies from this chapter can you use to address these issues in your practice?

- Think about what you perceive as the noisiest decision in your classroom. How does reflecting on the variability of this decision make you feel? How do you think it might feel to your students? What strategies from this chapter can you implement in order to quiet the noise and ensure that this decision is in greater alignment with your values and principles for increased consistency and equitable conditions for your students?

Questions for Conversation

Consider the following questions to converse about the ideas in this chapter and to leverage these insights toward improving your school.

- Daniel Kahneman and his coauthors (2021b) explore how noisy decisions can result in reduced personal freedom and unfair outcomes. Name some of the noisy decisions that are apparent in your classroom, your school, and your district. As a group, how will you decide which of these decisions are the most critical area to reduce noise?

- Emily Oster (2021b) suggests that a way to reduce decision fatigue is to craft a mission statement that articulates your values and priorities and then use that statement to devise a schedule and inform more specific guiding principles. What are some of the ways these strategies might work in your classroom? Discuss your values and priorities, and play around with what a mission statement for your classroom might sound like.

- Barry Schwartz (2016) suggests that the abundance of choices available causes people to feel overwhelmed in the decision-making process and more uncertain about the decisions they ultimately make. Share a time in either your personal or professional life when you struggled to make a decision and were still dissatisfied with the outcome. In hindsight, how could you have both simplified this process and perhaps found a more satisfactory outcome?

- How can you reduce decision fatigue in order to cultivate more equitable learning environments? How does this understanding of decision fatigue inform your approach to student choice?

Jigsaw Questions Across Chapters

Consider the following questions for conversation with individuals who read a different chapter. Share insights and discover how the intersection of these ideas might spark creative solutions to both impact student learning and improve your experiences as educators.

- Can you summarize an inspiring idea from this chapter in your own words? In what way did this idea cause you to think differently about your practice? How might this idea offer insight to you personally?

- What word or quote from this chapter resonates with you?

- What voices and perspectives are not represented in this text?

- What idea, introspective exercise, or strategy from the chapter holds the most promise for you, and why and how would you implement it in your classroom?

- What is one takeaway from this chapter that you'd like to share with students, colleagues, or your team?

- What additional readings can you bring to the conversation? What other texts or articles could further advance everyone's thinking on this topic?

Conclusion

Decision fatigue is inevitable in a profession as important and impactful as education. But there are concrete steps you can take to release its hold and, in the process, make better, more equitable decisions for your students. To understand the great promise and risk that your decisions can hold for your students, we encourage you to visit https://bit.ly/3UfaX1i to watch Deborah Loewenberg Ball's presidential keynote address at the 2018 AERA convention and to learn more about her concept of discretionary spaces.

CHAPTER 6

TELLING STORIES THAT LEAD TO LIBERATION

Estimated Read Time:
50 Minutes

Those little stories we tell ourselves make us what we are,
and too often, what we're not.

—Anna Quindlen

As we became increasingly aware of the impact of the language we use on the people we serve, we've supported each other to rewrite the old scripts that have repeatedly played in our heads. We have learned to ask ourselves, again and again, "Does this way of thinking align with who I am as a person? With who I am as an educator? With what I believe about students?" For Katie, these questions surfaced most poignantly when working with students who were working to read at grade level. She knew she could not work with them to improve their skills without discarding narratives that labeled them as *struggling, low,* or *behind*. Similarly, Beth began to notice that the way she talked to students about their performance had the power to either highly motivate or completely discourage. She wondered then, If our words have this dramatic effect on ourselves and others, how can we learn to rely more on words that will build people up rather than knock them down?

The thinkers in this chapter have guided us to change our habits and reframe the narratives and the words we use so they more accurately reflect our mission and beliefs about what is best for our students. We invite you to join us in exploring this topic, along with Trabian Shorters, Elizabeth Gilbert, and Adam Grant, and think about how it may resonate with you.

Ideas to Consider

Imagine that it is the beginning of the school year, and you've spent the prior days and weeks preparing for your students' arrival. Maybe you've created seating charts, identified students who have accommodations and require preferential seating, and decided on welcoming rituals and activities to get to know your students and build community. This year, you may have a preassessment to help you understand your students' proficiency and skills and inform how you might most effectively meet their needs. As your days together unfold, you begin to notice nuances about your students. You observe which students seem to be quieter, and wonder, Is it a tendency toward introversion? Is it social anxiety? Is it a lack of academic confidence? You identify which students tend to be impulsive, calling out answers and touching classmates who are close by. Then there are the students who consistently approach you with enthusiasm, boldly sharing about their lives outside of school and actively engaging in the life of the classroom.

As a community of learners begin to differentiate themselves, we educators begin, as is our tendency, to attach labels to our students and create stories about them based on our years of experience, conventional wisdom, or even stereotypes. These stories are generally designed to help us harness students' differences in an effort to unite them toward the common goal of building a community that will master the knowledge, skills, and dispositions required to succeed in our course or at our current grade level. Yet, we have been taught and conditioned to categorize and label our students in well-intentioned ways that actually hinder instead of help them. The perceptions we form create student narratives that, although we may not communicate it explicitly, can subtly hinder students' progress or place an artificial ceiling on what they are capable of achieving (Grujiters & Kurian, 2023).

This chapter explores ideas from an activist, a writer, and an organizational psychologist that concern how we can leverage the power of narrative, curiosity, and a willingness to rethink our preconceived ideas in order to let go of the student stories we tell ourselves and empower students to become the authors of their own stories. This subject intersects with the other chapters in this book in that our role as educators is to provide scaffolds and supports to create an equitable learning environment so students can each flourish and become who and what they want to be. Chapter 4 (page 113) seeks to support teachers' growth as leaders to be responsive to students' needs, which may require teachers to let go of the labels in their minds. Chapter 5 (page 143) focuses on teachers' decision fatigue and how teachers can be more present for their students when they are less inundated by myriad decisions.

This shift in mindset creates the possibility for students to define and redefine their views of themselves and their future possibilities toward academic success and overall wellness so *they* can determine their own life trajectories. For us, this is liberation.

Trabian Shorters on Why the Stories We Tell Matter

Trabian Shorters is a social entrepreneur and the founder and CEO of BMe, which is dedicated to defining Black people not by the barriers they may face but by their aspirations and contributions so that organizations can partner to effectively support Black communities in accessing their fundamental freedoms and opportunities. Shorters's work has implications for educators because we have a tendency to define students according to their challenges, whether they are learning or behavioral issues, content-specific competencies, or factors in their home lives. This tendency is, of course, well meaning; if we can identify where our students are struggling, we can focus our attention on filling in these learning gaps or working with the realities that we perceive as defining their lives.

The problem, as Shorters indicates, is that the stories we construct about people and their lives, particularly when framed in the negative or by what people can't do or don't have, place an artificial limit on what is actually possible for them. Shorters further illustrates the power of narrative by describing his philosophy, which is based on cognitive scientific research:

> *Narrative actually matters more than facts. Clearly. Our minds are always forming mental narratives. That is how we make our decisions. . . . It's really important that for those of us that are in the narrative business, in the communication business, you need to credit how powerful your role is in every decision anyone makes. . .* [*We are hardwired to create narratives and make our decisions based on [these] narratives.*] *(The Communications Network, 2020)*

As explored in chapter 5, anchoring our decisions in our values and reflecting on the narratives we tell ourselves help us ensure that our decisions align with who we want to be and what our desired outcomes are. And although it might seem counterintuitive, the narratives we construct about our students are similarly powerful in affecting outcomes. We are not explicitly telling our students these narratives, but it is true that we are communicating these stories to them in subtler ways that impact what they believe they can do or accomplish and even how they see themselves. Think about it from our students' perspective: Are our more vulnerable readers pulled out of our classes for remediation? Are they grouped differently or even reading a different stimulus than the rest of the class? Do we single them out more often, or ask them noticeably different questions? When students graduate from high school, don't the labels that followed them in school adhere to their sense of identity far into adulthood? And if this is the case, how does this impact the kinds of decisions students make for themselves in school and beyond, and what can we do differently at the individual, programmatic, and organizational levels?

Archbishop Desmond Tutu (as cited in *Bill Moyers Journal*, 2007) says, "Language is very powerful. Language does not just describe reality. Language creates the reality it describes." The danger here is that we don't want to trap our students in a narrative where they are cast as the struggling reader or the weak writer, because in doing so, we actually run the risk of upholding that reality. Educational management professor Olubukola James (2018) drives this point home by concluding from research that the "attitude of a teacher, consciously or unconsciously, directly or indirectly affects students' academic performance" (p. 2). With this being the case, we must be mindful of how we speak to students and about students, and even how we think about students.

As author and business adviser Daniel Coyle (2018) writes in his book *The Culture Code: The Secrets of Highly Successful Groups*:

> We tend to use the word story casually, as if stories and narratives were ephemeral decorations for some unchanging underlying reality. The deeper neurological truth is that stories do not cloak reality but create it, triggering cascades of perception and motivation. . . . Stories are not just stories; they are the best invention ever created for delivering mental models that drive behavior. (p. 182)

As educators, we must consider that when we attempt to attach fixed narratives to students' identity and achievement, we are actually creating deficit models that have the capacity to hinder rather than foster their progress.

Shorters (as cited in Fotias, 2018) also explores what he views as the intersection of narrative and identity:

> Narrative tells us which facts to even credit, which facts to ignore, which things are real, which things are false. Narrative literally tells you who you are, it tells you who matters, it tells you where you should go and where you should not go. . . . Narrative is really the key to how we frame our lives. Identity is then a subset of narrative. Identity is the role you play in the story you believe is your life.

According to Shorters's explanation, it then follows that when we define students by their challenges, it directly impacts the formation of their identities. It is therefore critical to explore the ways we think and speak about our students, because in our efforts to support them, we may be causing them harm. Consider the danger of deficit-framed narratives and, as an alternative, asset-framing in the following sections.

The Danger of Deficit-Framed Narratives

It may be our tendency to frame things negatively, and sometimes with judgment, but our main purpose in doing so is usually to define a problem with the goal of finding a solution. Shorters illustrates this kind of hopeful but fruitless deficit-framing when he talks about the money the United States has spent to disrupt oppressive conditions. Although the goal is to eradicate these issues, focusing on the challenges of the people who are suffering—and not who they are and what they aspire to become—has failed. Shorters explains:

> We've spent, over the last 50 years, trillions on our wars on poverty and our wars on crime and our wars on drugs and our wars on illiteracy. . . . And when you look at the very populations who we say we care the most about, the very populations who might self-mobilize around this stuff . . . when those groups organize, they don't even count us as allies . . . . How wrong do you have to get it to spend that much money on an issue, call yourself an ally, and those who have lived the experience know better? People know when they're being denigrated, and they know by whom. (Shorters, as cited in The Communications Network, 2020)

This begs the question, How do we work alongside our vulnerable populations while ensuring that they feel we are *with* them, and even more importantly, that they feel a sense of agency on their journey toward growth and improvement? When we are the architects of deficit-framed stories, we reflect these ideas back to our students, who very likely are already crafting stories of their own that hinder their ability to thrive. Vulnerability researcher Brené Brown (2017) writes, "Sometimes the most dangerous thing for kids is the silence that allows them to construct their own stories—stories that almost always cast them as alone and unworthy of love and belonging" (p. 15).

Knowing the consequences of the stories we tell more fully, we see that we have a responsibility to reconsider how we think and talk about students and to begin to

construct narratives that resonate with inclusivity, hope, and possibilities. To reiterate Shorters's point, "you need to credit how powerful your role is in every decision anyone makes" (The Communications Network, 2020).

This notion of defining other people's stories for them, particularly with a focus on their shortcomings or trauma, reminded us (Beth and Katie) of hearing poet Ada Limón on the podcast *The Slowdown* in an episode titled "They'll Ask You Where It Hurts the Most" (the title of which comes from the title of the poem by Kwame Opoku-Duku). During the podcast, Limón (2021) explains:

> Does it ever seem to you that what gets the most currency these days is pain? Art about pain? Writing about pain? I'll admit I love a sad poem that breaks me open, moves me to tears. But sometimes it worries me when the saddest art gets the most praise. It feels like the world is telling people that the saddest story will win, that the saddest story is the most important story. . . . I worry about the commodification of suffering. I can't tell you how many things I've turned down because they'd rather focus on my pain rather than my resilience or my generational trauma rather than my generational magic. I want to write about trees. I want to write about joy and praise and the interconnectedness of the world. I want to write about those things because I want to feel those things.

Limón's words inspired us to think more about how we can similarly decide to view our students through a strengths-based lens and focus less on their struggles and more on what educator and author Gholdy Muhammad (2020) refers to as their *genius and joy.*

Asset-Framing

Trabian Shorters offers a strengths-based approach to empowering the people we work alongside called *asset-framing*, which is "defining people by their aspirations and contributions before noting their challenges" (The Communications Network, 2020). Shorters maintains that this doesn't mean we should ignore people's struggles or negative attributes, but we shouldn't lead with speaking about people in terms of their challenges, nor define them that way. Shorters elucidates why this is essential:

> Once you recognize that "I want to be a scientist or a leader," or maybe "I just aspire to graduate high school" . . . whatever that aspiration is, if you acknowledge that aspiration before you go into my

various challenges, you're telling a truer story about me. I don't run around believing I'm an "at-risk this" or a "low-income that" or "high poverty, high crime." . . . No one carries around those labels thinking, "That's how I'm going to face the world." People think about it as "I want to maybe go to school" or "I want to maybe someday own a home." . . . Whatever that person's aspiration is, if you haven't bothered to acknowledge that aspiration before you engage them, then you have made them an object in the sentence. They are a thing to be dealt with, to be moved or manipulated. They are not a person. (as cited in Fotias, 2018)

If we apply this to our work with students, how might defining a student first by their aspiration to attend nursing school or the volunteer work they engage in after school, rather than thinking about them as a weak writer, alter our approach? We might be more likely to meet them where they are with high-interest, relevant materials that would lead to higher levels of engagement, and perhaps motivate them to have more to write about. If we focus on a student's strengths first, instead of being the author of a deficit-framed narrative, we can work alongside the student and partner with them in this context toward continual growth and improvement.

It makes logical sense that if we define people primarily by their strengths and contributions, we can best meet their needs and at the same time have them feel that we are allies who will work alongside them. Shorters's deeper examination of asset-framing clarifies how this approach is clearly an issue of equity:

Equity, in essence, is always about value. Whether you're talking about equity in the financial markets, or equity in social impact spaces, you're always talking about value. . . . So defining people in ways that devalue them from the jump categorically undermines the quest for equity. If you want to believe that people should make greater investments in people, use investment language. Talk about their worth. Talk about their assets. Talk about their aspirations. Talk about their contributions. Talk about their strengths. And, by the way, we never say ignore any of the negative stuff. Don't ignore it, but don't define people by it. (as cited in Fotias, 2018)

Equity is a word that's often used in schools, but we don't generally use the words *value*, *asset*, and *worth*. That doesn't mean we don't feel or recognize these things, but for some reason, it's not the place where we typically begin—not in our own thinking, our discussions with colleagues, or our relationships with students. And based on our understanding that the stories we tell have the power to shape identity, learning how to use asset-framing language more effectively can ensure that students begin to similarly define themselves by their strengths, and not internalize the labels we assign or the ways we may unknowingly further marginalize them.

Shorters considers asset-framing a cognitive skill in that it's more than what we say about people; it's what we think about them. And it's a skill we can, and must, practice. Shorters says, "If you're about liberating people, if you're about justice, if you're about freedom, then you have to have a language about liberation and justice and freedom, and that begins by valuing all members of the human family" (The Communications Network, 2020). If as educators we are committed to equity, our language—the language we use internally when thinking about our students, and the language we use externally when talking about or with them—needs to demonstrate and honor that commitment.

We explore asset-framing more deeply later in the chapter, but for now, let's consider how we can make simple shifts in our language. Perhaps we replace the word *remedial* with *developmental*, and we view our students' progress on a continuum of improvement focusing on what they *can do* rather than what they *can't do*. We know enough not to tell children who can't yet swim that they are *struggling swimmers* or below an arbitrary norm for their age. Instead, we describe what they *can do* in the water, and we mark their progress as they become increasingly more proficient. Similarly, as the stories we tell about our students' behavior and ability have the power to shape their identity, it is equally important to consider how we can have an impact on the kinds of stories our students are telling themselves. One way we can do this, as explored by Elizabeth Gilbert, is by examining the stories we tell ourselves that hinder our own well-being so we can model for our students how telling a truer story is the path to personal freedom.

Elizabeth Gilbert on Telling Truer Stories

Elizabeth Gilbert is an author whose life and work has centered on helping herself and others find what is true about themselves. She began this journey most publicly with her 2006 memoir, *Eat, Pray, Love*, and has continued her pursuit to discover how we can all live our lives more authentically, in abundance, and with abandon. In her quest, Gilbert (2015) has examined how the stories we tell ourselves about who we are and what our lives should look like can lead us to make choices that at best are personally unfulfilling, and at worst are suffocating. Her works offer insight into how we can learn to question and challenge the stories we tell ourselves about our lives, internalized from outside forces such as parents and teachers as well as societal definitions and expectations of what happiness is supposed to look like. Gilbert (2015) proposes that the path to a happier and more fulfilling life lies in what she terms *creative living*, which she defines as "a life that is driven more strongly by curiosity than by fear" (p. 9). Consider leading with courage, not fear, and giving yourself permission to follow your curiosities.

Leading With Courage, Not Fear

Gilbert (2015) acknowledges the difficulty of transcending your fears because as a child, she was frightened by so many things that her father began calling her *Pitiful Pearl*. She shares:

> *Growing up, I was afraid not only of all the commonly recognized and legitimate childhood dangers (the dark, strangers, the deep end of the swimming pool), but I was also afraid of an extensive list of completely benign things (snow, perfectly nice babysitters, cars, playgrounds, stairs, Sesame Street, the telephone, board games, the grocery store, sharp blades of grass, any new situation whatsoever, anything that dared to move, etc., etc., etc.). (Gilbert, 2015, p. 16)*

Fortunately for Gilbert (2015), her mother insisted that she was much more capable than she realized, and her mother's determination and willfulness served to help Gilbert revise the story she had been telling herself, one in which she characterized herself as "emotionally and physically totally enfeebled" (p. 18).

She began to learn that she could move forward courageously, and at the same time continue to respect her very real fears. Gilbert (2015) describes how she has learned to invite fear along with her on the journey to creative living, which again is "a life that is driven more strongly by curiosity than by fear." The story Gilbert (2015) now tells goes like this:

> *Dearest Fear: Creativity and I are about to go on a road trip together. I understand you'll be joining us, because you always do. I acknowledge that you believe you have an important job to do in my life, and that you take your job seriously. Apparently, your job is to induce complete panic whenever I'm about to do anything interesting—and, may I say, you are superb at your job. . . . There's plenty of room in this vehicle for all of us, so make yourself at home, but understand this: Creativity and I are the only ones who will be making any decisions along the way. (p. 25)*

ilbert clearly indicates, the stories we tell ourselves can ensnare us in a prison of our own making, if we let them. Our commitment to rewriting these stories we tell ourselves truly has the power to liberate us.

Gilbert further clarifies that her definition of creativity is simply about living a life in which you follow your curiosity, and that being a creative person is not limited to being an artist type. She asserts:

> *If you're alive, you're a creative person. You and I and everyone you know are descended from tens of thousands of years of makers. Decorators, tinkerers, storytellers, dancers, explorers, fiddlers, drummers, builders, growers, problem-solvers, and embellishers—these are our common ancestors. (Gilbert, 2015, p. 89)*

Sadly, fear is not the only barrier that stands in our way of feeling free enough to explore our curiosities. Many of us may also struggle with issues of worthiness, so we doubt our ability to create or express something that is valuable or somehow beneficial. Gilbert addresses how we can more fully liberate ourselves and tell ourselves a different story by directly confronting and addressing these issues.

Giving Ourselves Permission

There are many reasons we may come up with for not following our curiosities. Gilbert (2015) offers an extensive list of excuses we may use, ranging from "you're afraid you'll be rejected or criticized" to "maybe you have no talent" or "perhaps it's just not worth pursuing for any number of reasons" (p. 13). Yet, if we succumb to our fears and don't pursue what excites us or quenches our curiosity, are we really living our fullest lives? Gilbert (2015) writes about what she calls *creative entitlement*, which she defines as "believing that you are allowed to be here, and that—merely by being here—you are allowed to have a voice and a vision of your own" (p. 92) and then elaborates:

> *Often what keeps you from creative living is your self-absorption (your self-doubt, your self-disgust, your self-judgment, your crushing sense of self-protection). The arrogance of belonging pulls you out of the darkest depths of self-hatred—not by saying "I am the greatest!" but merely by saying "I am here!" (p. 93)*

One thing we can all agree on is that we are all here! And if that is all that is required to follow our curiosities, we likely should ask ourselves the question, "What do I most need to give myself permission to do?" And for educators, maybe the question is, "What permission do my students need to give to themselves, and in what ways can I support them to do so?" Answers to these questions do not come easily, and all of us are continually contemplating how to best answer these questions for ourselves.

Gilbert shares a story about her friend Susan, who had competed as a figure skater when she was young, but quit when she realized that she didn't have the skills to be an award-winning skater. As an adult, when she was seeking something that would bring her joy, Susan remembered how transcendent she felt when she skated. She ultimately decided to resume skating for the sheer pleasure it brought her. Gilbert (2015) reminds us that we all have this same opportunity to pursue what brings us joy.

We all deserve to engage in pursuits that bring us joy, such as playing an instrument (whether or not it's pleasing to any listener other than ourselves), creating art (regardless of the quality of the outcome), or playing a sport (whether or not we can play competitively or even marginally well). When we rethink the stories we tell ourselves about what we can't do, or what we shouldn't do, we are free to create the space to live a more expansive and fulfilling life. Kurt Vonnegut (2006, as cited in Usher, 2021) expresses this well when he urges high school students to:

> practice any art, music, singing, dancing, acting, drawing, painting, sculpting, poetry, fiction, essays, reportage, no matter how well or badly, not to get money and fame, but to experience becoming, to find out what's inside you, to make your soul grow.

We all deserve to experience the power of creativity to lift our spirits and transcend our everyday lives. We just need to give ourselves permission that we're worth it.

Adam Grant on the Power of Rethinking

Adam Grant is an author, an organizational psychologist, and a professor at the Wharton School at the University of Pennsylvania. As described on his website (https://adamgrant.net/about/biography), Grant's work focuses on "how we can find motivation and meaning, rethink assumptions, and live more generous and creative lives." Through his work, Grant reminds us how, over time, our most strongly held ideas and beliefs are often proven to be misguided or just plain false. He posits that if we could remember this undeniable truth, it might enable us to remain more flexible in our present thinking, more apt to listen to and consider the opinions of others, and therefore more willing to change our minds (Grant, 2021b). In his book *Think Again: The Power of Knowing What You Don't Know*, Grant (2021b) writes:

> I can't think of a more vital time for rethinking. As the coronavirus pandemic unfolded . . . we've all had to put our mental pliability to the test. We've been forced to question assumptions that we had long taken for granted: That it's safe to go to the hospital, eat in a restaurant, and hug our parents or grandparents. That live sports will always be on TV and most of us will never have to work remotely or homeschool our kids. That we can get toilet paper and hand sanitizer whenever we need them. . . . If you can master the art of rethinking, I believe you'll be better positioned for success at work and happiness in life. Thinking again can help you generate new solutions to old problems and revisit old solutions to new problems. It's a path to learning more from the people around you and living with fewer regrets. (pp. 9–10, 12)

Grant's work connects the ideas of Shorters and Gilbert: we need to consistently be open to rethinking our beliefs, and let go of narratives that no longer serve us. Further, we need to positively frame any stories we tell about ourselves and others, and these stories must reflect the present and evolving truth about ourselves and our lives. Consider the ways that relying too heavily on intellect can be a barrier to rethinking and the joy of rethinking.

Intellect as a Barrier to Rethinking

Grant (2021b) writes extensively about how U.S. society tends to value conviction and decisiveness as hallmarks of strong leadership or an entrepreneurial spirit. Although it may seem counterintuitive, these precise traits can trap us in our certainty, hampering our ability to make the most optimal decisions:

> Mental horsepower doesn't guarantee mental dexterity. No matter how much brainpower you have, if you lack the motivation to change your mind, you'll miss many occasions to think again. Research reveals that the higher you score on an IQ test, the more likely you are to fall for stereotypes, because you're faster at recognizing patterns. And recent experiments suggest that the smarter you are, the more you might struggle to update your beliefs. (Grant, 2021b, p. 24)

As educators, we may have difficulty internalizing this; we'd like to believe that mental acuity translates into our ability to think flexibly. Yet, if you engage in self-reflection (and perhaps call to mind some of your most esteemed colleagues), you will quickly notice how firmly we often hold onto our beliefs without close examination or a sense of urgency to update them, regardless of the evidence to the contrary. For example, although research about personalized learning and student-centered classrooms indicates otherwise, we might still be clinging to our favorite lengthy lectures, waxing poetic about when students sat quietly in rows and took notes, railing against notions of student-centeredness, and feeling defensive about our district initiatives—even those that are grounded in the latest psychological and educational research. This might sound like, "A new way to teach math?" Perhaps you're certain that the old way is the most effective. "A departure from teaching whole-class texts from the literary canon?" You may be sure that it is not in the best interest of your students. As Grant (2021b) writes, "the brighter you are, the harder it can be to see your own limitations. Being good at thinking can make you worse at rethinking" (p. 25).

Grant advocates that we adopt the philosophy of thinking more like scientists. He describes this mode of thinking as "being actively open-minded. It requires searching for reasons why we might be wrong—not for reasons why we must be right—and revising our views based on what we learn" (Grant, 2010b, p. 25). Grant (2021b) does acknowledge that many scientists also become trapped by their intellect, particularly when they are certain about a well-researched outcome, and that they, too, must be reminded to approach all aspects of thinking and rethinking as a scientist engaged in discovery: "We move into scientist mode when we're searching for the truth" (p. 20).

Another barrier to our ability to rethink involves situations "where it's easy to confuse experience for expertise, like driving, typing, trivia, and managing emotions" (Grant, 2021b, p. 43). Since we engage proficiently in these areas so often, we fool ourselves into thinking we have achieved mastery. This is supported by the Dunning–Kruger effect, which is a "cognitive bias in which people wrongly overestimate their knowledge or ability in a specific area. This tends to occur because a lack of self-awareness prevents them from accurately assessing their own skills" (Psychology Today Staff, n.d.). Some of us think we can text while driving because we've driven for years with few incidents; we may feel confident speaking on the nuances of a moment in history solely because we were alive when it happened. Yet this false belief in our infallibility leads to our resistance to accept criticism or consider another point of view, and consequently an unwillingness to rethink and change our minds.

Grant (2021b) suggests that the remedy to knock down this barrier is to approach all our opinions with what he terms *confident humility*. He cites blogger Tim Urban's definition: "humility is a permeable filter that absorbs life experience and converts it into knowledge and wisdom" (Grant, 2021b, p. 45). If we remain confident in our ability to achieve our goals, yet bathe that confidence in the understanding that we might be wrong, therein lies the invitation to change our minds without the sense that a change in our beliefs or choices somehow compromises our intellect, integrity, overall competence, or self-worth. If we consider ourselves life scientists who change our minds based on the evidence presented, we can boldly revise the stories we tell ourselves and move assuredly toward our ever-evolving truths. The good news here is that the ability to rethink our choices can be affirming and life giving for ourselves and others.

The Joy of Rethinking

One reason we struggle with being wrong is that for many of us, our identity is connected to our beliefs. Therefore, if our beliefs prove to be incorrect, what does that then say about who we are? *If I am a teacher who is committed to teaching history in a particular way, and the newest research indicates that my methods are not optimal, doesn't that make me a bad teacher?* It is natural to want to resist change if it's going to indicate that we are somehow inferior or even, in the best case, not as competent as we believe we are. Grant (2021b) suggests:

> Who you are should be a question of what you value, not what you believe. Values are your core principles in life—they might be excellence and generosity, freedom and fairness, or security and integrity. Basing your identity on these kinds of principles enables you to remain open-minded about the best ways to advance them. You want the doctor whose identity is protecting health, the teacher whose identity is helping students learn, and the police chief whose identity is promoting safety and justice. (p. 64)

If we lead with our values and understand that, when we do, our identity is safe regardless of when and how often we change our opinions, we can embrace new concepts and ideas as the facts indicate otherwise and new truths become evident. With a firm sense of belonging that is grounded in who our values say we are, not what we believe at a particular moment, we can actually find joy in changing our mind. Grant (2021b) cites forecaster Kjirste Morrell, who has a doctorate from MIT in mechanical engineering, and describes it this way: "There's no benefit to me for ⸱⸱rong longer . . . and it's a good feeling to have that sense of a discovery, that ⸱" (p. 69).

Finding joy in rethinking is not an easy task, as we inevitably become attached to our beliefs, and we tend to surround ourselves with people whose beliefs are closely aligned with ours. When we do change our minds, we likely have others to whom we will need to justify our newly minted opinions. And yet, this is not a compelling reason for us to hold onto beliefs that don't serve us anymore. As educators, we know that students learn by approaching new concepts with curiosity, and then engaging in critical thought. So, if we want to truly continue to be students of life, we need to continually ask questions when faced with new information. We must show a willingness to change our minds. Based on the highly successful thinkers Grant has interviewed, he suggests that instead of being passionate about proving how right we are, we would be better served considering ways we might be wrong.

A wonder and joy of rethinking lies in the fact that if you are open to changing your mind, you will actually be right more of the time, and you will earn the respect of the people you lead and love. In *Think Again*, Grant recounts a situation from the early 1990s when the physicist Andrew Lyne was preparing to present on a major discovery at an astronomy conference; Lyne realized that he had made a grave error and his findings were incorrect. Grant (2021b) writes, "In front of hundreds of colleagues, Andrew walked onto the ballroom stage and admitted his mistake. When he finished his confession, the room exploded in a standing ovation. One astrophysicist called it 'the most honorable thing I've ever seen'" (p. 73). And Grant (2021b) concurs: when we admit that we were wrong, it doesn't make us look less competent; rather, "it's a display of honesty and a willingness to learn" (p. 73). Think about how much students appreciate it when teachers own up to their mistakes and display vulnerability. Think about how liberating and resonant our new stories can be, for either teachers or students, if they don't rely on the necessity of being right all the time.

Implications for the Classroom

As former language arts teachers, we (Beth and Katie) had long understood the power of story and the implications of the narratives we construct about ourselves. And yet, we hadn't applied this same understanding to consider that the type of narratives we construct about our students may actually perpetuate the precise problems we are trying to solve. In our roles as instructional coaches, we've identified with a more discerning eye that many rubrics categorize students as "inadequate," many default gradebook comments are framed in the negative, and conversations about students primarily reflect their shortcomings, oftentimes without an equal emphasis on their strengths. These practices are embedded in our educational system, a system that advocates that we rank and sort students at every turn, whether it be through a standardized testing continuum, a grading profile, a behavior chart, or a placement in a leveled course.

True, we often use these data to attempt to find logic-based solutions for students by identifying the problems presented. But people are not problems to be solved, and we need to place an emphasis on how to work alongside our students and their families toward academic and overall well-being. As we continue to think deeply about Trabian Shorters's definition of asset-framing (Skillman Foundation, 2018), we can't help but continue to correct each other as we fall into the familiar patterns we've become accustomed to as longtime public educators. We are heartened by Adam Grant's invitation to think again about the way we talk about students, and to examine if it is perhaps hindering our ability to both support them and have them see us as allies on their learning journey. For us, this quote on Shorters's website (https://trabianshorters.com) has been resonating very deeply: "You can't *lift people up* by putting them down."

The intersecting work of Shorters, Gilbert, and Grant has challenged us to rethink how we can more effectively support our students by (1) recognizing them by their strengths before considering their challenges and (2) creating an inquiry-based classroom culture in which asking questions and exploring curiosities with the freedom to change one's mind will increase personal growth and freedom for everyone. Consider practicing asset-framing, creating space for magic, and valuing questions over answers.

Practicing Asset-Framing

Shorters's philosophy reminds us of something we both already knew to be true as parents: we try (yet do not always succeed) to notice what our children are doing right and help them build on these strengths, rather than focusing too much on their shortcomings. When we are able to focus on their strengths, our children are empowered to tell more hopeful stories about themselves, whether those stories bolster their success in learning to tie their shoes independently or to pass geometry. Our children are much more likely to see the intrinsic benefits in building new habits when we emphasize skills they already possess.

Further, as parents and educators, we know that the words we use in our positions of authority have the power to guide those we lead toward positive change, yet also derail their progress and even shape their perception of who they are and what they are capable of doing and becoming. It is through this lens that we are developing a greater understanding of why, as educators, we must use language very intentionally when we talk *with* students and *about* students.

For example, in the case of a student who is chronically absent (which may be perplexing for us, because how can we help a student who does not come to school?), we might assume that this student and their family do not value education—that they don't care enough. We could instead attempt to learn what their hopes and aspirations are, and use that information to work together to create a game plan that does not ignore the problem of chronic absence. We can partner with guidance counselors and administrators to consider what assets the student and family can harness to address the root causes, whether they are logistical, psychological, or otherwise, and then work together to identify resources to support the family.

With asset-framing, no one is *behind* on a learning curve or *inadequate* on a rubric; every person is valued for who they are, and educators are here to work alongside them accordingly, without judgment. This mindset paves the way for telling truer stories about our students that are framed positively and focused on their strengths. These more expansive narratives create the space for our students to learn, grow, and flourish without being limited by our perspectives or the language we use. Shorters reminds us that when the language we use is inaccurate, it misdirects our actions and leads us to solve the wrong problems. Earlier, we discussed replacing the word *remedial* with *developmental* (page 180); the critical difference is that a remedial course presupposes we are remediating students until they are somehow "fixed," whereas a developmental course accepts students at their current skill level to develop and improve at their own pace. Our students are never the problem. Never. And we need to be wary of any language that indicates otherwise.

Spotlight On: Adopting an Asset-Based Rubric—Thesis Statements

Here's an example of a deconstructed rubric with affirmative indicators of student performance, about thesis statements, along a continuum.

- **Developing:** States an argument related to the topic
- **Achieving:** States an argument about the topic that answers the questions *why* or *how*
- **Exceeding:** States an argument about the topic that is central to the text and answers the questions *why* or *how*

Creating Space for Magic

In her book *Big Magic: Creative Living Beyond Fear*, Elizabeth Gilbert (2015) writes about the importance of living a life driven more by curiosity than by fear, and asks the question, "Do you have the courage to bring forth the treasures that are hidden within you?" (p. 8). She suggests that when you unleash these treasures, you open yourself to experiencing magic. Both of us, Beth and Katie, are intimately aware of how both our fears of not being good enough and the stories we tell ourselves can hinder or empower our ability to follow our curiosities. For Beth, her curiosity was the desire to become a writer. Even though she was told throughout high school and college that she had a talent for writing, she never fully believed it. She told herself that she was the kind of writer who could write a good essay, craft beautiful personal correspondence, or persuade someone through writing to change their mind. She told herself that hers was certainly not the kind of writing that was of publishable quality. As she got older, she further solidified this truth that, of course, she was a good writer. She was an English teacher! It wasn't until twenty years later that she began to rethink whether she might have something to say that could be worth reading and putting out into the world.

For Katie, overcoming a false narrative about identity helped her take a leap in a new career direction. The idea of leaving the classroom to do anything else but teach was unthinkable, even after a decade of teaching and leading from the classroom in both informal and formal teacher leadership roles. It wasn't until life (as it always does) threw her family some curveballs that she began to renegotiate her relationship to this narrative. In examining what made her define her identity only through her work in the classroom, she realized that her deep commitment to justice and excellence in education for every child was what mattered most. She also realized that some of the ways she had conceived of her identity were unhealthy, driven by ego, overwork, and at times saviorism. There were, in fact, plenty of ways to realize her commitment in the field of education, and she gave herself permission to look for new roles that served this commitment while respecting her and her family's needs for a different work-life balance. It was then that her curiosity led her to ultimately accept an instructional coach role, which has helped her grow and change in many surprisingly wonderful ways while remaining a teacher at heart. Beyond the benefits of telling yourself a truer story and embracing what is right for you, there are consequences if you do not. Poet Joy Harjo (2012) writes in her memoir, *Crazy Brave*, "I believe that if you do not answer the noise and urgency of your gifts, they will turn on you. Or drag you down with their immense sadness at being abandoned" (p. 135).

It is very likely that many of our students are isolated in the stories they tell themselves that might be inhibiting their willingness to take risks, seize opportunities, and build on strengths others have noted but they themselves fail to recognize. We can't help but think, Is there a way we can create a more affirming experience for our students so they can transcend their self-doubt to confidently explore their curiosities and share their voices and gifts with their world?

We do believe that we have the capacity to create this kind of magic for students in our classrooms. To us, it begins with recognizing the humanity and inherent worth of each of our students and designing learning experiences that offer them opportunities to engage with their curiosities and truly discover their boundless potential. It continues with offering tasks that are accessible to all the students in the classroom regardless of ability or learning differences. These tasks then enable students to pursue different pathways and reach heights that are commensurate with their skills and strengths. It is our job, then, to work alongside them to support them on their individual journeys and provide them with feedback and resources along the way. As we work alongside our students and learn more about them and the stories they are currently telling themselves, we can gently guide them to reframe their story arcs so they become more accurate and expansive. In the process, we might discover that *our* stories about them are likewise in need of revision.

In a language arts classroom, where our new stories resonate with the themes of equity, access, and belonging, magic might look like students engaging in a choice reading initiative where they are reading books across reading levels and genres, ranging from graphic novels to popular young adult fiction to literary classics. All these books enable students to engage in discussions across texts, identify quotes that resonate with them, and share insights they've learned, so they support increasing each student's reading level at their own pace. A culminating assignment based on these books can involve creative writing, written analysis, graphic design, or various art media that invite constructing meaning and demonstrating understanding. We've had students across grade levels convey their understandings through spoken-word poems, songs, computer code, design and engineering projects, and a combination of these. This variety of options increases student engagement, enables students to explore their curiosities, and creates the possibilities that they will reach higher levels of learning and discovery because they are engaged in pursuits that are personally meaningful and enable them to begin where they are.

In other content-area courses, this might look like regular opportunities to engage in independent research to explore personal passions or ideas from broader units of study that sparked personal interests or connections. These types of opportunities create much-needed time and space for instructors to experience the joy and surprise of rethinking when they discover the otherwise unknowable: the lesson or idea a student found wonder inducing; the deep, specific background knowledge a student brought to a topic; the passion a student had that was already emerging about a particular issue or challenge. When we're willing to accept the idea that there may be much to uncover about students' experience in our content area, regardless of their affect or participation in our class, we are welcoming the opportunity to delight together in the *genius and joy* Muhammad (2020) urges us to seek in the work of teaching and learning.

In this way, we create the possibility for both teachers and students to write and rewrite their own stories as they discover and extend their understanding about what they like, where their strengths lie, and what ignites their curiosity. To our minds, a teacher's job is to create opportunities for students to engage in this type of discovery so they can author their own stories, rather than be confined to stories they are told about themselves. When people are given the space to engage in self-discovery in an environment where they are accepted for who they are and offered the chance to start where they are, it enables them to begin to transcend their preconceived limitations. We believe the greatest gift we can give our students is to allow them to cultivate what Gilbert (2015) calls a *voice and vision* of their own.

Valuing Questions Over Answers

In her ninth-grade language arts classroom, Beth displayed posters featuring mantras that reminded her to continually ground her practice in the value of questioning and seeking answers that aligned with our ever-evolving personal truths. These mantras were as much for her as for her students, as it's often difficult to remain constant in our values when there are so many voices and distractions in a classroom, coupled with the reality that we operate within a system and a hierarchical power structure that value obedience and compliance. One of the posters displayed prominently in front of the room read, "The right answers will help you in school, but asking questions will help you in life" (a version of something said by Warren Berger, as cited in Ferlazzo, 2014). On the other side of the room was a quote from educator and author Clint Smith (2014) to remind students to use their voices toward freedom and justice: "Read critically, write consciously, speak clearly, tell your truth." Another critical message to students from Walt Whitman's (1892) poem "O Me! O Life!" reminded them why their lives and their voices matter:

> What good amid these, O me, O life?
> Answer.
> That you are here—that life exists and identity,
> That the powerful play goes on, and you may contribute a verse.

At pivotal points during lessons and activities, when students' comments and contributions reflected these values, Beth would direct students to the posters as affirmation of the work they were doing together. When students were writing opinion pieces, and she felt that they were holding back, she would direct their attention to Clint Smith's (2014) words, "Speak clearly, tell your truth." She always found that bringing in these other mentors and guides for her students helped to decenter herself in the classroom and to more authentically cultivate a classroom environment where everyone was equally a seeker of what was true for them.

Adam Grant's teachings about the power of rethinking remind us of how critical it is that we continually question our own firmly held beliefs if we want to ever get closer to the truth; this vulnerable stance is a powerful one to model for our students. We also note that our classrooms become richer and more equitable when there isn't one of us who is the all-knowing deliverer of knowledge, and students aren't present merely as recipients who are then literally assessed on how well they've internalized what we dispensed.

Regardless of how well we know our content or how skilled we are in our profession, we can attest that there are innumerable times when our students teach us. When we commit ourselves to the philosophy that all learning requires us to engage in a constant rethinking cycle, the stories we tell in our classrooms become about intellectual freedom and personal liberation. To us, these stories are framed by our aspirations and contributions, and they create the space for magic. In keeping with Grant's philosophy, what we've offered here is what we are thinking now, but we are open to rethinking our position!

Introspective Exercises for Teachers

Engage in the following exercises to examine how the ideas in this chapter could impact and inspire your teaching practice and inform your instructional decisions.

.rospective Exercise One: Using Asset-Framed Language in the Classroom

Consider how you can incorporate this asset-based terminology into your lesson plans, assignment sheets, and minilessons so you can begin to tell your students more empowering stories about what's possible. Then, make the commitment to use between five and eight new asset-framed words, like those listed in figure 6.1, each school year as you begin to rewrite any deficit-framed narratives you may unintentionally tell your students.

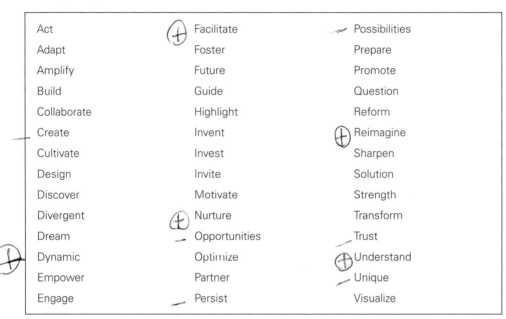

Act	Facilitate	Possibilities
Adapt	Foster	Prepare
Amplify	Future	Promote
Build	Guide	Question
Collaborate	Highlight	Reform
Create	Invent	Reimagine
Cultivate	Invest	Sharpen
Design	Invite	Solution
Discover	Motivate	Strength
Divergent	Nurture	Transform
Dream	Opportunities	Trust
Dynamic	Optimize	Understand
Empower	Partner	Unique
Engage	Persist	Visualize

FIGURE 6.1: Chart for using asset-framed language in the classroom.

*Visit **go.SolutionTree.com/teacherefficacy** for a free reproducible version of this figure.*

Introspective Exercise Two: Rethinking the Story You Tell Yourself

Some people may be trapped in the stories they tell themselves, and the rest may not even know what their stories are. Elizabeth Gilbert speaks and writes extensively about how the way to find your purpose, and perhaps achieve solace and liberation, is to follow your curiosities. The exercise in figure 6.2 is an intersection of Gilbert's philosophy and Grant's assertion that people continually rethink their assumptions. When you are happier and more fulfilled, you have more to give to students and are less likely to deplete your resources.

Directions: Part one invites you to reflect on a series of questions. Part two challenges you to make a commitment to try something new. When you are happier and more fulfilled personally, you have more to give to your students. We encourage you to record your responses to create the space to unravel and plan what will very likely be a pathway to your truer story.

Part One

What did you like to do when you were younger? Why don't you do it now?

What would you do if you weren't afraid of failing?

What would you do if you weren't embarrassed or afraid of being criticized for trying?

What do you avoid doing because you feel you aren't very good at it, but you would like to do it anyway?

What do you admire when other people do it? Would you consider trying this for yourself? Why or why not?

What is something you'd most like to try but you've convinced yourself that you can't because it requires too much time, money, or effort?

Part Two

Make a commitment to try something you identified that you imagine will bring you joy, peace, or transcendence.

FIGURE 6.2: Chart for rethinking the story you tell yourself.

*Visit **go.SolutionTree.com/teacherefficacy** for a free reproducible version of this figure.*

Classroom Strategies

These strategies are inspired by the ideas in this chapter and designed for immediate classroom use. Use these strategies with your students to increase their awareness of themselves and society in order to empower them to tell truer stories.

Classroom Strategy One: Creating an Identity Map

The more awareness that students build about their identities, the less likely that their choices and sense of self will be impacted by the stories that are told about them. Use the activity in figure 6.3 to have students explore their identities through completing an identity map so they can consider revising the stories they tell themselves.

Step one: Create a list of things that make you who you are (your identity). In order to help you think about your identity, what follows is a list of some of the things that make up a person's identity. Please do *not* feel limited by this list. Remember, your identity is simply *who you are* and *you* are the person who gets to define yourself! *Developing a deeper understanding of ourselves builds confidence and self-efficacy. Understanding the identities of the people around us builds community.*

Our identity is composed of the following (and more).

- Gender
- Race and ethnicity
- Family and pets
- Who we love
- Cultural background
- Work
- Strengths
- Challenges
- Aspirations
- Personality traits
- Tendencies
- Family role (sibling, grandchild, cousin, and so on)
- Where our family comes from
- Where we were born or our immigration status
- Home language
- Religion or spiritual practice
- Abilities
- Family structure (number of family members, parents, and roles)
- Hobbies or passions
- Hair color and texture
- Interests

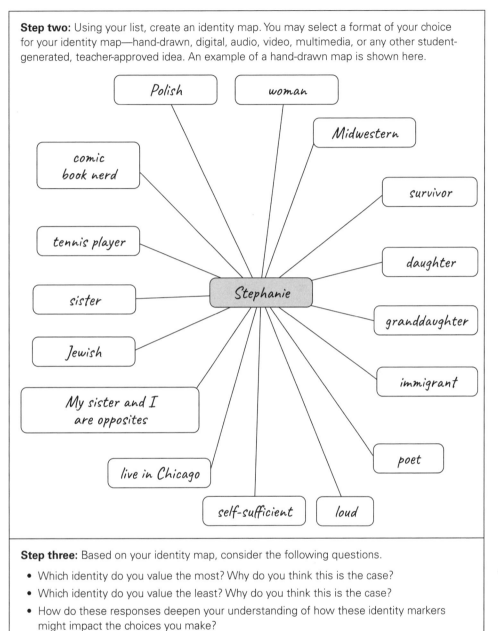

Step two: Using your list, create an identity map. You may select a format of your choice for your identity map—hand-drawn, digital, audio, video, multimedia, or any other student-generated, teacher-approved idea. An example of a hand-drawn map is shown here.

Polish

woman

Midwestern

comic book nerd

survivor

tennis player

daughter

sister

Stephanie

granddaughter

Jewish

immigrant

My sister and I are opposites

live in Chicago

poet

self-sufficient

loud

Step three: Based on your identity map, consider the following questions.

- Which identity do you value the most? Why do you think this is the case?
- Which identity do you value the least? Why do you think this is the case?
- How do these responses deepen your understanding of how these identity markers might impact the choices you make?

FIGURE 6.3: Identity map—Who am I?

*Visit **go.SolutionTree.com/teacherefficacy** for a free reproducible version of this figure.*

Consider completing this exercise yourself and modeling your thinking (to the extent you feel comfortable) to support students as they reflect on their identities with greater vulnerability.

Classroom Strategy Two: Imagining Possibilities Through Storytelling

Use the exercise in figure 6.4 with your students to help them redefine what is possible for them by having them rethink, redefine, and rewrite a story they've been telling themselves. Choose a mode, a format, and a length that align with your objectives, and communicate the parameters to your students. Consider modeling for students how you reframed a story you had been telling yourself.

Directions: What story do you tell about yourself and your life that prevents you from trying something new or following your curiosities because you feel you are somehow not skilled, capable, or worthy of doing so? Now imagine that you have given yourself permission to try. How would you rewrite the story using positive language to tell a more inspirational story about your future possibilities? Consider using some of the following words in your story. Follow the mode, format, and length guidelines as directed by your teacher.

Act	Facilitate	Possibilities
Adapt	Foster	Prepare
Amplify	Future	Promote
Build	Guide	Question
Collaborate	Highlight	Reform
Create	Invent	Reimagine
Cultivate	Invest	Sharpen
Design	Invite	Solution
Discover	Motivate	Strength
Divergent	Nurture	Transform
Dream	Opportunities	Trust
Dynamic	Optimize	Understand
Empower	Partner	Unique
Engage	Persist	Visualize

FIGURE 6.4: Chart for imagining possibilities through storytelling.

*Visit **go.SolutionTree.com/teacherefficacy** for a free reproducible version of this figure.*

Classroom Strategy Three: Thinking Again

Use this exercise to help deepen students' understanding that all stories change over time because people learn new information and hear differing perspectives and their thinking evolves. This truth is evident in everything from evolving historical narratives and scientific discoveries to relationship conflicts and changes in habits. In the rethinking cycle, you can rely on a series of questions to help you reach a more accurate version of the truth.

You can use the activity in figure 6.5 to analyze narratives in language arts tory classes, to challenge theories in science classes, to resolve interpersonal conflicts, and even to question the fairness of school or district policies and procedures.

What do you still need to know in order to get a more complete picture of the story being told? In other words, what facts are missing? Whose voices aren't being heard?

Did you learn something you didn't know before? If so, what? Does this new information make you think differently?

How does this apply to you?

Think about a conflict or challenge you are facing in your own life. List three ways that asking these kinds of questions can help you expand your perspective and, perhaps, think differently.

FIGURE 6.5: Chart for thinking again.

Visit **go.SolutionTree.com/teacherefficacy** *for a free reproducible version of this figure.*

Questions for Reflection and Discussion

In this section, you will find three different types of questions: questions for individual reflection, questions for conversation, and jigsaw questions across chapters. Each offers you a specific way to think through additional questions about concepts from the chapter.

Questions for Individual Reflection

One of the ways you can most impact your students is by modeling your thinking and doing what we call a *think-aloud* for your students. The following questions can help you think about the ideas in this chapter and consider what personal anecdotes you feel comfortable sharing with your students to demonstrate to them how everyone, regardless of age, has similar personal struggles. This kind of sharing can both normalize their experiences and create an opening for them to feel more connected to you. And by preparing these anecdotes in advance, you can ensure that you will be appropriately vulnerable in a way that includes boundaries but also feels cathartic and instructive.

Consider the following questions.

- Can you think of a story that you've been telling yourself that has somehow been holding you back, and can you share with your students how you've been working to reframe this narrative and how this has helped you?

- Can you think of a few things you might be willing to share with your students from the introspective exercises? How have you made a commitment to use more asset-framed language? What words have you decided to use in your personal life and in the classroom? (We have played around with substituting the word *opportunity* for *assignment* in our classrooms.) How have you become more forgiving with yourself and allowed yourself to explore your curiosities? What have you tried, and how has it felt for you?

Questions for Conversation

Consider the following questions to converse about the ideas in this chapter and to leverage these insights toward improving your school.

- Trabian Shorters believes that the language you use and the stories you tell have a profound impact on your life and your ability to partner with people in a meaningful way (The Communications Network, 2020). Can you think of a time when the way you spoke to a student—either framing an opportunity, encouraging the student in a particular direction, or offering critical feedback—was well received because of your delivery and the language you used?

- Elizabeth Gilbert (2015) suggests that bravely exploring your curiosities, wherever they may lead you, is the path toward more liberating narratives and personal freedom. Can you share an example you've either experienced or witnessed that illustrates the truth of Gilbert's philosophy?

- Adam Grant (2021b) explores the benefits of approaching your wealth of knowledge with a healthy dose of skepticism, a commitment to rethink your most fervent beliefs, and a willingness to change your mind. It is much easier to accept Grant's invitation when you reflect on your life and consider what you used to believe and how you've altered your beliefs over time. Can you share a specific anecdote that illustrates something you used to believe, how you changed your mind over time, and the factors that led to this change?

- Take turns sharing stories you used to tell yourself that hindered your ability to live your life to the fullest, and answer, How were you able to rewrite these stories toward greater personal freedom? How can you apply these life lessons in a way that could empower your students to do the same?

Jigsaw Questions Across Chapters

Consider the following questions for conversation with individuals who read a different chapter. Share insights and discover how the intersection of these ideas might spark creative solutions to both impact student learning and improve your experiences as educators.

- Can you summarize an inspiring idea from this chapter in your own words? In what way did this idea cause you to think differently about your practice? How might this idea offer insight to you personally?

- What word or quote from this chapter resonates with you?

- What voices and perspectives are not represented in this text?

- What idea, introspective exercise, or strategy from the chapter holds the most promise for you, and why and how would you implement it in your classroom?

- What is one takeaway from this chapter that you'd like to share with students, colleagues, or your team?

- What additional readings can you bring to the conversation? What other texts or articles could further advance everyone's thinking on this topic?

Conclusion

The thought leaders in this chapter have inspired us to believe that, through our words and actions, we have the power to create an environment in which students can prosper intellectually, emotionally, and creatively. Shorters taught us to be ever more mindful about the language we use, Grant gave us permission to be wrong because we can always think again, and Gilbert expanded our view of how following our curiosity and encouraging our students to do the same can lead to magic. If you are interested in seeking out more ideas that can impact your and your students' personal freedom and liberation, we have recommendations. Visit https://bit.ly/3KeLLDI to watch or read the transcript of "12 Truths I Learned From Life and Writing," a short TED Talk by Anne Lamott (2017). Lamott is one of our favorite authors and one of our go-tos when we're looking for inspiration and a shift in mindset. Search through the archives of the *On Being* podcast with Krista Tippett (https://onbeing.org/series/podcast); let your curiosity guide you to listen to and learn from thinkers across disciplines. Finally, visit https://bit.ly/3GnaFQt to learn more about Elizabeth Gilbert's idea of living a life driven by curiosity.

EPILOGUE

Thank you for joining us on this journey through a landscape of thinkers who have pushed us to examine innovative ways to positively impact teaching and learning in our classrooms and schools. A point of frustration for us is that it seems to take years for emerging ideas across disciplines to trickle down into schools, and even when they do, they are often filtered by and reported through the lens of an educational researcher. At worst, these ideas are so watered down as to be unrecognizable. We feel strongly that educators should have direct access to progressive ideas that can empower them to better serve learners and create more humane and just educational communities. We hope this reading experience inspires you to bring some of the most exciting emerging ideas, research, and approaches to bear on your practice *now*.

By providing you direct access to thinkers across disciplines whose ideas have relevance to educators, we hope we have supplied the stimulus and insight that will ultimately lead you to your best ideas for how to most effectively serve your students. One of our motivations in writing this book was that we feel passionately that our best ideas arise when we expand our thinking through exploring new ideas and stretching our minds in conversation with each other. As science writer Annie Murphy Paul (2021) writes in *The Extended Mind: The Power of Thinking Outside the Brain*:

> For one thing: thought happens not only inside the skull but out in the world, too; it's an act of continuous assembly and reassembly that

*draws on resources external to the brain. For another: the kinds of mate-
rials available to "think with" affect the nature and quality of the thought
that can be produced. . . . Researchers have found, experts are less
likely to "use their heads" and more inclined to extend their minds—a
habit that the rest of us can learn to emulate on our way to achieving
mastery. (pp. 11, 16)*

It is our hope that you will consider some of these ideas in the way Paul (2021)
describes as a "plainly practical invitation to think differently and better" (p. xii).
Perhaps these ideas and subsequent reflections and conversations can help you extend
your mind to find solutions that you have never before imagined. We invite you to
continue exploring the seeds planted here once you put down this book, and to follow your instinct and intuition as you "find your way to the rainbow by the sound
of your own voice" (Shange, 2010, p. 16).

REFERENCES AND RESOURCES

Ackerman, C. E. (2018, April 20). *What is positive psychology and why is it important?* Accessed at https://positivepsychology.com/what-is-positive -psychology-definition on April 4, 2023.

Aguilar, E. (2018). *The onward workbook: Daily activities to cultivate your emotional resilience and thrive.* San Francisco: Jossey-Bass.

Aguilar, E. (2020). *Coaching for equity: Conversations that change practice.* San Francisco: Jossey-Bass.

Allen, K.-A., Kern, M. L., Vella-Brodrick, D., Hattie, J., & Waters, L. (2018). What schools need to know about fostering school belonging: A meta-analysis. *Educational Psychology Review, 30*(1), 1–34.

American Academy of Child and Adolescent Psychiatry. (2020, February). *Screen time and children.* Accessed at www.aacap.org/AACAP/Families_and _Youth/Facts_for_Families/FFF-Guide/Children-And-Watching-TV-054 .aspx on June 30, 2022.

American Educational Research Association. (2018, May 4). *AERA 2018 presidential address: Deborah Loewenberg Ball* [Video file]. Accessed at www.youtube.com/watch?v=JGzQ7O_SIYY&t on February 21, 2023.

Anderson, M., & Jiang, J. (2018, November 28). *Teens, friendships and online groups*. Washington, DC: Pew Research Center. Accessed at www.pewresearch.org/internet/2018/11/28/teens-friendships-and-online -groups on July 25, 2022.

Andersson, H. (2018, July 4). *Social media apps are "deliberately" addictive to users*. BBC News. Accessed at www.bbc.com/news/technology-44640959 on March 1, 2023.

Arain, M., Haque, M., Johal, L., Mathur, P., Nel, W., Rais, A., et al. (2013). Maturation of the adolescent brain. *Neuropsychiatric Disease and Treatment, 9*, 449–461. https://doi.org/10.2147/NDT.S39776

Associated Press. (2019, August 6). *Notable quotes by Toni Morrison, who died Monday at age 88*. Accessed at https://apnews.com/article/entertainment -celebrities-toni-morrison-7631ae6223894408b4fca49ab1874f4f on February 4, 2022.

Australian Institute of Family Studies. (2016, September). *Growing up in Australia: The longitudinal study of Australian children*. Melbourne, Victoria, Australia: Author. Accessed at https://aifs.gov.au/research/commissioned -reports/childrens-screen-time on March 15, 2023.

Baldwin, J. M. (1897). *Social and ethical interpretations in mental development*. New York: Macmillan.

Barrett, L. F. (2018, June 21). *Try these two smart techniques to help you master your emotions*. Accessed at https://ideas.ted.com/try-these-two-smart -techniques-to-help-you-master-your-emotions on April 12, 2023.

Barshay, J. (2018, May 7). *20 judgments a teacher makes in 1 minute and 28 seconds*. Accessed at https://hechingerreport.org/20-judgments-a-teacher-makes-in -1-minute-and-28-seconds on August 10, 2022.

Barshay, J. (2019, August 12). *Evidence increases for reading on paper instead of screens*. Accessed at https://hechingerreport.org/evidence-increases-for -reading-on-paper-instead-of-screens on August 1, 2022.

Baumeister, R. F., Vohs, K. D., & Tice, D. M. (2007). The strength model of self-control. *Current Directions in Psychological Science, 16*(6), 351–355. Accessed at http://assets.csom.umn.edu/assets/166733.pdf on August 10, 2022.

Beyers, W., & Luyckx, K. (2016). Ruminative exploration and reconsideration of commitment as risk factors for suboptimal identity development in adolescence and emerging adulthood. *Journal of Adolescence, 47,* 169–178. Accessed at https://psycnet.apa.org/record/2015-52340-001 on August 1, 2022.

Bill Moyers Journal. (2007, December 28). *Excerpt from Bill Moyers' conversation with Archbishop Tutu, April 27, 1999.* PBS. Accessed at www.pbs.org /moyers/journal/12282007/transcript2.html on June 29, 2022.

BMe Community. (2016, January 28). *Trabian Shorters Aspen Institute talk: Who do you think we are?* [Video file]. Accessed at www.youtube.com /watch?v=lDiPy1ik2UU on June 30, 2022.

Bouygues, H. L. (2019). *Does educational technology help students learn? An analysis of the connection between digital devices and learning.* Accessed at https://reboot-foundation.org/wp-content/uploads/2022/05/Does_Ed _Tech_Help_Students_Learn.pdf on June 19, 2023.

Brackett, M. (2019). *Permission to feel: Unlocking the power of emotions to help our kids, ourselves, and our society thrive.* New York: Celadon Books.

Brigham and Women's Hospital. (2014, December 22). *Light-emitting e-readers before bedtime can adversely impact sleep.* Accessed at www.brighamandwomens.org/about-bwh/newsroom/press-releases -detail?id=1962 on March 15, 2023.

Brill, S. (2021, May 18). For a fairer world, it's necessary first to cut through the "noise." *The New York Times.* Accessed at www.nytimes.com/2021/05/18 /books/review/noise-daniel-kahneman-olivier-sibony-cass-sunstein.html on July 26, 2022.

brown, a. m. (2017). *Emergent strategy: Shaping change, changing worlds.* Chico, CA: AK Press.

Brown, B. (2017). *Braving the wilderness: The quest for true belonging and the courage to stand alone.* New York: Random House.

Brown, B. (2018). *Dare to lead: Brave work. Tough conversations. Whole hearts.* New York: Random House.

Brown, B. (2021). *Atlas of the heart: Mapping meaningful connection and the language of human experience.* New York: Random House.

Brown, B. (Host). (2022, February 23). The four pivots: Reimagining justice, reimagining ourselves with Dr. Shawn Ginwright [Audio podcast episode]. In *Unlocking us*. Accessed at https://brenebrown.com/podcast /the-four-pivots-reimagining-justice-reimagining-ourselves on April 4, 2023.

Cameron, N. (2020, August 13). *Brené Brown: What it takes to be a brave leader right now*. Accessed at www.cmo.com.au/article/682135/brene-brown -what-it-takes-brave-leader-right-now on January 7, 2022.

Carlson, J. A., Engelberg, J. K., Cain, K. L., Conway, T. L., Mignano, A. M., Bonilla, E. A., et al. (2015). Implementing classroom physical activity breaks: Associations with student physical activity and classroom behavior. *Preventive Medicine, 81*, 67–72. Accessed at www.sciencedirect.com /science/article/abs/pii/S0091743515002583 on March 15, 2023.

Carothers, T., & O'Donohue, A. (Eds.). (2019a). *Democracies divided: The global challenge of political polarization*. Washington, DC: Brookings Institution Press.

Carothers, T., & O'Donohue, A. (2019b, October 1). *How to understand the global spread of political polarization*. Washington, DC: Carnegie Endowment for International Peace. Accessed at https://carnegieendowment.org /2019/10/01/how-to-understand-global-spread-of-political-polarization -pub-79893 on March 15, 2023.

Carr Center for Human Rights Policy. (2022). *Reimagining rights and responsibilities in the United States*. Accessed at https://carrcenter.hks.harvard.edu /reimagining-rights-responsibilities-united-states on June 1, 2022.

Center for Self-Determination Theory. (n.d.). *Overview*. Accessed at https://self determinationtheory.org/theory on December 27, 2021.

Clear, J. (2018). *Atomic habits: An easy and proven way to build good habits and break bad ones*. New York: Avery.

Clifton, J. (2018, July 2). *10 things you need to know from Gallup for July 4th*. Washington, DC: Gallup. Accessed at https://news.gallup.com/opinion /gallup/236411/things-need-know-gallup-july4th.aspx on June 1, 2022.

Clinton, V. (2019). Reading from paper compared to screens: A systematic review and meta-analysis. *Journal of Research in Reading, 42*(2), 288–325.

Coelho, P. (1988). *The alchemist*. New York: HarperCollins.

Collaborative for Academic, Social, and Emotional Learning. (n.d.). *What is the CASEL framework?* Accessed at https://casel.org/fundamentals-of-sel/what-is-the-casel-framework on April 4, 2023.

Commonwealth Club of California. (2020, February 19). *Ezra Klein: Why we're polarized* [Video file]. Accessed at www.youtube.com/watch?v=CZXb2pKcU5k on February 18, 2023.

The Communications Network. (2020, October 14). *Trabian Shorters, founder and CEO of BMe Community and expert on asset-framing* [Video file]. Accessed at www.youtube.com/watch?v=f3t1DJV0xfI on June 29, 2022.

Cornell University Center for Teaching Innovation. (n.d.). *Getting started with establishing ground rules.* Accessed at https://teaching.cornell.edu/resource/getting-started-establishing-ground-rules on August 20, 2022.

Costello, B., Wachtel, J., & Wachtel, T. (2009). *The restorative practices handbook for teachers, disciplinarians and administrators.* Bethlehem, PA: International Institute for Restorative Practices.

Cowen, A. S., & Keltner, D. (2017). Self-report captures 27 distinct categories of emotion bridged by continuous gradients. *Proceedings of the National Academy of Sciences of the United States of America, 114*(38), E7900–E7909.

Coyle, D. (2018). *The culture code: The secrets of highly successful groups.* New York: Bantam Books.

Crone, E. A., & Konijn, E. A. (2018). Media use and brain development during adolescence. *Nature Communications, 9,* 588. Accessed at www.nature.com/articles/s41467-018-03126-x on August 1, 2022.

Csikszentmihalyi, M. (1990). *Flow: The psychology of optimal experience.* New York: Harper & Row.

Dakanalis, A., Carrà, G., Calogero, R., Fida, R., Clerici, M., Zanetti, M. A., et al. (2015). The developmental effects of media-ideal internalization and self-objectification processes on adolescents' negative body-feelings, dietary restraint, and binge eating. *European Child and Adolescent Psychiatry, 24*(8), 997–1010.

David, S. (2017). *The gift and power of emotional courage* [Video file]. TED Conferences. Accessed at www.ted.com/talks/susan_david_the_gift_and_power_of_emotional_courage/transcript?language=en on April 4, 2023.

de Hoog, N. (2013). Processing of social identity threats: A defense motivation perspective. *Social Psychology, 44*(6), 361–372.

Delgado, P., Vargas, C., Ackerman, R., & Salmerón, L. (2018). Don't throw away your printed books: A meta-analysis on the effects of reading media on reading comprehension. *Educational Research Review, 25*, 23–38.

Edmondson, A. C. (2012). *Teaming: How organizations learn, innovate, and compete in the knowledge economy.* San Francisco: Wiley.

Ehrenreich, S. E., & Underwood, M. K. (2016). Adolescents' internalizing symptoms as predictors of the content of their Facebook communication and responses received from peers. *Translational Issues in Psychological Science, 2*(3), 227–237.

Eichhorn, K. (2019). *The end of forgetting: Growing up with social media.* Cambridge, MA: Harvard University Press.

Epstein, D. (2019). *Range: Why generalists triumph in a specialized world.* New York: Riverhead Books.

Ferlazzo, L. (2014, July 16). "A more beautiful question": An interview with Warren Berger. *Education Week.* Accessed at www.edweek.org/teaching -learning/opinion-a-more-beautiful-question-an-interview-with-warren -berger/2014/07 on February 20, 2023.

Fotias, N. (2018, September 24). *The power of asset framing: A conversation with Trabian Shorters* [Blog post]. Accessed at www.skillman.org/blog /the-power-of-asset-framing on June 25, 2022.

Gallagher, K. (n.d.). *Article of the week.* Accessed at www.kellygallagher.org /article-of-the-week on August 19, 2022.

Gaspard, H., Dicke, A.-L., Flunger, B., Brisson, B. M., Häfner, I., Nagengast, B., et al. (2015). Fostering adolescents' value beliefs for mathematics with a relevance intervention in the classroom. *Developmental Psychology, 51*(9), 1226–1240.

Gates, M. (2019). *The moment of lift: How empowering women changes the world.* New York: Flatiron Books.

Gerber, M. (Ed.). (1979). *The RIE manual for parents and professionals.* Los Angeles: Resources for Infant Educarers.

Gilbert, E. (2006). *Eat, pray, love: One woman's search for everything across Italy, India and Indonesia.* New York: Viking.

Gilbert, E. (2015). *Big magic: Creative living beyond fear.* New York: Riverhead Books.

Ginwright, S. A. (2022). *The four pivots: Reimagining justice, reimagining ourselves.* Berkeley, CA: North Atlantic Books.

Gordon, S. (2022, May 13). What are the 24 character strengths? *VeryWellMind.* Accessed at www.verywellmind.com/what-are-character-strengths -4843090 on January 4, 2023.

Grant, A. (Host). (2021a, March 16). Taken for granted: Daniel Kahneman doesn't trust your intuition [Podcast transcript]. *Taken for Granted.* Accessed at www.ted.com/podcasts/taken-for-granted-daniel-kahneman -doesnt-trust-your-intuition-transcript on July 25, 2022.

Grant, A. (2021b). *Think again: The power of knowing what you don't know.* New York: Viking.

Groysberg, B., Lee, J., Price, J., & Cheng, J. Y.-J. (2018). The leader's guide to corporate culture. *Harvard Business Review.* Accessed at https://hbr.org /2018/01/the-leaders-guide-to-corporate-culture on January 2, 2022.

Grujiters, R. J., & Kurian, N. (2023). *Deficit-oriented teacher beliefs inhibit poor students' learning and wellbeing.* Accessed at www.ukfiet.org/2023/deficit -oriented-teacher-beliefs-inhibit-poor-students-learning-and-wellbeing on May 6, 2023.

Hale, L., & Guan, S. (2015). Screen time and sleep among school-aged children and adolescents: A systematic literature review. *Sleep Medicine Reviews, 21,* 50–58.

Hall, E. T. (1976). *Beyond culture.* New York: Anchor Books.

Hari, J. (2022). *Stolen focus: Why you can't pay attention—And how to think deeply again.* New York: Crown.

Harjo, J. (2012). *Crazy brave: A memoir.* New York: Norton.

Hemphill, P. [@prentishemphill]. (2021, April 5). *Boundaries are the distance at which I can love you and me simultaneously* [Text post]. Instagram. Accessed at www.instagram.com/p/CNSzFO1A21C/?hl=enon on February 19, 2023.

Herrando, C., & Constantinides, E. (2021). Emotional contagion: A brief overview and future directions. *Frontiers in Psychology, 12.* Accessed at www.frontiersin.org/articles/10.3389/fpsyg.2021.712606/full on April 3, 2023.

Howie, E. K., Beets, M. W., & Pate, R. R. (2014). Acute classroom exercise breaks improve on-task behavior in 4th and 5th grade students: A dose–response. *Mental Health and Physical Activity*, *7*(2), 65–71. Accessed at www.sciencedirect.com/science/article/abs/pii /S1755296614000295 on March 15, 2023.

Hu, E., & Lee, J. W. (2021, August 9). *Get your family running more smoothly with tricks from running small businesses*. Accessed at www.npr.org /2021/08/06/1025447008/emily-oster-the-family-firm-decision-making -parenting on August 18, 2022.

James, O. (2018, Fall). Teachers' professional attitudes and students' academic performance in secondary schools in Ilorin Metropolis of Kwara State. *eJournal of Education Policy*. Accessed at https://files.eric.ed.gov/fulltext /EJ1203831.pdf on April 3, 2023.

James, W. (1918). *The principles of psychology*. New York: Holt.

Jordan, J. (1980). *Poem for South African women* [Poem]. Accessed at www.june jordan.net/poem-for-south-african-women.html on August 30, 2022.

Kahneman, D. (2013). *Thinking, fast and slow*. New York: Farrar, Straus and Giroux.

Kahneman, D., Sibony, O., & Sunstein, C. R. (2021a, May 15). Bias is a big problem. But so is "noise." *The New York Times*. Accessed at www.nytimes .com/2021/05/15/opinion/noise-bias-kahneman.html on July 25, 2022.

Kahneman, D., Sibony, O., & Sunstein, C. R. (2021b). *Noise: A flaw in human judgment*. New York: Little, Brown Spark.

Kamenetz, A. (2022, April 29). *The education culture war is raging. But for most parents, it's background noise*. Accessed at www.npr.org/2022/04 /29/1094782769/parent-poll-school-culture-wars on June 1, 2022.

Kim, A. (2021, August 29). AP's equity face-plant. *Washington Monthly*. Accessed at https://washingtonmonthly.com/2021/08/29/aps-equity-face-plant on April 5, 2023.

Klein, A. (2021, December 6). 1,500 decisions a day (at least!): How teachers cope with a dizzying array of questions. *Education Week*. Accessed at www.edweek.org/teaching-learning/1-500-decisions-a-day-at-least -how-teachers-cope-with-a-dizzying-array-of-questions/2021/12 on January 2, 2022.

Klein, E. (2020). *Why we're polarized*. New York: Avid Reader Press.

Kostøl, E. M. F., & Cameron, D. L. (2021). Teachers' responses to children in emotional distress: A study of co-regulation in the first year of primary school in Norway. *Education 3–13*. Accessed at www.tandfonline.com/doi /full/10.1080/03004279.2020.1800062 on May 6, 2023.

Laidler, J. (2019, March 4). High tech is watching you. *Harvard Gazette*. Accessed at https://news.harvard.edu/gazette/story/2019/03/harvard-professor-says -surveillance-capitalism-is-undermining-democracy on July 25, 2022.

Lamott, A. (2017). *12 truths I learned from life and writing* [Video file]. TED Conferences. Accessed at www.ted.com/talks/anne_lamott_12_truths_i _learned_from_life_and_writing?language=en on April 12, 2023.

Lansbury, J. (2014). *Elevating child care: A guide to respectful parenting*. Malibu, CA: JLML Press.

LeBlanc, V. R., McConnell, M. M., & Monteiro, S. D. (2015). Predictable chaos: A review of the effects of emotions on attention, memory and decision making. *Advances in Health Sciences Education: Theory and Practice, 20*(1), 265–282.

Lerner, J. S., Li, Y., Valdesolo, P., & Kassam, K. S. (2015). Emotion and decision making. *Annual Review of Psychology, 66*. Accessed at www.annualreviews .org/doi/10.1146/annurev-psych-010213-115043 on March 1, 2023.

Lester, R. R., Allanson, P. B., & Notar, C. E. (2017). Routines are the foundation of classroom management. *Education, 137*(4). Accessed at https://go.gale .com/ps/i.do?p=AONE&u=googlescholar&id=GALE|A496083773& v=2.1&it=r&sid=AONE&asid=95511862 on April 6, 2023.

Levine, A., & Heller, R. S. F. (2012). *Attached: The new science of adult attachment and how it can help you find—and keep—love*. New York: TarcherPerigree.

Levine, E., & Patrick, S. (2019). *What is competency-based education? An updated definition*. Vienna, VA: Aurora Institute. Accessed at https://files.eric .ed.gov/fulltext/ED604019.pdf on April 4, 2023.

Levounis, P., & Sherer, J. (Eds.). (2022). *Technological addictions*. Washington, DC: American Psychiatric Association.

Lieberman, M. D. (2013). *Social: Why our brains are wired to connect*. New York: Oxford University Press.

Limón, A. (Host). (2021, October 6). They'll ask you where it hurts the most [Audio podcast transcript]. In *The slowdown*. Accessed at www.slowdownshow.org/episode/2021/10/06/517-theyll-ask-you-where -it-hurts-the-most on July 9, 2022.

Lissak, G. (2018). Adverse physiological and psychological effects of screen time on children and adolescents: Literature review and case study. *Environmental Research, 164*, 149–157.

Marsh, C. (2019, November 1). *Honoring the global Indigenous roots of restorative justice: Potential restorative approaches for child welfare.* Washington, DC: Center for the Study of Social Policy. Accessed at https://cssp.org /2019/11/honoring-the-global-indigenous-roots-of-restorative-justice on April 3, 2023.

Maslow, A. H. (1943). A theory of human motivation. *Psychological Review, 50*(4), 370–396.

McFarlane, G. (2022, December 2). How Facebook (Meta), Twitter, social media make money from you. *Investopedia*. Accessed at www.investopedia.com /stock-analysis/032114/how-facebook-twitter-social-media-make-money -you-twtr-lnkd-fb-goog.aspx on March 1, 2023.

Melville, H. (1856). Bartleby, the scrivener: A story of Wall Street. In *The piazza tales*. New York: Dix & Edwards.

Metcalf, S. (2020, March 11). Ezra Klein's "Why We're Polarized" and the drawbacks of explainer journalism. *The New Yorker*. Accessed at www.newyorker.com/books/under-review/ezra-kleins-why-were-polarized -and-the-drawbacks-of-explainer-journalism on August 15, 2022.

Mindful. (2018, February 2). *The tyranny of relentless positivity*. Accessed at www.mindful.org/real-gift-negative-emotions on May 7, 2022.

Mlodinow, L. (2022). *Emotional: How feelings shape our thinking*. New York: Pantheon.

Montag, C., Lachmann, B., Herrlich, M., & Zweig, K. (2019). Addictive features of social media/messenger platforms and freemium games against the background of psychological and economic theories. *International Journal of Environmental Research and Public Health, 16*(14), 2612.

Muhammad, G. (2020). *Cultivating genius: An equity framework for culturally and historically responsive literacy*. New York: Scholastic.

Newman, K. M. (2018, April 11). *Can self-awareness help you be more empathic?* Berkeley, CA: Greater Good Science Center at the University of California, Berkeley. Accessed at https://greatergood.berkeley.edu/article /item/can_self_awareness_help_you_be_more_empathic on April 4, 2023.

Newport, C. (2019). *Digital minimalism: Choosing a focused life in a noisy world.* New York: Portfolio.

Odell, J. (2019). *How to do nothing: Resisting the attention economy.* New York: Melville House.

The On Being Project. (2022). *The six grounding virtues of the On Being Project.* Accessed at https://onbeing.org/social-healing-at-on-being/the-six -grounding-virtues-of-the-on-being-project on August 20, 2022.

Osika, A., MacMahon, S., Lodge, J. M., & Carroll, A. (2022, March 18). Emotions and learning: What role do emotions play in how and why students learn? *The Times Higher Education.* Accessed at www.times highereducation.com/campus/emotions-and-learning-what-role-do -emotions-play-how-and-why-students-learn on March 26, 2023.

Oster, E. (2019). *Cribsheet: A data-driven guide to better, more relaxed parenting, from birth to preschool.* New York: Penguin.

Oster, E. (2021a). *Expecting better: Why the conventional pregnancy wisdom is wrong—and what you really need to know* (Updated ed.). New York: Penguin.

Oster, E. (2021b). *The family firm: A data-driven guide to better decision making in the early school years.* New York: Penguin.

OWN. (2015, November 20). *The advice Elizabeth Gilbert won't give anymore* [Video file]. Accessed at www.youtube.com/watch?v=Z7V-sXCY9Rk on February 15, 2023.

Pak, S. S., & Weseley, A. J. (2012). The effect of mandatory reading logs on children's motivation to read. *Journal of Research in Education, 22*(1), 251–265.

Parker, P. (2018). *The art of gathering: How we meet and why it matters.* New York: Riverhead Books.

Paul, A. M. (2021). *The extended mind: The power of thinking outside the brain.* Boston: Mariner Books.

Perel, E. [estherperelofficial]. (2022, July 18). *Finding yourself polarized around politics with: Those you love? People at work? Strangers on the internet? Let's talk about it* [Text post]. Instagram. Accessed at www.instagram.com/p/CgKg9xrvFMH/?igshid=YmMyMTA2M2Y%3Don on April 6, 2023.

Perel, E., & Miller, M. A. (n.d.). *Letters from Esther #36: Fighting with your partner about values?* [Blog post]. Accessed at www.estherperel.com/blog/letters-from-esther-36-fighting-with-your-partner-about-values on August 20, 2022.

Peterson, C., & Seligman, M. E. P. (2004). *Character strengths and virtues: A handbook and classification.* New York: Oxford University Press.

Pew Research Center. (2014, June). *Political polarization in the American public.* Washington, DC: Author. Accessed at www.pewresearch.org/politics/2014/06/12/political-polarization-in-the-american-public on March 15, 2023.

Porosoff, L., & Weinstein, J. (2023). *EMPOWER moves for social-emotional learning: Tools and strategies to evoke student values.* Bloomington, IN: Solution Tree Press.

Postman, N. (1985). *Amusing ourselves to death: Public discourse in the age of show business.* New York: Penguin.

Psychology Today Staff. (n.d.). *Dunning-Kruger effect.* Accessed at www.psychologytoday.com/us/basics/dunning-kruger-effect on April 4, 2023.

Quindlen, A. (n.d.). *Discussion guide:* Lots of Candles, Plenty of Cake. Accessed at www.penguinrandomhouseaudio.com/discussion-guide/203763/lots-of-candles-plenty-of-cake on July 12, 2022.

Ra, C. K., Cho, J., Stone, M. D., De La Cerda, J., Goldenson, N. I., Moroney, E., et al. (2018). Association of digital media use with subsequent symptoms of attention-deficit/hyperactivity disorder among adolescents. *Journal of the American Medical Association, 320*(3), 255–263. Accessed at https://jamanetwork.com/journals/jama/article-abstract/2687861 on August 1, 2022.

Readiness and Emergency Management for Schools Technical Assistance Center. (n.d.). *Student perceptions of safety and their impact on creating a safe school environment.* Accessed at https://rems.ed.gov/docs/Student_Perceptions_Safety_Fact_Sheet_508C.pdf on April 5, 2023.

Reber, A. S. (1985). *The Penguin dictionary of psychology*. London: Penguin.

Rhodes, L. (Producer), & Orlowski-Yang, J. (Director). (2020). *The social dilemma* [Film]. Boulder, CO: Exposure Labs.

Roy, A. (2022, September 18). *In pursuit of cultural freedom* [Video file]. Accessed at https://lannan.org/events/arundhati-roy-with-howard-zinn on July 15, 2022.

Santos, H. C., Varnum, M. E. W., & Grossman, I. (2017). Global increases in individualism. *Association for Psychological Science, 28*(9), 1228–1239.

Satullo, C. (2021, November 4). *Reflection on Loretta Ross and "Call in Culture."* Accessed at https://snfpaideia.upenn.edu/reflection-on-loretta-ross-call-in -culture on June 11, 2023.

Schaeffer, K. (2022, February 25). *State of the union 2022: How Americans view major national issues*. Washington, DC: Pew Research Center. Accessed at www.pewresearch.org/fact-tank/2022/02/25/state-of-the-union-2022-how -americans-view-major-national-issues on June 1, 2022.

Schwartz, B. (2005). *The paradox of choice* [Video file]. TED Conferences. Accessed at www.ted.com/talks/barry_schwartz_the_paradox_of _choice?language=en on July 26, 2022.

Schwartz, B. (2016). *The paradox of choice: Why more is less*. New York: HarperCollins.

Shange, N. (2010). *For colored girls who have considered suicide / when the rainbow is enuf: A choreopoem*. New York: Scribner.

Singer, L. M., & Alexander, P. A. (2017). Reading on paper and digitally: What the past decades of empirical research reveal. *Review of Educational Research, 87*(6), 1007–1041.

Singh, A. K., Srivastava, S., & Singh, D. (2015). Student engagement as the predictor of direct and indirect learning outcomes in the management education context. *Metamorphosis: A Journal of Management Research, 14*(2), 20–29.

Skillman Foundation. (2018, August 20). *Trabian Shorters: Define people by their aspirations, not their challenges* [Video file]. Accessed at www.youtube.com /watch?v=O04CuqStRvM on April 3, 2023.

Smith, C. (2014, July). *The danger of silence* [Video file]. TED Talk Lessons. Accessed at https://ed.ted.com/lessons/the-danger-of-silence-clint-smith on July 13, 2022.

Sofer, O. J. (2018). *Say what you mean: A mindful approach to nonviolent communication.* Boulder, CO: Shambhala.

Statistics Canada. (2019, April 17). *Physical activity and screen time among Canadian children and youth, 2016 and 2017.* Accessed at www150.statcan.gc.ca/n1/pub/82-625-x/2019001/article/00003-eng.htm on March 15, 2023.

Stolen focus. (2021). *Interviews.* Accessed at https://stolenfocusbook.com/audio on June 16, 2023.

Sturgis, C. (2018, May 16). *The code of culture: Establishing purpose in competency-based schools* (part 3). Accessed at https://aurora-institute.org/cw_post/the-code-of-culture-establishing-purpose-in-competency-based-schools-part-3 on July 19, 2022.

Tamana, S. K., Ezeugwu, V., Chikuma, J., Lefebvre, D. L., Azad, M. B., Moraes, T. J., et al. (2019). Screen-time is associated with inattention problems in preschoolers: Results from the CHILD birth cohort study. *PLoS One, 14*(4), e0213995.

Tang, Y., & Hu, J. (2022). The impact of teacher attitude and teaching approaches on student demotivation: Disappointment as a mediator. *Frontiers in Psychology, 13.* Accessed at www.frontiersin.org/articles/10.3389/fpsyg.2022.985859/full on April 3, 2023.

Taylor, L. K., Merrilees, C. E., Goeke-Morey, M. C., Shirlow, P., Cairns, E., & Cummings, E. (2014). Political violence and adolescent out-group attitudes and prosocial behaviors: Implications for positive inter-group relations. *Social Development, 23*(4), 840–859.

Thomas B. Fordham Institute. (2021, April 8). *Children learn best when they feel safe and valued.* Washington, DC: Author. Accessed at https://fordhaminstitute.org/national/commentary/children-learn-best-when-they-feel-safe-and-valued on April 5, 2023.

Tierney, J. (2011, August 17). Do you suffer from decision fatigue? *The New York Times Magazine.* Accessed at www.nytimes.com/2011/08/21/magazine/do-you-suffer-from-decision-fatigue.html on August 10, 2022.

Tippett, K. (Host). (2011, January 20). Frances Kissling: What is good in the position of the other [Audio podcast episode]. In *On being with Krista Tippett*. Accessed at https://onbeing.org/programs/frances-kissling-what-is -good-in-the-position-of-the-other-sep2018 on August 29, 2022.

Tippett, K. (Host). (2016, July 7). Elizabeth Gilbert: Choosing curiosity over fear [Audio podcast episode]. In *On being with Krista Tippett*. Accessed at https://onbeing.org/programs/elizabeth-gilbert-choosing-curiosity-over -fear-may2018 on August 5, 2022.

Tippett, K. (Host). (2022, February 3). Trabian Shorters: A cognitive skill to magnify humanity [Audio podcast episode]. In *On being with Krista Tippett*. Accessed at https://onbeing.org/programs/trabian-shorters-a -cognitive-skill-to-magnify-humanity on August 5, 2022.

Turkle, S. (2015). *Reclaiming conversation: The power of talk in a digital age*. New York: Penguin.

Turner, C., & Bhat, D. (2022). Practicing self-awareness to elevate teacher efficacy. *Journal of Social and Emotional Learning*, *3*(12). Accessed at www.crslearn .org/publication/empowering-educators/practicing-self-awareness-to -elevate-teacher-efficacy on April 4, 2023.

Usher, S. (2021, November 5). Make your soul grow. *Letters of Note*. Accessed at https://news.lettersofnote.com/p/make-your-soul-grow on April 6, 2023.

Varlas, L. (2018, June 1). Emotions are the rudder that steers thinking. *Educational Leadership*, *60*(6). Accessed at www.ascd.org/publications/newsletters /education-update/jun18/vol60/num06/Emotions-Are-the-Rudder-That -Steers-Thinking.aspx on December 29, 2022.

Visible Learning. (2018, March). *Collective teacher efficacy (CTE) according to John Hattie*. Accessed at https://visible-learning.org/2018/03/collective-teacher -efficacy-hattie on February 6, 2022.

Whitman, W. (1892). *O me! O life!* [Poem]. Accessed at www.poetryfoundation .org/poems/51568/o-me-o-life on July 13, 2022.

Wiseman, L. (2017). *Multipliers: How the best leaders make everyone smarter*. New York: Harper Business.

Zuboff, S. (2019). *The age of surveillance capitalism: The fight for a human future at the new frontier of power*. New York: PublicAffairs.

INDEX

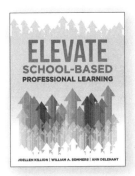

Elevate School-Based Professional Learning
Joellen Killion, William A. Sommers, and Ann Delehant
Collaborative staff development implemented in tandem with daily teacher practice has been proven to have a greater impact on student success. This practical resource illustrates the importance of school-based professional learning and offers guidance on how to implement it.
BKG085

I'm Listening
Beth Pandolpho
Rely on *I'm Listening* to help drive deeper, more meaningful learning by integrating relationship building into lesson design. Using the book's practical strategies will help you empower learners to succeed at all subjects by being proficient readers, writers, speakers, and listeners.
BKF926

EMPOWER Moves for Social-Emotional Learning
Lauren Porosoff and Jonathan Weinstein
Empower students to discover the values they want to live by. You will learn twenty-eight activities, as well as extensions and variations for each, that engage students and help them make school a source of meaning, vitality, and community in their lives.
BKG095

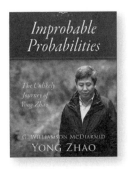

Improbable Probabilities
By G. Williamson McDiarmid and Yong Zhao
Improbable Probabilities is the story of the life and career of internationally acclaimed educator Yong Zhao. This powerful book follows Zhao's path from his impoverished boyhood in China to his emergence as one of the most influential educators of the 21st century.
BKG016

Solution Tree | Press
a division of
Solution Tree

Visit SolutionTree.com or call 800.733.6786 to order.